NORTH CAR

MUSEUM SEASCAPES SERIES

VOYAGE

OF

THE PAPER CANOE

VOYAGE

OF

THE PAPER CANOE

Nathaniel H. Bishop

A REPRINT OF THE 1878 CLASSIC

Coastal Carolina Press
Wilmington, North Carolina
in partnership with
North Carolina Maritime Museum
Beaufort, North Carolina

Published by

Coastal Carolina Press
4709 College Acres Drive, Suite 1
Wilmington, NC 28403 U.S.A.
www.coastalcarolinapress.org

Copyright © 2000 by North Carolina Maritime Museum

Lea & Shepard, First Edition 1878
Coastal Carolina Press, First Edition 2000

Printed in the United States of America

ISBN 1-928556-13-2

Library of Congress Cataloging-in Publication Data
Bishop, Nathaniel H. (Nathaniel Holmes), 1837–1902.
  Voyage of the paper canoe / Nathaniel H. Bishop.
    p. cm. — (North Carolina Maritime Museum's seascapes series)
  ISBN 1-928556-13-2 (pbk.)
    1. Atlantic Coast (U.S.) — Description and travel. 2. Atlantic Coast
(Canada) — Description and travel. 3. United States — Description and
travel. 4. Canada, Eastern — Description and travel. 5. Waterways —
United States — History — 19th century. 6. Waterways — Canada,
Eastern — History — 19th century. 7. Bishop, Nathaniel H. (Nathaniel
Holmes), 1837–1902 — Journeys — United States. 8. Bishop, Nathaniel H.
(Nathaniel Holmes), 1837–1902 — Journeys — Canada, Eastern. 9. Canoes
and canoeing — United States — History — 19th century. 10. Canoes and
canoeing — Canada, Eastern — History — 19th century.
  I. Title. II. Series
  F106.B62 2000
  917.1304'4 — dc21   00-034068

SEASCAPES SERIES

Introduction

George Ward Shannon, Jr., Ph.D.
Director, North Carolina Maritime Museum

It is with great pleasure and pride that the North Carolina Maritime Museum has formed an alliance with Coastal Carolina Press to introduce the North Carolina Maritime Museum's Seascapes Series. Readers of the series will find rich opportunities for learning more about North Carolina's maritime heritage and natural history. The North Carolina Maritime Museum was established in 1975 with the mission of preserving and documenting the maritime heritage and natural history of North Carolina. Over the past twenty-five years the North Carolina Maritime Museum has been driven by its mission. With the institution of this new series of volumes, the museum is taking a further step to educate the public about the critical role the sea has played in all our lives and in the economic well being of North Carolina. The images and text of the volumes of the series will paint a picture of North Carolina's seafaring past for the reader. Whatever the maritime subject matter, all Seascapes Series volumes will share two defining characteristics: they will be educational and designed to engage broad public audiences. We hope that this new series will help the museum preserve important documents and make accounts of historical events accessible to large numbers of interested readers.

INTRODUCTION

TO THE

NEW EDITION

The North Carolina Maritime Museum is proud to present Nathaniel Bishop's *Voyage of the Paper Canoe* as the first offering in its Seascapes Series. The book was chosen for its detailed examination of the Atlantic Coast's 19th century maritime geography, cultures, and waterways. Nathaniel Bishop was an early conservationist, adventurer, and recreational canoeist whose keen observations on native flora, fauna, and their habitats were competently documented. These observations alone would make the book valuable to modern students of this period's maritime environments, but its predominant significance comes from Bishop's insightful documentation of regional lifestyles, folklore, family names, traditions, and vernacular speech. Bishop exhibits a sensitivity, respect, and appreciation for the different cultures and characters he encounters on his voyage. From these encounters, he beautifully portrays the ambience and issues of everyday life in isolated coastal environs as well as in the accessible populated seaside communities.

Why a Paper Canoe?

The legendary sea captain and prolific maritime author Alan Villiers wrote in *Men, Ships, and the Sea*, "Give a man something that floats . . . he will make a boat." Cultural historians and maritime archaeologists have proven this statement true time and again. From the most primitive woven basket-boats and inflated animal hides to dugout canoes, man has found inventive, convenient, and economical ways to traverse bodies of water. The Western World's view of a society's evolution generally assumes the more advanced a culture, the bigger, more durable and complicated their modes of transportation. So, the use of paper as a small craft building material in 19th-century America seems crude to most 20th and 21st-century thinkers. However, this was not the case.

Increased industrialization in both Europe and America during the Victorian Period (1837–1901) created an exponential need for large quantities of paper and prompted needed improvements in paper's then-primitive production methods. These fundamental production changes around the mid-1800s permitted abundant and economical manufacturing of this previously limited raw material. Industrialized nations went wild for this newly available, lightweight, and versatile 'high tech' medium. They made *paper* collars, *paper* suits, *paper* dolls, *paper* railroad-car wheels, *paper* observatory domes, *paper* boats, and inspired Victorian music hall songs such as "The Age of Paper."

Nathaniel Holmes Bishop, III

In 1838, twenty-two years before this 'age of paper,' Nathaniel Bishop was born in Medford, Massachusetts. Bishop became a lifelong adventurer, outdoorsman, and author whose first expedition was to South America as a quiet, redheaded youth of seventeen. His thousand-mile trek across that country was recounted in his first book, *The Pampas and Andes: A Thousand Mile Walk Across South America*, published in 1869. Five years prior to this first publication, he had moved to an area close to Hanover, New Jersey to pursue a livelihood as a cranberry farmer, and by 1872 he had moved to Manahawkin just southwest of Barnegat Bay. It was while living in Manahawkin that Bishop began a plan to emulate another celebrated adventurer and author.

John A. MacGregor

Bishop was greatly influenced by the writings of John A. Mac-Gregor (1825–1892), an English canoeist, outdoorsman, and author. MacGregor wrote three significant books on canoe voyages starting in 1866 with *A Thousand Miles in A Rob Roy Canoe on Rivers and Lakes of Europe* which initiated a world-wide canoe craze that Bishop would eventually augment.

In MacGregor's Victorian England, the rise of the middle class brought with it the new concept of leisure time and tourism. For the Victorians, leisure had to be respectable, productive, and good for both the individual and the country as a whole. This Victorian philosophy can be seen in the dedication of MacGregor's first book,

> *The author's profits from the first and second edition were given to the Royal National Lifeboat Institution and to the Shipwrecked Mariner's Society,*

and is reflected by Bishop in his book's dedication,

> *To the Superintendent, Assistants, Aids and all Employe[e]s of the United States Coast Survey Bureau, for their intelligent efforts and self-denying labors in the service of their country, so patiently and skillfully performed, under many difficulties and dangers.*

MacGregor felt that fledgling tourists visited all the same places and had indistinguishable experiences, when their greatest encounters should be in the unexplored regions along the rivers, streams, and lakes of their own countries.

> *But a mine of rich beauty remains there to be explored, and fresh gems of life and character are waiting there to be gathered. These are not mapped and labeled and ticketed in any handbook yet; and far better so, for the enjoyment of such treasures is enhanced to the best traveler by the energy and pluck required to get at them.*

Energy and Pluck

Bishop answered MacGregor's challenge of 'energy and pluck' by ordering an 18-foot, 300-pound wooden canoe, *Mayeta*, from J.S. Lamson in Bordentown, New Jersey and starting his journey for the Gulf of Mexico from Quebec in 1874. After logging 400 miles, Bishop came to Troy, New York. By chance or fate, he discovered and bought a 58-pound paper canoe from E. Waters & Sons and christened her *Maria Theresa*.

Bishop's paper canoe voyage ended a year later in Florida, and his account was published in 1878. During this period, Bishop was already initiating his next adventure: a cruise down the Ohio and Mississippi Rivers to the Gulf of Mexico in a Barnegat Bay sneakboat or box. This culminated in his third book entitled *Four Months in a Sneak-Box*, published in 1879.

American Canoe Association

After his adventures afield and their subsequent published documentaries, Bishop corresponded with fellow canoe enthusiasts through *Forest and Stream* magazine and suggested the formation of a common organization of American canoe clubs. The formation of sporting clubs was a trait of the Victorian Age, but Bishop's proposal was conceivably a salute to MacGregor, the founder of England's Royal Canoe Club. Nevertheless, whether following in the wake of his English counterpart or in step with the trends of the times, Bishop formed the American Canoe Association in 1880 and served as its secretary for the first six years. The American Canoe Association is today the largest and most active nonprofit paddle sports organization.

Bishop's Later Years

Sometime during the latter half of the 1880s Bishop moved to Toms River, New Jersey and, in spite of all his travels, managed to fall in love and marry Mary Ball. Bishop also found time to become a highly successful cranberry farmer, owning properties in California and Florida, as well as in Toms River. However, he regarded East Water Street, Toms River as his home and lived there the remainder of his life. Bishop died in 1902 and is buried beside his beloved wife, Mary, in Riverside Cemetery.

Bishop's Legacy

Bishop willed the bulk of his estate to Dover Township, New Jersey for a municipal library. Because of legal provisions made by Bishop, the library project was delayed for four decades and not completed until 1941. The Bishop Memorial Library is now part of the Ocean County Library System and houses a vast collection of 'Jerseyana,' the Ocean County Vocational School's Marine Biology Program and, naturally, all of Bishop's books, private papers, photographs, and maps.

In 1983, another young canoeist, Chris Cunningham of Edmonds, Washington, duplicated Bishop's historic voyage in a paper canoe. Even though Bishop's route can be retraced, his ex-

periences cannot be duplicated. Fortunately, we can relive them
through this book and can learn of an earlier maritime America
from the water level perspective of a paper canoe.

—Connie Mason
NORTH CAROLINA MARITIME MUSEUM

ACKNOWLEDGEMENTS, RESOURCES, AND FURTHER READING

American Canoe Association, 7432 Alban Station Blvd., Suite B-232, Springfield, VA 22150.

Bishop Memorial Library, Lois Brown, Librarian, c/o Toms River Branch Library, 101 Washington St., Toms River, NJ 08753.

Ken Cupery, "19th Century Paper Boat Technology; Pasting Together Shreds of Evidence," 1990, unpublished research paper.

Peter J. Guthorn, *The Sea Bright Skiff and Other Jersey Shore Boats*, 1971, Rutgers University Press.

John A. MacGregor, *A Thousand Miles in A Rob Roy Canoe on Rivers and Lakes of Europe*, 1866, London: Sampson, Low, Marston & Company Limited.

Home of the Alligator.

VOYAGE

OF

THE PAPER CANOE:

A GEOGRAPHICAL JOURNEY OF 2500 MILES, FROM
QUEBEC TO THE GULF OF MEXICO,
DURING THE YEARS 1874–5.

BY

NATHANIEL H. BISHOP,

AUTHOR OF "ONE THOUSAND MILES' WALK ACROSS SOUTH AMERICA,"
AND CORRESPONDING MEMBER OF THE BOSTON SOCIETY
OF NATURAL HISTORY, AND OF THE NEW
YORK ACADEMY OF SCIENCES.

BOSTON:
LEE AND SHEPARD, PUBLISHERS.
NEW YORK: CHARLES T. DILLINGHAM.
EDINBURGH: DAVID DOUGLAS.

TO THE

SUPERINTENDENT, ASSISTANTS, AIDS, AND ALL
EMPLOYÉS OF THE

UNITED STATES COAST SURVEY BUREAU,

THE

"VOYAGE OF THE PAPER CANOE"

IS RESPECTFULLY DEDICATED,

AS A SLIGHT EVIDENCE OF THE APPRECIATION BY ITS AUTHOR FOR
THEIR INTELLIGENT EFFORTS AND SELF-DENYING LABORS
IN THE SERVICE OF THEIR COUNTRY, SO PATIENTLY
AND SKILFULLY PERFORMED, UNDER MANY
DIFFICULTIES AND DANGERS.

INTRODUCTION.

THE author left Quebec, Dominion of Canada, July 4, 1874, with a single assistant, in a wooden canoe eighteen feet in length, bound for the Gulf of Mexico. It was his intention to follow the natural and artificial connecting watercourses of the continent in the most direct line southward to the gulf coast of Florida, making portages as seldom as possible, to show how few were the interruptions to a continuous water-way for vessels of light draught, from the chilly, foggy, and rocky regions of the Gulf of St. Lawrence in the north, to the semi-tropical waters of the great Southern Sea, the waves of which beat upon the sandy shores of the southernmost United States. Having proceeded about four hundred miles upon his voyage, the author reached Troy, on the Hudson River, New York state, where for several years E. Waters & Sons had been perfecting the construction of paper boats.

The advantages in using a boat of only fifty-eight pounds weight, the strength and durability of which had been well and satisfactorily tested, could not

be questioned, and the author dismissed his assistant, and "paddled his own canoe" about two thousand miles to the end of the journey. Though
frequently lost in the labyrinth of creeks and marshes
which skirt the southern coast of his country, the
author's difficulties were greatly lessened by the use
of the valuable and elaborate charts of the United
States Coast Survey Bureau, to the faithful exe-
cuters of which he desires to give unqualified and
grateful praise.

To an unknown wanderer among the creeks, rivers,
and sounds of the coast, the courteous treatment of
the Southern people was most gratifying. The
author can only add to this expression an extract
from his reply to the address of the Mayor of St.
Mary's, Georgia, which city honored him with an
ovation and presentation of flags after the completion of his voyage :

"Since my little paper canoe entered southern
waters upon her geographical errand, — from the
capes of the Delaware to your beautiful St. Mary's,
— I have been deeply sensible of the value of
Southern hospitality. The oystermen and fishermen
living along the lonely beaches of the eastern shore
of Maryland and Virginia; the surfmen and light-
house keepers of Albemarle, Pamplico, and Core
sounds, in North Carolina; the ground-nut planters
who inhabit the uplands that skirt the network of
creeks, marshes, ponds, and sounds from Bogue
Inlet to Cape Fear; the piny-woods people, lum-

bermen, and turpentine distillers on the little bluffs
that jut into the fastnesses of the great swamps of the
crooked Waccamaw River; the representatives of
the once powerful rice-planting aristocracy of the
Santee and Peedee rivers; the colored men of the
beautiful sea-islands along the coast of Georgia;
the Floridians living between the St. Mary's River
and the Suwanee — the wild river of song; the
islanders on the Gulf of Mexico where I terminated
my long journey; — all have contributed to make the
'Voyage of the Paper Canoe' a success."

After returning from this paper-canoe voyage, the
author embarked alone, December 2, 1875, in a cedar
duck-boat twelve feet in length, from the head of
the Ohio River, at Pittsburgh, Pennsylvania, and
followed the Ohio and Mississippi rivers over two
thousand miles to New Orleans, where he made a
portage through that city eastwardly to Lake Pont-
chartrain, and rowed along the shores of the Gulf
of Mexico six or seven hundred miles, to Cedar
Keys, Florida, the terminus of his paper-canoe
voyage.

While on these two voyages, the author rowed over
five thousand miles, meeting with but one accident,
the overturning of his canoe in Delaware Bay.
He returned to his home with his boats in good
condition, and his note-books, charts, &c., in an
excellent state of preservation.

At the request of the "Board on behalf of the
United States Executive Department" of the Cen-

tennial Exhibition at Philadelphia, the paper canoe
" Maria Theresa," and the cedar duck-boat " Centennial Republic," were deposited in the Smithsonian
Department of the United States Government building, during the summer and fall of 1876.

The maps, which show the route followed by
the paper canoe, have been drawn and engraved
by contract at the United States Coast Survey Bureau, and are on a scale of $\frac{1}{1.500,000}$. As the work
is based on the results of actual surveys, these
maps may be considered, for their size, the most
complete of the United States coast ever presented
to the public.

Much credit is due to Messrs. Waud and Merrill
for the artistic results of their pencils, and to Messrs.
John Andrew & Son for their skill in engraving the
illustrations.

To the readers of the author's first book of travels, " The Pampas and Andes : a Thousand Miles'
Walk across South America," which journey was
undertaken when he was but seventeen years of
age, the writer would say that their many kind and
appreciative letters have prompted him to send forth
this second book of travels — the " Voyage of the
Paper Canoe."

LAKE GEORGE, WARREN COUNTY, N. Y.,
JANUARY 1, 1878.

CONTENTS.

———•◦•———

CHAPTER I.

THE APPROACHES TO THE WATER-WAY OF THE CONTINENT.

CHAPTER II.

FROM QUEBEC TO SOREL.

CHAPTER III.

FROM THE ST. LAWRENCE RIVER TO TICONDEROGA, LAKE CHAMPLAIN.

CHAPTER IV.

FROM LAKES GEORGE AND CHAMPLAIN TO THE HUDSON RIVER.

CHAPTER V.

THE AMERICAN PAPER BOAT AND ENGLISH CANOES.

CHAPTER VI.

FROM TROY TO PHILADELPHIA.

CHAPTER VII.

FROM PHILADELPHIA TO CAPE HENLOPEN.

CHAPTER VIII.

FROM CAPE HENLOPEN TO NORFOLK, VIRGINIA.

CHAPTER IX.

FROM NORFOLK TO CAPE HATTERAS.

CHAPTER X.

FROM CAPE HATTERAS TO CAPE FEAR, NORTH CAROLINA.

CHAPTER XI.

FROM CAPE FEAR TO CHARLESTON, SOUTH CAROLINA.

CHAPTER XII.

FROM CHARLESTON TO SAVANNAH, GEORGIA.

CHAPTER XIII.

FROM THE SAVANNAH RIVER TO FLORIDA.

CHAPTER XIV.

ST. MARY'S RIVER AND THE SUWANEE WILDERNESS.

CHAPTER XV.

DOWN UPON THE SUWANEE RIVER.

LIST OF MAPS

DRAWN AND ENGRAVED AT THE

UNITED STATES COAST SURVEY BUREAU,

FOR THE "VOYAGE OF THE PAPER CANOE."

———◆◆———

ILLUSTRATIONS.

MAP OF ROUTES
FOLLOWED BY N.H.BISHOP
IN PAPER CANOE "MARIA THERESA"
AND DUCK BOAT "CENTENNIAL REPUBLIC"
1874-1876

Statute Miles

VOYAGE OF THE PAPER CANOE.

CHAPTER I.

THE APPROACHES TO THE WATER-WAY OF THE CONTINENT.

ISLAND OF ST. PAUL. — THE PORTALS OF THE GULF OF ST. LAWRENCE. — THE EXTINCT AUK. — ANTICOSTI ISLAND. — ICEBERGS. — SAILORS' SUPERSTITIONS. — THE ESTUARY OF THE ST. LAWRENCE. — TADOUSAC. — THE SAGUENAY RIVER. — WHITE WHALES. — QUEBEC.

WHILE on his passage to the ports of the St. Lawrence River, the mariner first sights the little island of St. Paul, situated in the waste of waters between Cape Ray, the southwestern point of Newfoundland on the north, and Cape North, the northeastern projection of Cape Breton Island on the south. Across this entrance to the Gulf of St. Lawrence from cape to cape is a distance of fifty-four nautical miles; and about twelve miles east-northeast from Cape North the island of St. Paul, with its three hills and two light-towers, rises from the sea with deep waters on every side.

This wide inlet into the gulf may be called the

I

middle portal, for at the northern end of Newfoundland, between the great island and the
coast of Labrador,. another entrance exists,
which is known as the Straits of Belle Isle,
and is sometimes called "the shorter passage
from England." Still to the south of the middle entrance is another and a very narrow one,
known as the Gut of Canso, which separates
the island of Cape Breton from Nova Scotia.
Through this contracted thoroughfare the tides
run with great force.

One hundred years ago, as the seaman approached the dangerous entrance of. St. Paul,
now brightened at night by its light-towers, his
heart was cheered by the sight of immense
flocks of a peculiar sea-fowl, now extinct.
When he saw upon the water the Great Auk
(*Alca impennis*), which he ignorantly called
"a pengwin," he knew that land was near at
hand, for while he met other species far out
upon the broad Atlantic, the Great Auk, his
"pengwin," kept near the coast. Not only was
this now extinct bird his indicator of proximity
to the land, but so strange were its habits, and
so innocent was its nature, that it permitted
itself to be captured by boat-loads; and thus
were the ships re-victualled at little cost or
trouble. Without any market-value a century
ago, the Great Auk now, as a stuffed skin, rep-
resents a value of fifteen hundred dollars in

gold.   There are but seventy-two specimens of
this bird in the museums of Europe and America, besides a few skeletons, and sixty-five of its
eggs.   It was called in ancient days Gare-fowl,
and was the *Geirfugl* of the Icelander.

Captain Whitbourne, who wrote in the reign
of James the First, quaintly said: "These Pen-
gwins are as bigge as Geese, and flye not, for
they have but a little short wing, and they mul-
tiply so infinitely upon a certain flat island that
men drive them from thence upon a board into
their boats by hundreds at a time, as if God had
made the innocency of so poor a creature to
become such an admerable instrument for the
sustenation of man."

In a copy of the English Pilot, "fourth book,"
published in 1761, which I presented to the
library of the United States Coast Survey, is
found this early description of this now extinct
American bird: "They never go beyond the
bank [Newfoundland] as others do, for they are
always on it, or in it, several of them together,
sometimes more but never less than two together.   They are large fowls, about the size
of a goose, a coal-black head and back, with a
white belly and a milk-white spot under one of
their eyes, which nature has ordered to be under
their right eye."

Thus has the greed of the sailor and pot-
hunter swept from the face of the earth an old

pilot — a trusty aid to navigation. Now the light-house, the fog-gun, and the improved chart have taken the place of the extinct auk as aids to navigation, and the sailor of to-day sees the bright flashes of St. Paul's lights when nearly twenty miles at sea. Having passed the little isle, the ship enters the great Gulf of St. Lawrence, and passes the Magdalen Islands, shaping its course as wind and weather permit towards the dreaded, rocky coast of Anticosti. From the entrance of the gulf to the island of Anticosti the course to be followed is northwesterly about one hundred and thirty-five nautical miles. The island which divides an upper arm of the gulf into two wide channels is one hundred and twenty-three miles long, and from ten to thirty miles wide. Across the entrance of this great arm, or estuary, from the high cape of Gaspé on the southern shore of the mainland to Anticosti in the narrowest place, is a distance of about forty miles, and is called the South Channel. From the north side of the island and near its west end to the coast of Labrador the North Channel is fifteen miles wide. The passage from St. Paul to Anticosti is at times dangerous. Here is an area of strong currents, tempestuous winds, and dense fogs. When the wind is fair for an upward run, it is *the* wind which usually brings misty weather. Then, from the icy regions of the Arctic circle, from the Land of Desolation,

come floating through the Straits of Belle Isle
the dangerous bergs and ice-fields. Early in the
spring these ice rafts are covered with colonies
of seals which resort to them for the purpose of
giving birth to their young. On these icy cra-
dles, rocked by the restless waves, tens of thousands of young seals are nursed for a few days;
then, answering the loud calls of their mothers,
they accompany them into the briny deep, there
to follow the promptings of their instincts. The
loud roarings of the old seals on these ice rafts
can be heard in a quiet night for several miles,
and strike terror into the heart of the superstitious sailor who is ignorant of the origin of
the tumult.

Frequently dense fogs cover the water, and
while slowly moving along, guided only by the
needle, a warning sound alarms the watchful
master. Through the heavy mists comes the
roar of breaking waters. He listens. The dull,
swashy noise of waves meeting with resistance
is now plainly heard. The atmosphere becomes
suddenly chilled: it is the breath of the iceberg!

Then the shrill cry of "All hands on deck!"
startles the watch below from the bunks. Anxiously now does the whole ship's company lean
upon the weather-rail and peer out into the thick
air with an earnestness born of terror. "Surely,"
says the master to his mate, "I am past the Mag-

dalens, and still far from Anticosti, yet we have
breakers; which way can we turn?" The riddle
solves itself, for out of the gloom come whitened
walls, beautiful but terrible to behold.

Those terror-stricken sailors watch the slowly
moving berg as it drifts past their vessel, fearing
that their own ship will be drawn towards it
from the peculiar power of attraction they believe
the iceberg to possess. And as they watch,
against the icy base of the mountain in the sea
the waves beat and break as if expending their
forces upon a rocky shore. Down the furrowed
sides of the disintegrating berg streamlets trickle,
and miniature cascades leap, mingling their
waters with the briny sea. The intruder slowly
drifts out of sight, disappearing in the gloom,
while the sailor thanks his lucky stars that he has
rid himself of another danger. The ill-omened
Anticosti, the graveyard of many seamen, is yet
to be passed. The ship skirts along its southern
shore, a coast destitute of bays or harbors of
any kind, rock-bound and inhospitable.

Wrecks of vessels strew the rocky shores, and
four light-houses warn the mariner of danger.
Once past the island the ship is well within the
estuary of the gulf into which the St. Lawrence
River flows, contributing the waters of the great
lakes of the continent to the sea. As the north
coast is approached the superstitious sailor is
again alarmed if, perchance, the compass-needle

shows sympathy with some disturbing element, the cause of which he believes to exist in the mountains which rise along the shore. He repeats the stories of ancient skippers, of vessels having been lured out of their course by the deviation of the guiding-needle, which succumbed to the potent influence exerted in those hills of iron ore; heeding not the fact that the disturbing agent is the iron on board of his own ship, and not the magnetic oxide of the distant mines.

The ship being now within the estuary of the St. Lawrence River, must encounter many risks before she reaches the true mouth of the river, at the Bic Islands.

The shores along this arm of the gulf are wild and sombre. Rocky precipices frown upon the swift tidal current that rushes past their bases. A few small settlements of fishermen and pilots, like Metis, Father Point, and Rimousky, are discovered at long intervals along the coast.

In these St. Lawrence hamlets, and throughout Lower Canada, a patois is spoken which is unintelligible to the Londoner or Parisian; and these villagers, the descendants of the French colonists, may be said to be a people destitute of a written language, and strangers to a literature.

While holding a commission from Francis the First, king of France, Jacques Cartier discovered the Gulf of St. Lawrence, during his first voyage of exploration in the new world. He entered the gulf on St. Lawrence's day, in the spring of 1534, and named it in honor of the event. Cartier explored no farther to the west than about the mouth of the estuary which is divided by the island of Anticosti. It was during his second voyage, in the following year, that he discovered and explored the great river. Of the desolate shores of Labrador, on the north coast, he said, "It might as well as not be taken for the country assigned by God to Cain."

The distance from Quebec to Cape Gaspé, measured upon a course which a steamer would be compelled to take, is four hundred and seven statute miles. The ship first enters the current of the river St. Lawrence at the two Bic Islands, where it has a width of about twenty miles. By consulting most maps the reader will find that geographers carry the *river* nearly two hundred miles beyond its usual current. In fact, they appropriate the whole estuary, which, in places, is nearly one hundred miles in width, and call it a river — a river which lacks the characteristics of a river, the currents of which vary with the winds and tidal influences, and the waters of which are as salt as those of the briny deep.

Here, in the mouth of the river, at the Bics,

secure anchorage for vessels may be found; but below, in the estuary, for a distance of more than two hundred and forty-five miles, to Gaspé, there is but one port of refuge, that of Seven Islands, on the north coast.

As the ship ascends the river from Bic Islands, a passage of about one hundred and sixty statute miles to Quebec, she struggles against a strong current. Picturesque islands and little villages, such as St. André, St. Anne, St. Rogue, St. Jean, and St. Thomas, relieve the monotony. But very different is the winter aspect of this river, when closed to navigation by ice from November until spring. Of the many tributaries which give strength to the current of the St. Lawrence and contribute to its glory, the Saguenay River with its remarkable scenery is counted one of the wonders of our continent. It joins the great river from the north shore, about one hundred and thirty-four statute miles below Quebec. Upon the left bank, at its mouth, nestles the little village of Tadousac, the summer retreat of the governor-general of the Dominion of Canada.

American history claims for the Roman Catholic church of this settlement an age second only to that of the old Spanish cathedral at St. Augustine, Florida. For three hundred years the storms of winter have beaten upon its walls, but it stands a silent yet eloquent monument of

the pious zeal of the ancient Fathers, who came
to conquer Satan in the wilderness of a new
world.   The Saguenay has become the "Mecca"
of northern tourists, ever attracting them with
its wild and fascinating scenery.   Capes Eternity
and Trinity guard the entrance to Eternity Bay.
The first towers sublimely to a height of eighteen hundred feet, the other is only a little
lower.   A visit to this mysterious river, with its
deep, dark waters and picturesque views, will
repay the traveller for the discomforts of a long
and expensive journey.

Where the turbulent current of the Saguenay
mingles angrily with that of the St. Lawrence,
there may be seen disporting in the waves the
white whale of aquariums, which is not a whale
at all, but a true porpoise (*Delphinopterus ca-
todon*, as he is now called by naturalists), having
teeth in the jaws, and being destitute of the
fringed bone of the whalebone whales.   This
interesting creature is very abundant in the Arctic Ocean on both the Atlantic and Pacific sides,
and has its southern limits in the Gulf of St.
Lawrence, although one is occasionally seen in
the Bay of Fundy, and it is reported to have
been observed about Cape Cod, on the Massachusetts coast.

As the ship nears the first great port of the
St. Lawrence River, the large and well cultivated island of Orleans is passed, and the bold

fortifications of Quebec, high up on the face of
Point Diamond, and flanked by the houses of the
French city, break upon the vision of the mariner. To the right, and below the city, which
Champlain founded, and in which his unknown
ashes repose, are the beautiful Falls of Montmo-
rency, gleaming in all the whiteness of their
falling waters and mists, like the bridal veil of a
giantess. The vessel has safely made her passage, and now comes to anchor in the Basin of
Quebec. The sails are furled, and the heart of
the sailor is merry, for the many dangers which
beset the ship while approaching and entering
the great water-way of the continent are now
over.

GREAT AUK.

CHAPTER II.

FROM QUEBEC TO SOREL.

THE WATER-WAY INTO THE CONTINENT. — THE WESTERN AND
THE SOUTHERN ROUTE TO THE GULF OF MEXICO.—THE MAYETA.
— COMMENCEMENT OF THE VOYAGE. — ASCENT OF THE RIVER
ST. LAWRENCE. — LAKE OF ST. PETER. — ACADIAN TOWN OF
SOREL.

THE canoe traveller can ascend the St. Lawrence River to Lake Ontario, avoiding the
rapids and shoals by making use of seven canals
of a total length of forty-seven miles.   He may
then skirt the shores of Lake Ontario, and enter
Lake Erie by the canal which passes around the
celebrated Falls of Niagara.   From the last great
inland sea he can visit lakes Huron, Michigan,
and, with the assistance of a short canal, the
grandest of all, Superior.   When he has reached
the town of Duluth, at the southwestern end of
Superior, which is the terminus of the Northern
Pacific Railroad, our traveller will have paddled
(following the contours of the land) over two
thousand miles from salt water into the American continent without having been compelled to
make a portage with his little craft.   Let him
now make his first portage westward, over the

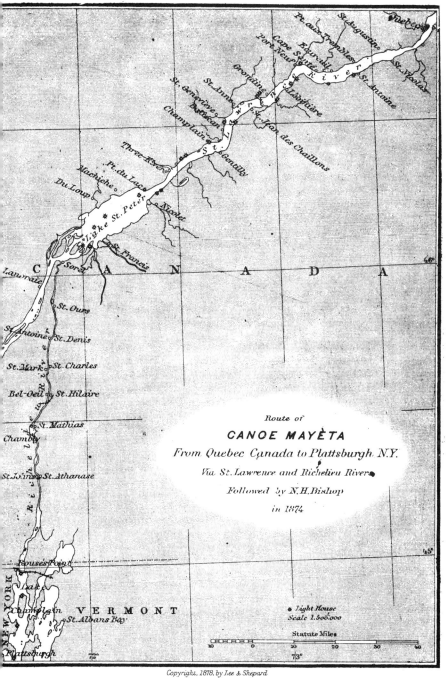

Route of

CANOE MAYÈTA

From Quebec Canada to Plattsburgh, N.Y.

Via St. Lawrence and Richelieu Rivers

Followed by N.H.Bishop

in 1874

⁕ *Light House*
Scale 1.500.000

Statute Miles

railroad one hundred and fifteen miles from Duluth, to the crossing of the Mississippi River at
Brainerd, and launch his boat on the Father of
Waters, which he may descend with but few
interruptions to below the Falls of St. Anthony,
at Minneapolis; or, if he will take his boat by
rail from Duluth, one hundred and fifty-five miles,
to St. Paul, he can launch his canoe, and follow
the steamboat to the Gulf of Mexico. This is
the longest, and may be called the canoeist's
western route to the great Southern Sea. In
St. Louis County, Minnesota, the water from
" Seven Beaver Lakes " flows south-southwest,
and joins the Flood-Wood River; there taking
an easterly course towards Duluth, it empties
into Lake Superior. This is the St. Louis River,
the first tributary of the mighty St. Lawrence
system. From the head waters of the St. Louis
to the mouth of the St. Lawrence at Bic Islands,
where it enters the great estuary, the length of
this great water system, including the great
Lakes, is about two thousand miles. The area thus
drained by the St. Lawrence River is nearly six
millions of square miles. The largest craft can
ascend it to Quebec, and smaller ones to Montreal; above which city, navigation being im-
peded by rapids, the seven canals before mentioned have been constructed that vessels may
avoid this danger while voyaging to Lake Ontario.

The southern and shorter coast route to the gulf leaves the great river at the Acadian town of Sorel, where the quiet Richelieu flows into the St. Lawrence River. Of the two long routes offered me I selected the southern, leaving the other to be traversed at some future time. To follow the contours of rivers, bays, and sounds, a voyage of at least twenty-five hundred miles was before me. It was my intention to explore the connecting watercourses southward, without making a single portage, as far as Cape Henlopen, a sandy headland at the entrance of Delaware Bay; there, by making short portages from one watercourse to another, to navigate along the interior of the Atlantic coast to the St. Mary's River, which is a dividing line between Georgia and Florida. From the Atlantic coast of southern Georgia, I proposed to cross the peninsula of Florida by way of the St. Mary's River, to Okefenokee Swamp; thence, by portage, to the Suwanee River, and by descending that stream (the boundary line of a geographical division — eastern and middle Florida), to reach the coast of the Gulf of Mexico, which was to be the terminal point of my canoe journey. Charts, maps, and sea-faring men had informed me that about twenty-three hundred miles of the trip could be made upon land-locked waters, but about two hundred miles of voyaging must be done upon the open Atlantic Ocean.

As I now write, I smilingly remember how erroneous were my advisers; for, while prosecuting my voyage, I was but once upon the open sea, and then through mistake and for only a few minutes. Had I then known that I could have followed the whole route in a small boat upon strictly interior waters, I should have paddled from the Basin of Quebec in the light paper canoe which I afterwards adopted at Troy, and which carried me alone in safety two thousand miles to the warm regions of the Gulf of Mexico. The counsels of old seamen had influenced me to adopt a large wooden clinker-built, decked canoe, eighteen feet long, forty-five inches beam, and twenty-four inches depth of hold, which weighed, with oars, rudder, mast and sail, above three hundred pounds. The Mayeta was built by an excellent workman, Mr. J. S. Lamson, at Bordentown, New Jersey. The boat was sharp at each end, and the lines from amidships to stem, and from amidships to sternpost, were alike. She possessed that essential characteristic of seaworthiness, abundant sheer. The deck was pierced for a cockpit in the centre, which was six feet long and surrounded by a high combing to keep out water The builder had done his best to make the Mayeta serve for rowing and sailing — a most difficult combination, and one not usually successful.

On the morning of July 4, 1874, I entered

the Basin of Quebec with my wooden canoe and my waterman, one David Bodfish, a "shoreman" of New Jersey. After weeks of preparation and weary travel by rail and by water, we had steamed up the Gulf and the River of St. Lawrence to this our most northern point of departure. We viewed the frowning heights upon which was perched the city of Quebec with unalloyed pleasure, and eagerly scrambled up the high banks to see the interesting old city. The tide, which rises at the city piers eighteen feet in the spring, during the neaps reaches only thirteen feet. Late in the afternoon the incoming tide promised to assist us in ascending the river, the downward current of which runs with torrent-like velocity, and with a depth abreast the city of from sixteen to twenty fathoms. Against this current powerful steamers run one hundred and eighty miles up the river to Montreal in eighteen hours, and descend in fourteen hours, including two hours' stoppages at Sorel and Three Rivers. At six o'clock P. M. we pushed off into the river, which is about two-thirds of a mile wide at this point, and commenced our voyage; but fierce gusts of wind arose and drove us to the shelter of Mr. Hamilton's lumber-yard on the opposite shore, where we passed the night, sleeping comfortably upon cushions which we spread on the narrow floor of the boat. Sunday was to be spent in camp;

but when dawn appeared we were not allowed
to build a fire on the lumber pier, and were
forced to ascend the St. Lawrence in quest of a
retired spot above the landing of St. Croix, on
the right bank of the river. The tide had been
a high one when we beached our boat at the foot
of a bluff. Two hours later the receding tide
left us a quarter of a mile from the current.
The river was fully two miles wide at this point,
and so powerful was its current that steamers
anchored in it were obliged to keep their wheels
slowly revolving to ease the strain on their
anchors. Early on Monday morning we beheld
with consternation that the tide did not reach
our boat, and by dint of hard labor we constructed a railroad from a neighboring fence,
and moved the Mayeta on rollers upon it over
the mud and the projecting reef of rocks some
five hundred feet to the water, then embarking,
rowed close along the shore to avoid the current.
A deep fog settled down upon us, and we were
driven to camp again on the left bank, where a
cataract tumbled over the rocks fifty or more
feet. Tuesday was a sunny day, but the usual
head wind greeted us. The water would rise
along-shore on the flood three hours before the
downward current was checked in the channel
of the river. We could not place any depend-
ence in the regularity of the tides, as strong
winds and freshets in the tributaries influence

them.   Earlier in the season, as a writer remarks, "until the upland waters have all run
down, and the great rivers have discharged the
freshets caused by thawing of the snows in the
spring of the year, this current, in spite of tides,
will always run down."   To the uninitiated the
spectacle is a curious one, of the flood tide rising
and swelling the waters of a great river some
eight to ten feet, while the current at the surface
is rapidly descending the course of the stream.

Finding that the wind usually rose and fell
with the sun, we now made it a rule to anchor
our boat during most of the day and pull against
the current at night.   The moon and the bright
auroral lights made this task an agreeable one.
Then, too, we had Coggia's comet speeding
through the northern heavens, awakening many
an odd conjecture in the mind of my old salt.

In this high latitude day dawned before three
o'clock, and the twilight lingered so long that
we could read the fine print of a newspaper
without effort at a quarter to nine o'clock P. M.
The lofty shores that surrounded us at Quebec
gradually decreased in elevation, and the tides
affected the river less and less as we approached
Three Rivers, where they seemed to cease alto-
gether.   We reached the great lumber station
of Three Rivers, which is located on the left
bank of the St. Lawrence, on Friday evening,
and moved our canoe into quiet waters near the

entrance of Lake of St. Peter. Rain squalls
kept us close under our hatch-cloth till eleven
o'clock A. M. on Saturday, when, the wind being
fair, we determined to make an attempt to reach
Sorel, which would afford us a pleasant camping-
ground for Sunday.

Lake of St. Peter is a shoal sheet of water
twenty-two miles long and nearly eight miles
wide, a bad place to cross in a small boat in
windy weather. We set our sail and sped mer-
rily on, but the tempest pressed us sorely, com-
pelling us to take in our sail and scud under
bare poles until one o'clock, when we double-
reefed and set the sail. We now flew over the
short and swashy seas as blast after blast struck
our little craft. At three o'clock the wind slack-
ened, permitting us to shake out our reefs and
crowd on all sail. A labyrinth of islands closed
the lake at its western end, and we looked with
anxiety to find among them an opening through
which we might pass into the river St. Lawrence again. At five o'clock the wind veered
to the north, with squalls increasing in intensity.
We steered for a low, grassy island, which
seemed to separate us from the river. The wind
was not free enough to permit us to weather it,
so we decided to beach the boat and escape the
furious tempest. But when we struck the marshy
island we kept moving on through the rushes
that covered it, and fairly sailed over its sub-

merged soil into the broad water on the other
side.   Bodfish earnestly advised the propriety of
anchoring here for the night, saying, " It is too
rough to go on; " but the temptation held out
by the proximity to Sorel determined me to
take the risk and drive on.   Again we bounded
out upon rough water, with the screeching tempest upon us.   David took the tiller, while I sat
upon the weather-rail to steady the boat.   The
Mayeta was now to be put to a severe test; she
was to cross seas that could easily trip a boat of
her size; but the wooden canoe was worthy of
her builder, and flew like an affrighted bird over
the foaming waves across the broad water, to
the shelter of a wooded, half submerged island,
out of which rose, on piles, a little light-house.
Under this lee we crept along in safety.   The
sail was furled, never to be used in storm again.
The wind went down with the sinking sun, and
a delightful calm favored us for our row up the
narrowing river, eight miles to the place of destination.

Soon after nine o'clock we came upon the
Acadian town, Sorel, with its bright lights cheerily flashing out upon us as we rowed past its
river front.   The prow of our canoe was now
pointed southward toward the goal of our ambition, the great Mexican Gulf; and we were about
to ascend that historic stream, the lovely Richelieu, upon whose gentle current, two hundred

and sixty-six years before, Champlain had ascended to the noble lake which bears his name,
and up which the missionary Jogues had been
carried an unwilling captive to bondage and to
torture.

We ascended the Richelieu, threading our
way among steam-tugs, canal-boats, and rafts,
to a fringe of rushes growing out of a shallow
flat on the left bank of the river, just above
the town. There, firmly staking the Mayeta
upon her soft bed of mud, secure from danger,
we enjoyed a peaceful rest through the calm
night which followed; and thus ended the rough
passage of one week's duration — from Quebec
to Sorel.

CHAPTER III.

FROM THE ST. LAWRENCE RIVER TO TICONDE-ROGA, LAKE CHAMPLAIN.

THE RICHELIEU RIVER. — ACADIAN SCENES. — ST. OURS. — ST ANTOINE. — ST. MARKS. — BELŒIL. — CHAMBLY CANAL. — ST. JOHNS. — LAKE CHAMPLAIN. — THE GREAT SHIP-CANAL. — DAVID BODFISH'S CAMP. — THE ADIRONDACK SURVEY. — A CANVAS BOAT. — DIMENSIONS OF LAKE CHAMPLAIN. — PORT. KENT. — AUSABLE CHASM. — ARRIVAL AT TICONDEROGA.

QUEBEC was founded by Champlain, July 3, 1680. During his first warlike expedition into the land of the Iroquois the following year, escorted by Algonquin and Montagnais Indian allies, he ascended a river to which was afterwards given the name of Cardinal Richelieu, prime minister of Louis XIII. of France. This stream, which is about eighty miles long, connects the lake (which Champlain discovered and named after himself) with the St Lawrence River at a point one hundred and forty miles above Quebec, and forty miles below Montreal. The waters of lakes George and Champlain flow northward, through the Richelieu River into the St. Lawrence. The former stream flows through a cultivated country, and upon its banks, after leaving Sorel, are situate the little towns of St. Ours, St. Rock, St. Denis, St. Antoine, St. Marks, Belœil, Chambly, and St. Johns.   Small steamers, tug-boats, and rafts pass from the St. Lawrence to Lake Champlain (which lies almost wholly within the United States), following the Richelieu to Chambly, where it is necessary, to avoid rapids and shoals, to take the canal that follows the river's bank twelve miles to St. Johns, where the Canadian custom-house is located. Sorel is called William Henry by the Anglo-Saxon Canadians.   The paper published in this town of seven thousand inhabitants is *La Gazette de Sorel.*   The river which flows past the town is called, without authority, by some geographers, Sorel River, and by others St. Johns, because the town nearest its source is St. Johns, and another town at its mouth is Sorel.   There are about one hundred English-speaking families in Sorel.   The American Waterhouse Machinery supplies the town with water pumped from the river at a cost of one ton of coal per day.   At ten o'clock on Monday morning we resumed our journey up the Richelieu, the current of which was nothing compared with that of the great river we had left.   The average width of the stream was about a quarter of a mile, and the grassy shores were made picturesque by groves of trees and quaintly constructed farm-houses.

It was a rich, pastoral land, abounding in fine herds of cattle.   The country reminded me of

the Acadian region of Grand Pré, which I had
visited during the earlier part of the season.
Here, as there, were delightful pastoral scenes
and rich verdure; but here we still had the Acadian peasants, while in the land of beautiful
Evangeline no longer were they to be found.
The New Englander now holds the titles to
those deserted old farms of the scattered colonists.   Our rowing was frequently interrupted
by heavy showers, which drove us under our
hatch-cloth for protection.   The same large,
two-steepled stone churches, with their unpaint-
ed tin roofs glistening like silver in the sunlight,
marked out here, as on the high banks of the
St. Lawrence River, the site of a village.

Twelve miles of rowing brought us to St. Ours,
where we rested for the night, after wandering
through its shaded and quaint streets.   The village boys and girls came down to see us off the
next morning, waving their kerchiefs, and shouting *"Bon voyage!"* Two miles above the town
we encountered a dam three feet high, which
deepened the water on a shoal above it.   We
passed through a single lock in company with
rafts of pine logs which were on the way to New
York, to be used for spars.   A lockage fee of
twenty-five cents for our boat the lock-master
told us would be collected at Chambly Basin.
It was a pull of nearly six miles to St. Denis,
where the same scene of comfort and plenty pre-

vailed. Women were washing clothes in large iron pots at the river's edge, and the hum of the spinning-wheels issued from the doorways of the farm-houses. Beehives in the well-stocked gardens were filled with honey, and the straw-thatched barns had their doors thrown wide open, as though waiting to receive the harvest. At intervals along the highway, over the grassy hills, tall, white wooden crosses were erected; for this people, like the Acadians of old, are very religious. Down the current floated " pin-flats," a curious scow-like boat, which carries a square sail, and makes good time only when running before the wind. St. Antoine and St. Marks were passed, and the isolated peak of St. Hilaire loomed up grandly twelve hundred feet on the right bank of the Richelieu, opposite the town of Belœil. One mile above Belœil the Grand Trunk Railroad crosses the stream, and here we passed the night. Strong winds and rain squalls interrupted our progress. At Chambly Basin we tarried until the evening of July 16, before entering the canal. Chambly is a watering-place for Montreal people, who come here to enjoy the fishing, which is said to be fair.

We had ascended one water-step at St. Ours. Here we had eight steps to ascend within the distance of one mile. By means of eight locks, each one hundred and ten feet long by twenty-two wide, the Mayeta was lifted seventy-five feet and one inch in height to the upper level of the canal. The lock-masters were courteous, and wished us the usual " *bon voyage!* " This canal was built thirty-four years prior to my visit. By ten o'clock P. M. we had passed the last lock, and went into camp in a depression in the bank of the canal. The journey was resumed at half past three o'clock the following morning, and the row of twelve miles to St. Johns was a delightful one. The last lock (the only one at St. Johns) was passed, and we had a full clearance at the Dominion custom-house before noon.

We were again on the Richelieu, with about twenty-three miles between us and the boundary line of the United States and Canada, and with very little current to impede us. As dusk approached we passed a dismantled old fort, situated upon an island called Ile aux Noix, and entered a region inhabited by the large bull-frog, where we camped for the night, amid the dolorous voices of these choristers. On Saturday, the 18th, at an early hour, we were pulling for the United States, which was about six miles from our camping-ground. The Richelieu widened, and we entered Lake Champlain, passing Fort Montgomery, which is about one thousand feet south of the boundary line. Champlain has a width of three fourths of a mile at Fort Montgomery, and at Rouse's Point expands to two miles and three quarters. The erection of the fort was commenced soon after 1812, but in 1818 the work was suspended, as some one discovered that the site was in Canada, and the cognomen of Fort Blunder was applied. In the Webster treaty of 1842, England ceded the ground to the United States, and Fort Montgomery was finished at a cost of over half a million of dollars.

At Rouse's Point, which lies on the west shore of Lake Champlain about one and one-half miles south of its confluence with the Richelieu, the Mayeta was inspected by the United States custom-house officer, and nothing contraband being discovered, the little craft was permitted to continue her voyage.

At the northern end of the harbor of Rouse's Point is the terminus of the Ogdensburg and the Champlain and St. Lawrence railroads. The Vermont Central Railroad connects with the above by means of a bridge twenty-two hundred feet in length, which crosses the lake. Before proceeding further it may interest the reader of practical mind to know that a very important movement is on foot to facilitate the navigation of vessels between the great Lakes, St. Lawrence River, and Champlain, by the construction of a ship-canal. The Caughnawaga Ship Canal Company, "incorporated by special act of the Dominion of Parliament of Canada, 12th May, 1870," (capital, three million dollars; shares, one hundred dollars each,) with a board of directors composed of citizens of the United States and Canada, has issued its prospectus, from which I extract the following:

" The commissioners of public works, in their report of 1859, approved by government, finally settled the question of route, by declaring that, ' after a patient and mature consideration of all the surveys and reports, we are of opinion that the line following the Chambly Canal and then crossing to Lake St. Louis near Caughnawaga, is that which combines and affords in the greatest degree all the advantages contemplated by this improvement, and which has been approved by Messrs. Mills, Swift, and Gamble.'

" The company's Act of Incorporation is in every respect complete and comprehensive in its details. It empowers the company to survey, to take, appropriate, have and hold, to and for the use of them and their successors, the line and boundaries of a canal between the St. Lawrence and Lake Champlain, to build and erect the same, to select such sites as may be necessary for basins and docks, as may be considered expedient by the directors, and to purchase and dispose of same, with any water-power, as may be deemed best by the directors for the use and profit of the company.

" It also empowers the company to cause their canal to enter into the Chambly Canal, and to widen, deepen, and enlarge the same, not less in size than the present St. Lawrence canals; also the company may take, hold, and use any portion of the Chambly Canal, and the works therewith connected, and all the tolls, receipts, and revenues thereof, upon terms to be settled and agreed upon between the company and the governor in council.

" The cost of the canal, with locks of three hundred feet by forty-five, and with ten feet six inches the mitre-sill, is now estimated at two million five hundred thousand dollars, and the time for its construction may not exceed two years after breaking ground.

" Probably no question is of more vital importance to Canada and the western and eastern United States than the subject of transportation. The increasing commerce of the Great West, the rapidity with which the population has of late flowed into that vast tract of country to the west and northwest of lakes Erie, Michigan, Huron, and Superior, have served to convince all well-informed commercial men that the means of transit between that country and the seaboard are far too limited even for the present necessities of trade; hence it becomes a question of universal interest how the products of the field, the mine, and the forest can be most cheaply forwarded to the consumer. Near the geographical centre of North America is a vast plateau two

thousand feet above the level of the sea, drained
by the Mississippi to the south, by the St. Lawrence to the east, and by the Saskatchewan and
McKenzie to the north. This vast territory
would have been valueless but for the water
lines which afford cheap transport between it
and the great markets of the world.

"Canada has improved the St. Lawrence by
canals round the rapids of the St. Lawrence, and
by the Welland Canal, connecting lakes Erie and
Ontario, twenty-eight miles in length with a fall
of two hundred and sixty feet, capable of passing vessels of four hundred tons. The St. Lawrence, from the east end of Lake Ontario, has a
fall of two hundred and twenty feet, overcome
by seven short canals of an aggregate length of
forty-seven miles, capable of passing vessels of
six hundred and fifty tons. The Richelieu River
is connected with Lake Champlain by a canal
of twelve miles from Chambly. A canal of one
mile in length, at the outlet of Lake Superior,
connects that lake with Lake Huron, and has
two locks, which will pass vessels of two thousand tons. New York has built a canal from
Buffalo, on Lake Erie, and from Oswego, on
Lake Ontario, to Albany, on the Hudson River,
of three hundred and sixty and of two hundred
and nine miles, capable of passing boats of two
hundred and ten tons; and she has also constructed a canal from the Hudson River into

Lake Champlain of sixty-five miles, which can pass boats of eighty tons.

"Such is the nature of the navigation between tide-water on the Hudson and St. Lawrence and the upper lakes. The magnitude of the commerce of the Northwest has compelled the enlargement of the Erie and Oswego canals from boats of seventy-eight to two hundred and ten tons, while the St. Lawrence and Welland canals have also been enlarged since their first construction. A further enlargement of the Erie and Champlain canals is now strongly urged in consequence of the want of the necessary facilities of transport for the ever increasing western trade. The object of the Caughnawaga Ship-canal is to connect Lake Champlain with the St. Lawrence by the least possible distance, and with the smallest amount of lockage. When built, it will enable the vessel or propeller to sail from the head of lakes Superior or Michigan without breaking bulk, and will enable such vessels to land and receive cargo at Burlington and Whitehall, from whence western freights can be carried to and from Boston, and throughout New England, by railway cheaper than by any other route.

"It will possess the advantage, when the Welland Canal is enlarged and the locks of the St. Lawrence Canal lengthened, of passing vessels of eight hundred and fifty tons' burden, and with that size of vessel (impossible on any other route) of improved model, with facilities for loading and discharging cargoes at both ends of the route, in the length of the voyage without transshipment, in having the least distance between any of the lake ports and a seaport, and in having the shortest length of taxed canal navigation. The construction of the Caughnawaga Canal, when carried out, will remedy the difficulties which now exist and stand in the way of an uninterrupted water communication between the western states and the Atlantic seaboard."

From Rouse's Point we proceeded to a picturesque point which jutted into the lake below Chazy Landing, and was sheltered by a grove of trees into which we hauled the Mayeta. Bodfish's woodcraft enabled him to construct a wigwam out of rails and rubber blankets, where we quietly resided until Monday morning. The owner of the point, Mr. Trombly, invited us to dinner on Sunday, and exhibited samples of a ton of maple sugar which he had made from the sap of one thousand trees.

On Monday, July 20th, we rowed southward. Our route now skirted the western shore of Lake Champlain, which is the eastern boundary of the great Adirondack wilderness. Several of the tributaries of the lake take their rise in this region, which is being more and more visited by the hunter, the fisherman, the artist, and the tourist, as its natural attractions are becoming known to the public.   The geodetical survey of the northern wilderness of New York state, known as the Adirondack country, under the efficient and energetic labors of Mr. Verplanck Colvin, will cover an area of nearly five thousand square miles.   In his report of the great work he eloquently says:

" The Adirondack wilderness may be considered the wonder and the glory of New York. It is a vast *natural* park, one immense and silent forest, curiously and beautifully broken by the gleaming waters of a myriad of lakes, between which rugged mountain-ranges rise as a sea of granite billows.   At the northeast the mountains culminate within an area of some hundreds of square miles; and here savage, treeless peaks, towering above the timber line, crowd one another, and, standing gloomily shoulder to shoulder, rear their rocky crests amid the frosty clouds.   The wild beasts may look forth from the ledges on the mountain-sides over unbroken woodlands stretching beyond the reach of sight — beyond the blue, hazy ridges at the horizon. The voyager by the canoe beholds lakes in which these mountains and wild forests are reflected like inverted reality; now wondrous in their dark grandeur and solemnity, now glorious in resplendent autumn color of pearly beauty.   Here — thrilling sound to huntsman --

echoes the wild melody of the hound, awakening the solitude with deep-mouthed bay as he pursues the swift career of deer. The quavering note of the loon on the lake, the mournful hoot of the owl at night, with rarer forest voices, have also to the lover of nature their peculiar charm, and form the wild language of this forest.

"It is this region of lakes and mountains — whose mountain core is well shown by the illustration, 'the heart of the Adirondacks' — that our citizens desire to reserve forever as a public forest park, not only as a resort of rest for themselves and for posterity, but for weighty reasons of political economy. For reservoirs of water for the canals and rivers; for the amelioration of spring floods by the preservation of the forests sheltering the deep winter snows; for the salvation of the timber, — our only cheap source of lumber supply should the Canadian and western markets be ruined by fires, or otherwise lost to us, — its preservation as a state forest is urgently demanded. To the number of those chilly peaks amid which our principal rivers take their rise, I have added by measurement a dozen or more over four thousand feet in height, which were before either nameless, or only vaguely known by the names given them by hunters and trappers.

"It is well to note that the final hypsometrical computations fully affirm my discovery that in Mount Haystack we have another mountain of five thousand feet altitude. It may not be uninteresting also to remark that the difference between the altitudes of Mount Marcy and Mount Washington of the White Mountains of New Hampshire is found to be quite eight hundred feet. Mount Marcy, Mount MacIntyre, and Mount Haystack are to be remembered as the three royal summits of the state.

"The four prominent peaks are —

Mount Marcy { Mount *Tahawus* — " I cleave the clouds," . . . }	5,402.65
Mount Haystack, ...	5,006.73
Mount MacIntyre, ...	5,201.80
Mount Skylight, ...	4,977.76."

If the general reader will pardon a seeming digression to gratify the curiosity of some of my boating friends, I will give from the report of the Adirondack Survey Mr. Colvin's account of his singular boat, — one of the lightest yet constructed, and weighing only as much as a hunter's double-barrelled gun.

Mr. Colvin says:

"I also had constructed a canvas boat, of my own invention, for use in the interior of the wilderness on such of the mountain lakes as were inaccessible to boats, and which it would be necessary to map. This boat was peculiar; no more frame being needed than could be readily cut in thirty minutes in the first thicket. It was twelve feet long, with thin sheet brass prows, riveted on, and so fitted as to receive the keelson, prow pieces, and ribs (of boughs), when required; the canoe being made water-proof with pure rubber gum, dissolved in naphtha, rubbed into it."

Page 43 of Mr. Colvin's report informs the reader how well this novel craft served the purpose for which it was built.

" September 12 was devoted to levelling and topographical work at Ampersand Pond, a solitary lake locked in by mountains, and seldom visited. There was no boat upon its surface, and in order to complete the hydrographical work we had now, of necessity, to try my portable canvas boat, which had hitherto done service as bed or tent. Cutting green rods for ribs, we unrolled the boat and tied them in, lashing poles for gunwales at the sides, and in a short time our canvas canoe, buoyant as a cork, was floating on the water. The guides, who had been unable to believe that the flimsy bag they carried could be used as a boat, were in ecstasies.   Rude but efficient paddles were hastily hewn from the nearest tree, and soon we were all gliding in our ten-pound boat over the waves of Ampersand, which glittered in the morning sunlight.   To the guides the boat was something astonishing; they could not refrain from laughter to find that they were really afloat in it, and pointed with surprise at the waves, which could be seen *through* the boat, rippling against its sides. With the aid of the boat, with prismatic compass and sextant, I was able to secure an excellent map of the lake; and we almost succeeded in catching a deer, which was driven into the lake by a strange hound. The dog lost the trail at the water, and desiring to put him on the track, we paddled to him. He scrambled into the boat with an air of satisfaction, as if he had always travelled in just such a thing. Soon we had regained the trail, and making the mountains echo to his voice, he again pursued the deer on into the trackless forest.

" Continuing our work, we passed down into the outlet, where, in trying to effect a landing, we suddenly came face to face with a large panther, which had evidently been watching us. He fled at our approach.

" Our baggage was quickly packed, and the temporary frame of the canoe having been taken out and thrown away, we rolled up our boat and put it in the bottom of a knapsack. . . . The same day by noon we reached Cold Brook again, here navigable. In an hour and a half we had reframed the canvas, cut out two paddles from a dry cedar-tree, had dinner, loaded the boat, and were off, easily gliding down stream to the Saranac River. Three men, the heaped baggage in the centre, and the solemn hound, who seemed to consider himself part of the company, sitting upright near the prow, forming in all a burden of about one third of a ton, was a severe test of the green boughs of which we had made the frame.

"Ascending the Saranac River, we struck out into the broad Saranac Lake, some six miles in length, and though the winds and the waves buffeted us, the canvas sides of the boat responding elastically to each beat of the waves, we got safely along till near the Sister Islands, when, the wind blowing very fresh, the white-capped rollers began to pitch into the boat. The exertions of the guides brought us under the lee shore, and at evening we disembarked at Martin's."

Geographies, guide-books, and historical works frequently give the length of Lake Champlain as one hundred and fifty, or at the least one hundred and forty miles. These distances are not correct. The lake proper begins at a point near Ticonderoga and ends not far from the boundary line of the United States and Canada. Champlain is not less than one hundred nor more than one hundred and twelve miles long. The Champlain Canal, which connects the river that flows from Whitehall into the lake with the Hudson River, is sixty-four miles long, ending at the Erie Canal at Junction Lock, near Troy. From Junction Lock to Albany, along the Erie Canal, it is six miles: or seventy miles from Whitehall to Albany by canal route. This distance has frequently been given as fifty-one miles.

From the United States boundary line southward it is a distance of seven miles to Isle la
Motte, which island is five and a half miles long
by one and three quarters wide, with a light-
house upon its northwest point.   From the New
York shore of Monti Bay, across the end of Isle
la Motte to St. Albans, Vermont, is a distance of
thirteen and a half miles.   Two miles south of
the island, on the west shore, is Point au Roche
light; and two miles and three quarters south of
it is Rocky Point, the terminus of Long Point.
Next comes Treadwell Bay, three miles across;
then two miles further on is Cumberland Head
and its light-house.   West from Cumberland,
three miles across a large bay, is Plattsburgh, at
the mouth of the Saranac River, a town of five
thousand inhabitants.   In this vicinity Commodore Macdonough fought the British fleet in 1814.
These are historic waters, which have witnessed
the scene of many a bloody struggle between
French, English, and Indian adversaries.   Off
Cumberland Head, and dividing the lake, is
Grand Isle, twelve miles in length and from
three to four in width.

The village of Port Kent is near the mouth of
the Ausable River, which flows out of the northern Adirondack country.   A few miles from the
lake is the natural wonder, the Ausable Chasm,
which is nearly two miles in length.   The river
has worn a channel in the Potsdam sandstone

formation to a depth, in places, of two hundred
feet. Between high walls of rock the river is
compressed in one place to ten feet in breadth,
and dashes wildly over falls and rapids on its
way to Lake Champlain. It is said to rival the
famous Swiss Gorge du Triant.

Schuyler's Island, upon the shore of which we
passed Tuesday night, is nearly in the latitude of
Burlington, Vermont. The distance from Port
Douglass on the west, to Burlington on the east
side of Champlain, over an open expanse of
water, is nine miles and three quarters. We
breakfasted by starlight, and passed Ligonier's
Point early in the day. One mile and a half east
of it is the group of little islands called Four
Brothers. The lake grew narrower as we rowed
southward, until, after passing Port Henry Iron
Works, and the high promontory of Crown Point,
upon which are the ruins of the French Fort
Frederic, built in 1731, it has a width of only
two miles.

At eight o'clock P. M. we dropped anchor under the banks of Ticonderoga, not far from the
outlet of Lake George. It is four miles by road
between the two lakes. The stream which connects them can be ascended from Champlain
about two miles to the Iron Works, the remainder of the river being filled with rapids.

A railroad now (1867) connects lakes George
and Champlain, over which an easy portage can

be made. The ruined walls of Fort Ticonderoga are near the railroad landing. A little
south of this the lake grows so narrow as to resemble a river. At its southern end, twenty-
four miles from Ticonderoga, is situated the
town of Whitehall, where the Champlain and
Hudson River Canal forms a junction with Lake
Champlain. This long river-like termination of
Champlain gave to the Indians the fancy of calling it *Tisinondrosa* — " the tail of the lake; "
which in mouths inexperienced with the savage
tongue became corrupted into Ticonderoga.

Wednesday broke upon us a glorious day.
Proceeding three miles to Patterson's Landing,
into the " tail of the lake," I left the Mayeta to
explore on foot the shores of Lake George,
promising Bodfish to join him at Whitehall when
my work should be finished.

CHAPTER IV.

FROM LAKES GEORGE AND CHAMPLAIN TO THE HUDSON RIVER.

THE DISCOVERY OF LAKE GEORGE BY FATHER JOGUES. — A PE-
DESTRIAN JOURNEY. — THE HERMIT OF THE NARROWS. —
CONVENT OF ST. MARY'S OF THE LAKE. — THE PAULIST
FATHERS. — CANAL–ROUTE FROM LAKE CHAMPLAIN TO AL-
BANY. — BODFISH RETURNS TO NEW JERSEY. — THE LITTLE
FLEET IN ITS HAVEN OF REST.

IN the last chapter I gave, from seemingly
good authority, the appellation of the narrow
terminal water of the southern end of Lake
Champlain, "the tail of the lake." Another
authority, in describing Lake George, says:
" The Indians named the lake, on account of the
purity of its waters, *Horican,* or 'silvery water;'
they also called it *Canderi-oit,* or 'the tail of
the lake,' on account of its connecting with Lake
Champlain." Cooper, in his "Last of the Mo-
hicans," says: "It occurred to me that the
French name of the lake was too complicated,
the American too commonplace, and the Indian
too unpronounceable for either to be used fa-
miliarly in a work of fiction." So *he* called it
Horican.

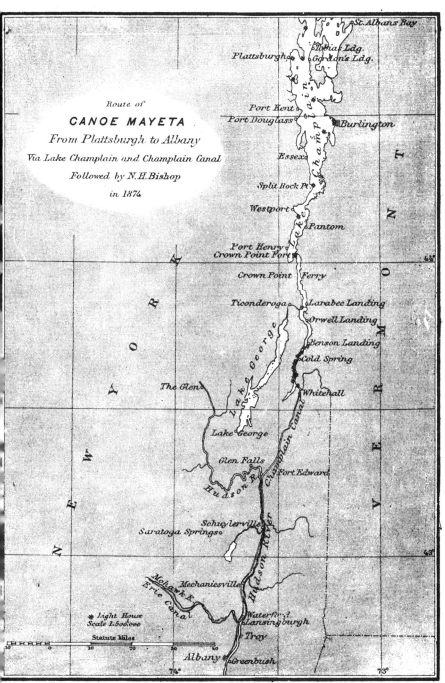

Route of

CANOE MAYETA

From Plattsburgh to Albany

Via Lake Champlain and Champlain Canal

Followed by N. H. Bishop

in 1874

St. Albans Bay

Tobias Ldg.

Plattsburgh

Gordon's Ldg.

Port Kent

Port Douglass

Burlington

Essex

Split Rock Pt.

Westport

Pantom

Port Henry

Crown Point Fort

Crown Point   Ferry

Ticonderoga

Larabee Landing

Orwell Landing

Benson Landing

Cold Spring

Lake George

Whitehall

The Glen

Lake George

Glen Falls

Fort Edward

Hudson R.

Champlain Canal

Schuylerville

Saratoga Springs

Mohawk R.

Mechanicsville

Erie Canal

Hudson River

Waterford

Lansingburgh

Troy

Albany

Greenbush

★ light House

Scale 1:500,000

Statute Miles

10   0   10   20   30   40

NEW YORK

VERMONT

History furnishes us with the following facts
in regard to the discovery of the lake. While
journeying up the St. Lawrence in a fleet of
twelve canoes, on a mission to the friendly Huron aborigines, Father Isaac Jogues and his two
friends, *donnés* of the mission, René Goupil and
Guillaume Couture, with another Frenchman,
were captured at the western end of Lake of
St. Peter by a band of Iroquois, which was on a
marauding expedition from the Mohawk River
country, near what is now the city of Troy. In
the panic caused by the sudden onslaught of the
Iroquois, the unconverted portion of the thirty-
six Huron allies of the Frenchmen fled into the
woods, while the christianized portion defended
the white men for a while. A reinforcement of
the enemy soon scattered these also, but not
until the Frenchmen and a few of the Hurons
were made captive. This was on the 2d of
August, 1642.

According to Francis Parkman, the author of
" The Jesuits in North America," the savages
tortured Jogues and his white companions, strip-
ping off their clothing, tearing out their finger-
nails with their teeth, and gnawing their fingers
with the fury of beasts. The seventy Iroquois
returned southward, following the River Richelieu, Lake Champlain, and Lake George, *en
route* for the Mohawk towns. Meeting a war
party of two hundred of their own nation on

one of the islands of Champlain, the Indians formed two parallel lines between which the captives were forced to run for their lives, while the savages struck at them with thorny sticks and clubs.   Father Jogues fell exhausted to the ground, bathed in his own blood, when fire was applied to his body.   At night the young warriors tormented the poor captives by opening their wounds and tearing out their hair and beards.   The day following this night of torture the Indians and their mangled captives reached the promontory of Ticonderoga, along the base of which flowed the limpid waters, the outlet of Lake George.   Here the party made a portage through the primeval forests, carrying their canoes and cargoes on their backs, when suddenly there broke upon their view the dark blue waters of a beautiful lake, which Mr. Parkman thus eloquently describes:

"Like a fair naiad of the wilderness it slumbered between the guardian mountains that breathe from crag and forest the stern poetry of war.   But all then was solitude; and the clang of trumpets, the roar of cannon, and the deadly crack of the rifle had never as yet awakened their angry echoes.   Again the canoes were launched and the wild flotilla glided on its way, now in the shadow of the heights, now on the broad expanse, now among the devious channels of the Narrows, beset with woody islets where the hot air was redolent of the pine, the spruce, and the cedar, — till they neared that tragic shore where, in the following century, New England rustics baffled the soldiers of Dieskau, where Montcalm planted his batteries, where the red cross waved so long amid the smoke, and where, at length, the summer night was hideous with carnage, and an honored name was stained with a memory of blood.   The Indians landed at or near the future site of Fort William Henry, left their canoes, and with their prisoners began their march for the nearest Mohawk town."

Father Jogues lived among his captors until the fall of 1643, when he escaped in a vessel from the Dutch settlement of Rensselaerswyck (Albany), to which place the Iroquois had gone to trade with the inhabitants.   He arrived at the Jesuit college of Rennes, France, in a most destitute condition, on the 5th of January, 1644, where he was joyfully received and kindly cared for.   When he appeared before Queen Anne of Austria, the woman who wore a diadem thought it a privilege to kiss his mutilated hands.   In the Roman Catholic church a deformed or mutilated priest cannot say mass; he must be a perfect man in body and mind before the Lord.   Father Jogues wished to return to his old missionary field; so, to restore to him his lost right of saying mass, the Pope granted his prayer by a special

dispensation. In the spring of 1643 he returned
to the St. Lawrence country to found a new mission, to be called the Mission of Martyrs. His
Superior at Montreal ordered him to proceed to
the country of the Mohawks, and in company
with Sieur Bourdon, a government engineer, and
six Indians, he followed the Richelieu and Champlain, which the savages called "the doorway
of the country," until the little party stood on
the northern end of Lake George, on the evening of Corpus Christi; and with the catholic
spirit of the Jesuit missionary he christened it
Lac St. Sacrement, and this name it bore for a
whole century. On the 18th of October, 1646,
the tomahawk of the savage ended the life
of Father Jogues, who, after suffering many tor-
tures and indignities from his Iroquois captors,
died in their midst while working for their salvation in his field of Christian labor.

The right of a discoverer to name new lakes
and rivers is old and unquestioned. A missionary of the cross penetrated an unexplored wilderness and found this noblest gem of the lower
Adirondacks, unknown to civilized man. Impressed with this sublime work of his Creator,
the martyred priest christened it St. Sacrement.
One hundred years later came troops of soldiers
with mouths filled with strange oaths, cursing
their enemies. What respect had *they* for the
rights of discoverers or martyred missionaries?

So General Johnson, " an ambitious Irishman," discarded the Christian name of the lake and replaced it with the English one of George. He did not name it after St. George, the patron saint of England, of whom history asserts that he " was identical with a native of either Cappadocia or Cilicia, who raised himself by flattery of the great from the meanest circumstances to be purveyor of bacon for the army, and who was put to death with two of his ministers by a mob, for peculations, A. D. 361; " but he took that of a sensual king, George of England, in order to advance his own interests with that monarch.

For more than a century Lake George was the highway between Canada and the Hudson River. Its pure waters were so much esteemed as to be taken regularly to Canada to be consecrated and used in the Roman Catholic churches in baptismal and other sacred rites. The lake was frequently occupied by armies, and the forts George and William Henry, at the southern end, possess most interesting historical associations. The novelist Cooper made Lake George a region of romance. To the young generation of Americans who yearly visit its shores it is an El Dorado, and the very air breathes love as they glide in their light boats over its pellucid waters, adding to the picturesqueness of the scene, and supplying that need ever felt, no matter what the natural beauty, — the presence of man. I believe even the Garden of Eden itself could not have been perfect till among its shady groves fell the shadows of our first parents. The cool retreats, the jutting promontories, the moss-covered rocks against which the waves softly break, — if these had tongues, they would, like Tennyson's Brook, " go on forever," for surely they would never have done telling the tender tales they have heard. Nor would it be possible to find a more fitting spot for the cultivation of love and sentiment than this charming lake affords; for Nature seems to have created Lake George in one of her happiest moments. This lake is about thirty-four miles long, and varies in width from one to four miles. Its greatest depth is about the same as that of Champlain. It possesses (like all the American lakes when used as fashionable watering-places) the usual three hundred and sixty-five islands.

When I left the Mayeta I followed a narrow footpath to a rough mountain road, which in turn led me through the forests towards Lake George. In an isolated dell I found the home of one Levi Smith, who piloted me through the woods to the lake, and ferried me in a skiff across to Hague, when I dined at the hotel, and resumed my journey along the shores to Sabbath Day Point, where at four o'clock P. M. a steamer on its trip from Ticonderoga to the south end of the lake stopped and took me on board. We steamed southward to where high mountains shut in the lake, and for several miles threaded the "Narrows" with its many pretty islands, upon one of which Mr. J. Henry Hill, the hermit-artist, had erected his modest home, and where he toiled at his studies early and late, summer and winter. Three goats and a squirrel were his only companions in this lonely but romantic spot.

During one cold winter, when the lake was frozen over to a depth of two feet, and the forests were mantled in snow, Mr. Hill's brother, a civil engineer, made a visit to this icy region, and the two brothers surveyed the Narrows, making a correct map of that portion of the lake, with all its islands carefully located. Mr. Hill afterwards made an etching of this map, surrounding it with an artistic border representing objects of interest in the locality.

Late in the afternoon the steamer landed me at Crosbyside, on the east shore, about a mile from the head of the lake, resting beneath the shady groves of which I beheld one of the most charming views of Lake George. Early the following morning I took up my abode with a farmer, one William Lockhart, a genial and eccentric gentleman, and a relation of Sir Walter Scott's son-in-law. Mr. Lockhart's little cottage is half a mile north of Crosbyside, and near the high bluff which Mr. Charles O'Conor, the distinguished lawyer of New York city, presented to the Paulist Fathers, whose establishment is on Fifty-ninth Street in that metropolis. Here the members of the new Order come to pass their summer vacations, bringing with them their theological students. The Paulists are hard workers, visiting and holding "missions" in Minnesota, California, and other parts of the United States. They seem to feel forcibly the truth expressed in these lines, which are to be found in "Aspirations of Nature," a work written by the founder of their order, Father Hecker: "Existence is not a dream, but a solemn reality. Life was not given to be thrown away on miserable sophisms, but to be employed in earnest search after truth."

Mr. Lockhart kindly offered to escort me to the convent of St. Mary's of the Lake; and after following the mountain road for a quarter of a mile to the north of the cottage of my companion, we entered the shady grounds of the convent and were kindly received on the long piazza by the Father Superior, Rev. A. F. Hewit, who introduced me to several of his co-laborers, a party of them having just returned from an excursion to the Harbor Islands at the northern end of the Narrows, which property is owned by the Order. I was told that the members of this new religious establishment numbered about thirty, and that all but four were converts from our Protestant faith.

'Their property in New York city is probably worth half a million of dollars, and the Sunday schools under their charge contain about fifteen hundred scholars.   Here, among others, I saw Father D——, who gave up his distinguished position as instructor of the art of war at the Military Academy of West Point, to become a soldier of the Cross, preferring to serve his Master by preaching the gospel of peace to mankind.   Under an overhanging rock at a little distance were conversing, most happily, two young priests, who a few years before had fought on opposite sides during the civil strife which resulted in the preservation of the Great Republic.

A mathematician and astronomer from the Cambridge and also from a government observatory, who had donned the cassock, gave me much valuable information in regard to the mountain peaks of Lake George,* which he had care-

---

* Heights of mountains of Lake George, New York state, obtained by Rev. George M. Searle, C. S. P.

Finch, between Buck and Spruce, 1595 feet.

Cat-Head, near Bolton, 1640 feet.

Prospect Mountain, west of Lake George village, 1730 feet.

Spruce, near Buck Mountain, 1820 feet.

Buck, east shore, south of Narrows, 2005 feet.

Bear, between Buck and Black, 2200 feet.

Black, the monarch of Lake George, 2320 feet.

From another authority I find that Lake Champlain is ninety-three feet above the Atlantic tide-level, and that Lake George is two hundred and forty feet above Lake Champlain, or three hundred and thirty-three feet above the sea.

fully studied and accurately measured. Through his courtesy and generosity I am enabled to give on the preceding page the results of his labors.

The interesting conversation was here interrupted by the tolling of the convent bell. A deep silence prevailed, as, with uncovered heads and upon bended knees, the whole company most devoutly crossed themselves while repeating a prayer. I felt much drawn towards a young priest with delicate and refined features, who now engaged me in conversation. He was an adept in all that related to boats. He loved the beautiful lake, and was never happier than when upon its mirrored surface, except when laboring at his duties among the poor of the ninth district of New York. The son of a distinguished general, he inherited rare talents, which were placed at his Saviour's service. His Christianity was so liberal, his aspirations so noble, his sympathies so strong, that I became much interested in him; and when I left the lake, shortly after, he quietly said, "When you return next summer to build your cottage, let me help you plan the boat-house." But when I returned to the shores of Lake George, after the completion of my voyage to the Gulf of Mexico, no helping hand was there, and I built my boat-house unassisted; for the gentle spirit of the missionary Paulist had gone to God who gave it, and Father Rosencranz was receiving his reward.

When I joined my travelling companion, David Bodfish, he grievously inveighed against the community of Whitehall because some dishonest boatmen from the canal had appropriated the stock of pipes and tobacco he had laid in for his three or four days' voyage to Albany. " Sixty cents' worth of new pipes and tobacco," said David, in injured tones, " is a great loss, and a Bodfish never was worth anything at work without his tobacco. I used to pour *speerits* down to keep my speerits up, but of late years I have depended on tobacco, as the speerits one gets nowadays isn't the same kind we got when I was a boy and worked in old Hawkin Swamp."

Canal voyaging, after one has experienced the sweet influences of lakes George and Champlain, is indeed monotonous. But to follow connecting watercourses it was necessary for the Mayeta to traverse the Champlain Canal (sixty-four) and the Erie Canal (six miles) from Whitehall to Albany on the Hudson River, a total distance of seventy miles.

There was nothing of sufficient interest in the passage of the canal to be worthy of record save the giving way of a lock-gate, near Troy, and the precipitating of a canal-boat into the vortex of waters that followed. By this accident my boat was detained one day on the banks of the canal. On the fourth day the Mayeta ended her services by arriving at Albany, where, after a journey of four hundred miles, experience had taught me that I could travel more quickly in a lighter boat, and more conveniently and economically without a companion. It was now about the first week in August, and the delay which would attend the building of a new boat especially adapted for the journey of two thousand miles yet to be travelled would not be lost, as by waiting a few weeks, time would be given for the malaria on the rivers of New Jersey, Delaware, and Maryland, and even farther south, to be eradicated by the fall frosts. David returned to his New Jersey home a happy man, invested with the importance which attaches itself to a great traveller. I had unfortunately contributed to Mr. Bodfish's thirst for the marvellous by reading to him at night, in our lonely camp, Jules Verne's imaginative "Journey to the Centre of the Earth." David was in ecstasies over this wonderful contribution to fiction. He preferred fiction to truth at any time. Once, while reading to him a chapter of the above work, his credulity was so challenged that he became excited, and broke forth with, "Say, boss, how do these big book-men larn to lie so well? does it come nat'ral to them, or is it got by edication?" I have since heard that when Mr. Bodfish arrived in the pine-wood regions of New Jersey he related to his friends his adventures "in furrin parts," as he styled the Dominion of Canada,

and so interlaced the *facts* of the cruise of the
Mayeta with the *fancies* of the "Journey to the
Centre of the Earth," that to his neighbors the
region of the St. Lawrence has become a country of awful and mysterious associations, while
the more knowing members of the community
which David honors with his presence are firmly
convinced that there never existed such a boat
as the Mayeta save in the wild imagination of
David Bodfish.

Mr. Bodfish's fictitious adventures, as related
by him, covered many thousand miles of canoe
voyaging. He had penetrated the region of ice
beyond Labrador, and had viewed with com-
placency the north pole, which he found to be
a pitch-pine spar that had been erected by
the Coast Survey "to measure pints from."
He roundly censured the crews of whale-ships
which had mutilated this noble government
work by splitting much of it into kindling-wood.
Fortunately about two-thirds of Mr. Bodfish's
audience had no very clear conceptions of the
character of the north pole, some of them having
ignored its very existence. So they accepted
this portion of his narrative, while they rejected
the most reasonable part of his story.

The Mayeta was sent to Lake George, and
afterwards became a permanent resident. Two
years later her successor, the Paper Canoe, one
of the most happy efforts of the Messrs. Waters,

of Troy, was quietly moored beside her; and soon after there was added to the little fleet a cedar duck-boat, which had carried me on a second voyage to the great southern sea. Here, anchored safely under the high cliffs, rocked gently by the loving waters of Lake George, rest these faithful friends. They carried me over five thousand miles, through peaceful rivers and surging seas. They have shared my dangers; they now share my peace.

ANCHORED AT LAST.

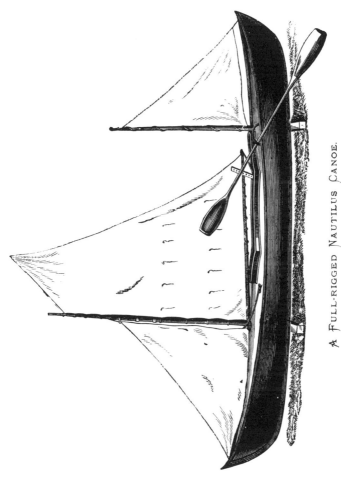

A Full-rigged Nautilus Canoe.

CHAPTER V.

THE AMERICAN PAPER BOAT AND ENGLISH CANOES.

THE PECULIAR CHARACTER OF THE PAPER BOAT. — THE HISTORY OF THE ADOPTION OF PAPER FOR BOATS. — A BOY'S INGENU- ITY. — THE PROCESS OF BUILDING PAPER BOATS DESCRIBED. — COLLEGE CLUBS ADOPTING THEM. — THE GREAT VICTORIES WON BY PAPER OVER WOODEN SHELLS IN 1876.

INQUIRIES regarding the history and dura- bility of paper boats occasionally reach me through the medium of the post-office. After all the uses to which paper has been put during the last twenty years, the public is yet hardly convinced that the flimsy material, paper, can successfully take the place of wood in the con- struction of light pleasure-boats, canoes, and racing shells. Yet the idea has become an ac- complished fact. The success of the victorious paper shells of the Cornell College navy, which were enlisted in the struggles of two seasons at Saratoga, against no mean antagonists, — the col- lege crews of the United States, — surely proves that in strength, stiffness, speed, and fineness of model, the paper boat is without a rival.

When used in its own peculiar sphere, the

improved paper boat will be found to possess the following merits: less weight, greater strength, stiffness, durability, and speed than a wooden boat of the same size and model; and the moulded paper shell will retain the delicate lines so essential to speed, while the brittle wooden shell yields more or less to the warping influences of sun and moisture. A comparison of the strength of wood and paper for boats has been made by a writer in the Cornell Times, a journal published by the students of that celebrated New York college:

" Let us take a piece of wood and a piece of paper of the same thickness, and experiment with, use, and abuse them both to the same extent. Let the wood be of one-eighth of an inch in thickness — the usual thickness of shell-boats, and the paper heavy pasteboard, both one foot square. Holding them up by one side, strike them with a hammer, and observe the result. The wood will be cracked, to say the least; the pasteboard, whirled out of your hand, will only be dented, at most. Take hold and bend them: the wood bends to a certain degree, and then splits; the pasteboard, bent to the same degree, is not affected in the least. Take a knife and strike them: the wood is again split, the pasteboard only pierced. Place them on the water: the wood floats for an indefinite time; the pasteboard, after a time, soaks, and finally sinks, as was to be expected. But suppose we soak the pasteboard in marine glue before the experiment, then we find the pasteboard equally as impervious to the water as wood, and as buoyant, if of the same weight; but, to be of the same weight, it must be thinner than the wood, yet even then it stands the before-mentioned tests as well as when thicker; and it will be found to stand all tests much better than wood, even when it weighs considerably less.

" Now, enlarging our pieces, and moulding them into boats of the same weight, we find the following differences: Wood, being stiff and liable to split, can only be moulded into comparative form. Paper, since it can be rendered perfectly pliable, can be pressed into any shape desirable; hence, any wished-for fineness of lines can be given to the model, and the paper will assume the identical shape, after which it can be water-proofed, hardened, and polished. Paper neither swells, nor shrinks, nor cracks, hence it does not leak, is always ready for use, always serviceable. As to cost, there is very little difference between the two; the cost being within twenty-five dollars, more or less, the same for both. Those who use paper boats think them very near perfection; and surely those who have the most to do with boats ought to know, prejudice aside, which is the best."

An injury to a paper boat is easily repaired by a patch of strong paper and a coating of shellac

put on with a hot iron. As the paper boat is
a novelty with many people, a sketch of its early
history may prove interesting to the reader. Mr.
George A. Waters, the son of the senior member
of the firm of E. Waters & Sons, of Troy, New
York, was invited some years since to a masquer-
ade party. The boy repaired to a toy shop to
purchase a counterfeit face; but, thinking the
price (eight dollars) was more than he could
afford for a single evening's sport, he borrowed
the mask for a model, from which he produced a
duplicate as perfect as was the original. While
engaged upon his novel work, an idea impressed
itself upon his ingenious brain. "Cannot," he
queried, "a paper shell be made upon the wooden
model of a boat? And will not a shell thus produced, after being treated to a coat of varnish,
float as well, and be lighter than a wooden boat?"

This was in March, 1867, while the youth was
engaged in the manufacture of paper boxes.
Having repaired a wooden shell-boat by covering the cracks with sheets of stout paper cemented
to the wood, the result satisfied him; and he immediately applied his attention to the further
development of his bright idea. Assisted by his
father, Mr. Elisha Waters, the enterprise was
commenced " by taking a wooden shell, thirteen
inches wide and thirty feet long, as a mould,
and covering the entire surface of its bottom and
sides with small sheets of strong Manila paper,

glued together, and superposed on each other, so that the joints of one layer were covered by the middle of the sheet immediately above, until a sheet of paper had been formed one-sixteenth of an inch in thickness. The fabric thus constructed, after being carefully dried, was removed from the mould and fitted up with a suitable frame, consisting of a lower keelson, two inwales, the bulkhead; in short, all the usual parts of the frame of a wooden shell, except the timbers, or ribs, of which none were used — the extreme stiffness of the skin rendering them unnecessary. Its surface was then carefully waterproofed with suitable varnishes, and the work was completed. Trials proved that, rude as was this first attempt compared with the elegant craft now turned out from paper, it had marked merits, among which were, its remarkable stiffness, the symmetry of the hull with respect to its long axis, and the smoothness of the water-surface."

A gentleman, who possesses excellent judgment and long experience in all that relates to paper boats, furnishes me with the following valuable information, which I feel sure will interest the reader.

"The process of building the paper shell-boat is as follows: The dimensions of the boat having been determined upon, the first step is to construct a wooden model, or form, an exact facsimile of the desired boat, on which to mould

the paper skin. For this purpose the lines of the
boat are carefully drawn out of the full size, and
from the drawings thus made the model is prepared. It is built of layers of well-seasoned
pine, securely fastened together to form one solid
mass; which, after having been laid up of the
general outline required, is carefully worked off,
until its surface, which is made perfectly smooth,
exactly conforms to the selected lines, and its
beam, depth, and length are those of the given
boat. During the process of its construction,
suitable rabbets are cut to receive the lower keelson, the two inwales, and the bow and stern
deadwoods, which, being put in position, are
worked off so that their surfaces are flush with
that of the model, and forming, as it were, an
integral part of it. It being important that these
parts should, in the completed boat, be firmly
attached to the skin, their surface is, at this part
of the process, covered with a suitable adhesive
preparation.

"The model is now ready to be covered with
paper. Two kinds are used: that made from the
best Manila, and that prepared from pure unbleached linen stock; the sheets being the full
length of the model, no matter what that may
be. If Manila paper is used, the first sheet is
dampened, laid smoothly on the model, and
securely fastened in place by tacking it to certain rough strips attached to its upper face.

Other sheets are now superposed on this and on each other, and suitably cemented together; the number depending upon the size of the boat and the stiffness required. If linen paper is used, but one sheet is employed, of such weight and dimensions that, when dry, it will give just the thickness of skin necessary. Should the surface of the model be concave in parts, as in the run of boats with square sterns for instance, the paper is made to conform to these surfaces by suitable convex moulds, which also hold the paper in place until, by drying, it has taken and will retain the desired form. The model, with its enveloping coat of paper, is now removed to the dry-room. As the paper skin dries, all wrinkles disappear, and it gradually assumes the desired shape. Finally, when all moisture has been evaporated, it is taken from the mould an exact fac-simile of the model desired, exceedingly stiff, perfectly symmetrical, and seamless.

"The paper is now subjected to the water-proof process, and the skin, with its keelson, inwales, and dead-woods attached, is then placed in the carpenter's hands, where the frame is completed in the usual manner, as described for wooden boats. The paper decks being put on, it is then ready for the brass, iron, and varnish work. As the skins of these boats (racing-shells) vary from one-sixteenth of an inch in the singles, to one-twelfth of an inch in the six-oared outriggers, the wooden frame becomes necessary to support and keep them in shape. In applying this invention to gigs, dingys, canoes, and skiffs, a somewhat different method is adopted. Since these boats are subjected to much hard service, and must be so constructed as to permit the occupant to move about in them as is usual in such craft, a light and strong frame of wood is prepared, composed of a suitable number of pairs of ribs, with stem and stern pieces cut from the natural crooks of hackmatack roots. These are firmly framed to two gunwales and a keelson, extending the length of the boat; the whole forming the skeleton shape of the desired model. The forms for these boats having been prepared, as already described for the racing-shells, and the frame being let into this form, so that the outer surface of the ribs, stem and stern pieces will conform with its outer surface, the paper skin is next laid upon it. The skin, manufactured from new, unbleached linen stock, is carefully stretched in place, and when perfectly dry is from one-tenth to three-sixteenths of an inch thick. Removed from the model, it is water-proofed, the frame and fittings completed, and the boat varnished. In short, in this class of boats, the shape, style, and finish are precisely that of wooden ones, of corresponding dimensions and class, except that for the usual wooden sheathing is substituted the paper skin as described.

" The advantages possessed by these boats over
those of wood are:

" By the use of this material for the skins of
racing-shells, where experience has demonstrated
the smooth bottom to be the best, under-water
lines of any degree of fineness can be developed,
which cannot successfully be produced in those
of wood, even where the streaks are so reduced
in thickness that strength, stiffness, and durability are either wholly sacrificed or greatly im-
paired.   In the finer varieties of ' dug-outs '
equally fine lines can be obtained; but so delicate
are such boats, if the sides are reduced to three-
sixteenths of an inch or less in thickness, that it
is found practically impossible to preserve their
original forms for any length of time.   Hence,
so far as this point is concerned, it only remains
for the builder to select those models which
science, guided by experience, points out as the
best.

" The paper skin, after being water-proofed, is
finished with hard varnishes, and then presents a
solid, perfectly smooth, and horny surface to the
action of the water, unbroken by *joint*, *lap*, or
seam.   This surface admits of being polished as
smooth as a coach-panel or a mirror.   Unlike
wood, *it has no grain to be cracked or split*, *it
never shrinks*, and, paper being one of the best
of non-conductors, no ordinary degree of heat
or cold affects its shape or hardness, and hence

these boats are admirably adapted for use in all climates.   As the skin absorbs no moisture, *these boats gain no weight by use*, and, having no moisture to give off when out of the water, they do not, like wooden boats, show the effect of exposure to the air by leaking.   They are, therefore, in this respect always prepared for service.

" The strength and stiffness of the paper shells are most remarkable.   To demonstrate it, a single shell of twelve inch beam and twenty-eight feet long, fitted complete with its outriggers, the hull weighing twenty-two pounds, was placed on two trestles eight feet apart, in such a manner that the trestles were each the same distance from the centre of the cockpit, which was thus entirely unsupported.   A man weighing one hundred and forty pounds then seated himself in it, and remained in this position three minutes.   The deflection caused by this strain, being accurately measured, was found to be one-sixteenth of an inch at a point midway between the supports.   If this load, applied under such abnormal conditions, produced so little effect, we can safely assume that, when thus loaded and resting on the water, supported throughout her whole length, and the load far more equally distributed over the whole frame, there would be no deflection whatever.

" Lightness, when combined with a proper, stiff-

ness and strength, being a very desirable quality,
it is here that the paper boats far excel their wood-
en rivals. If two shells are selected, the one of
wood and the other with a paper skin and deck,
as has been described, *of the same dimensions
and equally stiff*, careful experiment proves that
the wooden one will be *thirty per cent. the
heaviest*. If those of the *same dimensions and
equal weight* are compared, the paper one will
be found to exceed the wooden one in stiffness
and in capacity to resist torsional strains in the
same proportion. Frequent boasts are made that
wooden shells can be and are built much lighter
than paper ones; and if the quality of lightness
alone is considered, this is true; yet when the
practical test of *use* is applied, such extremely
light wooden boats have always proved, and will
continue to prove, failures, as here this quality
is only *one* of a number which combine to make
the boat serviceable. A wooden shell whose
hull weighs twenty-two pounds, honest weight,
is a very fragile, short-lived affair. A paper
shell of the same dimensions, and of the same
weight, will last as long, and do as much work,
as a wooden one whose hull turns the beam at
thirty pounds.

"An instance of their remarkable strength is
shown in the following case. In the summer of
1870, a single shell, while being rowed at full
speed, with the current, on one of our princi-

pal rivers, was run into the stone abutment of a bridge. The bow struck squarely on the obstacle, and such was the momentum of the mass that the oarsman was thrown directly through the flaring bow of the cockpit into the river. Witnesses of the accident who were familiar with wooden shells declared that the boat was ruined; but, after a careful examination, only the bow-tip was found to be twisted in a spiral form, and the washboard broken at the point by the oarsman as he passed between the sides. Two dollars covered the cost of repair. Had it been a wooden shell the shock would have crushed its stem and splintered the skin from the bow to the waist."

Old and cautious seamen tried to dissuade me from contracting with the Messrs. Waters for the building of a stout paper canoe for my journey. Harvard College had not adopted this " newfangled notion" at that time, and Cornell had only begun to think of attempting to out-row other colleges at Saratoga by using paper boats. The Centennial year of the independence of the United States, 1876, settled all doubts as to the value of the result of the years of toil of the inventors of the paper boat. During the same year the incendiary completed his revengeful work by burning the paper-boat manufactory at Troy. The loss was a heavy one; but a few weeks later these unflinching men were able to

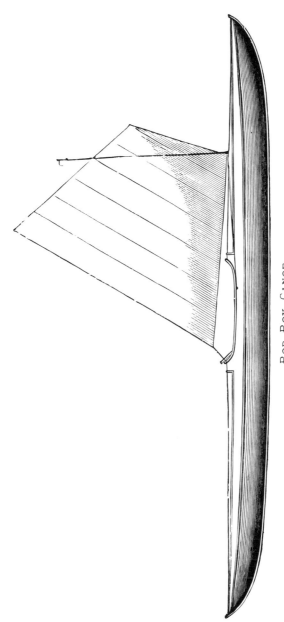

ROB ROY CANOE.

record the following victories achieved that single season by their boats.

The races won by the paper boats were:

The Intercollegiate Championship :
                    Freshmen and University.

The International Championship at Saratoga :
                    Singles, Doubles, and Fours.

The National Championship, N. A. of A. O. :
                    Singles, Doubles, and Fours.

The World's Championship at Centennial Exhibition :
                    Singles, Doubles, and Fours.

The Professional Championship of the United States.

And every other important race of the season, besides receiving the highest honors at the Centennial Exhibition. The right to make boats of paper in Canada and in the United States is exclusively held by the Messrs. Waters, and they are the only manufacturers of paper boats in the world.

It is not many years since Mr. Macgregor, of London, built the little Rob Roy canoe, and in it made the tour of interesting European waters. His example was followed by an army of tourists, and it is now a common thing to meet canoe voyagers in miniature flotillas upon the watercourses of our own and foreign lands. Mr. W. Baden-Powell, also an Englishman, perfected the model of the Nautilus type of canoe, which possesses a great deal of sheer with fullness of bow, and is therefore a better boat for rough

water than the Rob Roy.   The New York Canoe
Club, in 1874, had the Nautilus for their model.
We still need a distinctive American type for our
waters, more like the best Indian canoe than the
European models here presented.   These modern yacht-like canoes are really improved *kyaks*,
and in their construction we are much indebted
to the experience of the inhabitants of the Arctic
Circle.   Very few of the so-called Rob Roy canoes, built in the United States, resemble the
original perfected boat of Mr. Macgregor — the
father of modern canoe travelling.   The illustrations given of English canoes are from import-
ed models, and are perfect of their type.

NOTE TO PAGE 72. — The author has been criticised by technical
canoeists for using oars on a canoe. On this cruise, experience proved
that the paddle could be used effectively only two miles out of every
three. Head winds and seas frequently drive the paddler into camp,
while the adaptive cruiser pushes on with oar and outrigger, and avoids
the loss of many hours. Many canoeists exploring our broad watercourses have adopted the oar as an auxiliary, — the paddle properly
taking the precedence. We are progressing. The canoeist of 1882 may
follow the teachings of common-sense *vs.* unauthorized technical criticisms. Oars on a light paddling canoe are out of place; but are a
most effective power on a heavy cruising canoe, insuring a successful
voyage.

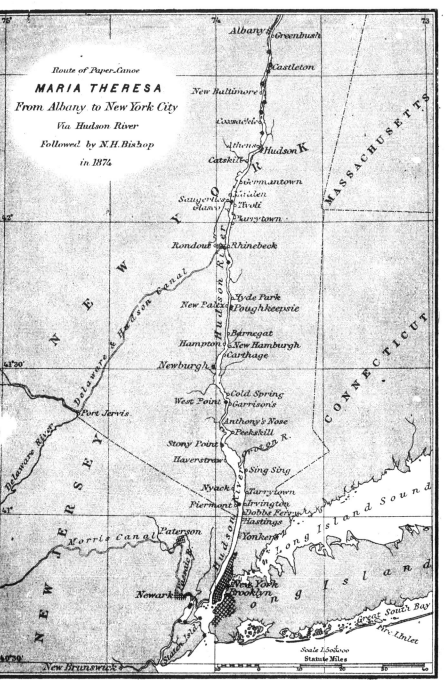

Route of Paper Canoe

MARIA THERESA

From Albany to New York City

Via Hudson River

Followed by N.H.Bishop

in 1874

Scale 1,500,000
Statute Miles

CHAPTER VI.

TROY TO PHILADELPHIA.

PAPER CANOE MARIA THERESA. — THE START. — THE DESCENT OF THE HUDSON RIVER. — CROSSING THE UPPER BAY OF NEW YORK. — PASSAGE OF THE KILLS. — RARITAN RIVER. — THE CANAL ROUTE FROM NEW BRUNSWICK TO THE DELAWARE RIVER. — FROM BORDENTOWN TO PHILADELPHIA.

MY canoe of the English "Nautilus" type was completed by the middle of October; and on the cold, drizzly morning of the 21st of the same month I embarked in my little fifty-eight pound craft from the landing of the paper-boat manufactory on the river Hudson, two miles above Troy. Mr. George A. Waters put his own canoe into the water, and proposed to escort me a few miles down the river. If I had any misgivings as to the stability of my paper canoe upon entering her for the first time, they were quickly dispelled as I passed the stately Club-house of the Laureates, which contained nearly forty shells, *all* of paper.

The dimensions of the Maria Theresa were: length, fourteen feet; beam, twenty-eight inches; depth, amidships, nine inches; height of bow from horizontal line, twenty-three inches; height of stern, twenty inches. The canoe was one-eighth of an inch in thickness, and weighed fifty-eight pounds. She was fitted with a pair of steel outriggers, which could be easily un-shipped and stowed away. The oars were of spruce, seven feet eight inches long, and weighed three pounds and a quarter each. The double paddle, which was seven feet six inches in length, weighed two pounds and a half. The mast and sail — which are of no service on such a miniature vessel, and were soon discarded — weighed six pounds. When I took on board at Philadelphia the canvas deck-cover and the rubber strap which secured it in position, and the outfit, — the cushion, sponge, provision-basket, and a fifteen-pound case of charts, — I found that, with my own weight included (one hundred and thirty pounds), the boat and her cargo, all told, provisioned for a long cruise, fell considerably short of the weight of three Saratoga trunks containing a very modest wardrobe for a lady's four weeks' visit at a fashionable watering-place.

The rain ceased, the mists ascended, and the sunlight broke upon us as we swiftly descended upon the current of the Hudson to Albany. The city was reached in an hour and a half. Mr. Waters, pointing his canoe northward, wished me *bon voyage*, and returned to the scene of the triumphs of his patient labors, while I settled down to a steady row southward. At Albany, the capital of the state, which is said to be one hundred and fifty miles distant from New York city, there is a tidal rise and fall of one foot.

A feeling of buoyancy and independence came over me as I glided on the current of this noble stream, with the consciousness that I now possessed the right boat for my enterprise. It had been a dream of my youth to become acquainted with the charms of this most romantic river of the American continent. Its sources are in the clouds of the Adirondacks, among the cold peaks of the northern wilderness; its ending may be said to be in the briny waters of the Atlantic, for its channel-way has been sounded outside of the sandy beaches of New York harbor in the bosom of the restless ocean. The highest types of civilized life are nurtured upon its banks. Noble edifices, which contain and preserve the works of genius and of mechanical art, rear their proud roofs from among these hills on the lofty sites of the picturesque Hudson. The wealth of the great city at its mouth, the metropolis of the young nation, has been lavished upon the soil of the river's borders to make it even more beautiful and more fruitful. What river in America, along the same length of coast-lines as from Troy to New York (one hundred and fifty-six miles), can rival in natural beauty and artificial applications of wealth the lovely Hudson? " The Hudson River," says its genial historian, Mr. Lossing, "from its birth among the mountains to its marriage with the ocean, measures a distance of full three hundred miles."

Captain John Smith's friend, the Englishman Henry Hudson, while in the employ of the Dutch East India Company, in his vessel of ninety tons, the Half-Moon, being in search of a northwest passage south of Virginia, cast anchor outside of Sandy Hook, September 3, 1609, and on the 11th passed up through the Narrows into the present bay of New York. Under the firm conviction that he was on his way to the long-sought Cathay, a day later he entered the Hudson River, where now stands the proud metropolis of America. As the Half-Moon ascended the river the water lost its saltness, and by the time they were anchored where the city of Albany now stands all hopes of Cathay faded from the heart of the mariner. Englishmen called this river in honor of its discoverer, but the Dutch gave it the name of North River, after the Delaware had been discovered and named South River. Thus, while in 1609 Samuel Champlain was exploring the lake which bears his name, Hudson was ascending his river upon the southern water-shed. The historian tells us that these bold explorers penetrated the wilderness, one from the north and the other from the south, to within one hundred miles of each other.

The Aboriginal Type (Kayak.)

The Improved Type (Maria Theresa Canoe.)

The same historian (Dr. Lossing) says: "The most remote source of the extreme western branch of our noble river is Hendricks Spring, so named in honor of Hendricks Hudson. We found Hendricks Spring in the edge of a swamp, cold, shallow, about five feet in diameter, — shaded by trees, shrubbery, and vines, and fringed with the delicate brake and fern. Its waters, rising within half a mile of Long Lake, and upon the same summit-level, flow southward to the Atlantic more than three hundred miles; while those of the latter flow to the St. Lawrence, and reach the same Atlantic a thousand miles away to the far northeast."

Since Dr. Lossing visited the western head of the Hudson River, the true and highest source of the stream has probably been settled by a gentleman possessing scientific acquirements and inflexible purpose. On the plateau south of Mount Marcy, State-Surveyor Colvin found the little Lake Tear-of-the-Clouds to be the loftiest sheet of water in the state, — four thousand three hundred and twenty-six feet above the sea, — and proved it to be the lake-head of the great river Hudson. A second little pond in a marsh on a high plateau, at the foot of Mount Redfield, was also discovered, — "margined and embanked with luxuriant and deep sphagnous moss," — which was named by the party Moss Lake. It was found to flow into the Hudson.

A beautiful little bivalve shell, three-sixteenths of an inch in diameter, of an undescribed species, was found in the pellucid water, and thus a new shell was handed over to conchology, and a new river source to geography, in the same hour. This pool is four thousand three hundred and twelve feet above tide-water, and only a few feet lower than its sister, Tear-of-the-Clouds — the highest source of the Hudson.

Should the state of New York adopt Mr. Colvin's suggestion, to reserve six hundred square miles of the Adirondack region for a public park, the pool Tear-of-the-Clouds will be within the reservation. The waters of these baby fountains are swollen by contributions from the streams, ponds, and lakes of the Adirondack wilderness, until along the banks of Fishing Brook, a tributary of the Hudson, the water is utilized at the first saw-mill. A few miles lower down the forests are vexed by the axe of the lumbermen, and logs are floated down the river one hundred miles to Glens Falls, where the State Dam and Great Boom are located. Half a million logs have been gathered there in a single spring.

It was upon the Hudson that the first successful steamboat, built by Robert Fulton, made its voyage to Albany, the engine having been built by Watt & Bolton, in England.

From Mr. Lossing we obtain the following.

" The Clermont was one hundred feet long, twelve feet wide, and seven feet deep. The following advertisement appeared in the Albany Gazette on the 1st of September, 1807:

"The North River steamboat will leave Paulus Hook (Jersey City) on Friday, the 4th of September, at 9 in the morning, and arrive at Albany on Saturday at 9 in the afternoon. Provisions, good berths, and accommodations are provided. The charge to each passenger is as follows :

To Newburgh, ...	3 Dollars. . .	Time, 14 hours.
" Poughkeepsie, . . .	4 "	" 17 "
" Esopus, ...	5 "	" 20 "
" Hudson, ...	5½ "	" 30 "
" Albany, ...	7 " . . . ·	" 36 " ."

The trip, which was made against a strong head wind, was entirely successful. The large steamers can now make the trip from New York to Albany in about twelve hours.

As I pulled easily along the banks of the river, my eyes feasted upon the gorgeous coloring of the autumnal foliage, which formed a scene of beauty never to be forgotten. The rapid absorption of oxygen by the leaves in the fall months produces, in northern America, these vivid tints which give to the country the appearance of a land covered with a varied and brilliant garment, " a coat of many colors." A soft, hazy light pervaded the atmosphere, while at the same time the October air was gently exhilarating to the nervous system. At six o'clock P. M. the canoe arrived at Hudson City, which is on the east bank of the river, and I completed a row of thirty-eight statute miles, according to local authority; but in reality forty-nine miles by the correct charts of the United States Coast Survey. After storing the Maria Theresa in a shed, I repaired to a dismal hotel for the night.

At seven o'clock the next morning the river was mantled in a dense fog, but I pushed off and guided myself by the sounds of the running trains on the Hudson River Railroad. This corporation does such an immense amount of freighting that, if their freight trains were connected, a continuous line of eighty miles would be constructed, of which sixteen miles are always in transit day and night. Steamboats and tugs with canal-boats in tow were groping about the river in the misty darkness, blowing whistles every few minutes to let people know that the pilot was not sleeping at the wheel. There was a grand clearing up at noon; and as the sun broke through the mist, the beautiful shores came into view like a vivid flame of scarlet, yellow, brown, and green. It was the death-song of summer, and her dying notes the tinted leaves, each one giving to the wind a sad strain as it softly dropped to the earth, or was quickly hurled into space.

A few miles south of Hudson City, on the west bank, the Catskill stream enters the river.

From this point the traveller may penetrate the picturesque country of the Appalachian range, where its wild elevations were called *Onti Ora*, or " mountains of the sky," by the aborigines.

Roundout, on the right bank of the Hudson, is the terminus of the Delaware and Hudson Canal, which connects it with Port Jervis on the Delaware, a distance of fifty-four miles. This town, the outlet of the coal regions, I passed after meridian. As I left Hudson on the first of the flood-tide, I had to combat it for several hours; but I easily reached Hyde Park Landing (which is on the left bank of the stream and, by local authority, thirty-five miles from Hudson City) at five o'clock P. M. The wharf-house sheltered the canoe, and a hotel in the village, half a mile distant on the high plains, its owner. I was upon the river by seven o'clock the next morning. The day was varied by strong gusts of wind succeeded by calms. Six miles south of Hyde Park is the beautiful city of Pough-keepsie with its eighteen thousand inhabitants, and the celebrated Vassar Female College. Eight miles down the river, and on the same side, is a small village called New Hamburg. The rocky promontory at the foot of which the town is built is covered with the finest arbor vitæ forest probably in existence. Six miles below, on the west bank, is the important city of Newburg, one of the termini of the New York and Erie

Railroad. Four miles below, the river narrows and presents a grand view of the north entrance of the Highlands, with the Storm King Mountain rising fully one thousand five hundred feet above the tide. The early Dutch navigators gave to this peak the name of *Boter-burg* (Butter-Hill), but it was rechristened Storm King by the author N. P. Willis, whose late residence, Idlewild, commands a fine view of Newburg Bay.

When past the Storm King, the Crow-Nest and the almost perpendicular front of Kidd's Plug Cliff tower aloft, and mark the spot where Kidd (as usual) was supposed to have buried a portion of that immense sum of money with which popular belief invests hundreds of localities along the watercourses of the continent. Now the Narrows above West Point were entered, and the current against a head-wind made the passage unusually exciting. The paper canoe danced over the boiling expanse of water, and neared the west shore about a mile above the United States Military Academy, when a shell, from a gun on the grounds of that institution, burst in the water within a few feet of the boat. I now observed a target set upon a little flat at the foot of a gravelly hill close to the beach. As a second, and finally a third shell exploded near me, I rowed into the rough water, much disgusted with cadet-practice and military etiquette. After dark the canoe was landed on the deck of a schooner which was discharging slag or cinder at Fort Montgomery Landing. I scrambled up the hill to the only shelter that could be found, a small country store owned by a Captain Conk who kept entertainment for the traveller. Rough fellows and old crones came in to talk about the spooks that had been seen in the neighboring hills. It was veritable " Sleepy Hollow " talk. The physician of the place, they said, had been " skert clean off a bridge the other night."

Embarking the following morning from this weird and hilly country, that prominent natural feature, Anthony's Nose, which was located on the opposite shore, strongly appealed to my imagination and somewhat excited my mirth. One needs a powerful imagination, I thought, to live in these regions where the native element, the hill-folk, dwell so fondly and earnestly upon the ghostly and mysterious. Three miles down the river, Dunderberg, " the thundering mountain," on the west bank, with the town of Peekskill on the opposite shore, was passed, and I entered Haverstraw Bay, the widest part of the river. " Here," says the historian, " the fresh and salt water usually contend, most equally, for the mastery; and here the porpoise is often seen in large numbers sporting in the summer sun. Here in the spring vast numbers of shad are caught while on their way to spawning-beds in fresh-water coves." Haverstraw Bay was crossed, and

Tarrytown passed, when I came to the picturesque little cottage of a great man now gone from among us. Many pleasant memories of his tales rose in my mind as I looked upon Sunnyside, the home of Washington Irving, nestled in the grove of living green, its white stuccoed walls glistening in the bright sunlight, and its background of grand villas looming up on every side. At Irvington Landing, a little further down the river, I went ashore to pass Sunday with friends; and on the Monday following, in a dense fog, proceeded on my route to New York.

Below Irvington the far-famed "Palisades," bold-faced precipices of trap-rock, offer their grandest appearance on the west side of the Hudson. These singular bluffs, near Hoboken, present a perpendicular front of three hundred or four hundred feet in height. Piles of broken rock rest against their base: the contribution of the cliffs above from the effects of frost and sun.

While approaching the great city of New York, strong squalls of wind, blowing against the ebb-tide, sent swashy waves into my open canoe, the sides of which, amidships, were only five or six inches above water; but the great buoyancy of the light craft and its very smooth exterior created but little friction in the water and made her very seaworthy, when carefully watched and handled, even without a deck of canvas or wood. While the canoe forged ahead through the troubled waters, and the breezes loaded with the saltness of the sea now near at hand struck my back, I confess that a longing to reach Philadelphia, where I could complete my outfit and increase the safety of my little craft, gave renewed vigor to my stroke as I exchanged the quiet atmosphere of the country for the smoke and noise of the city.   Every instinct was now challenged, and every muscle brought into action, as I dodged tug-boats, steamers, yachts, and vessels, while running the thoroughfare along the crowded wharves between New York on one side and Jersey City on the other.   I found the slips between the piers most excellent ports of refuge at times, when the ferry-boats, following each other in quick succession, made the river with its angry tide boil like a vortex. The task soon ended, and I left the Hudson at Castle Garden and entered the upper bay of New York harbor.   As it was dark, I would gladly have gone ashore for the night, but a great city offers no inducement for a canoeist to land as a stranger at its wharves.

A much more pleasant reception awaited me down on Staten Island, a gentleman having notified me by mail that he would welcome the canoe and its owner.   The ebb had ceased, and the incoming tide was being already felt close in shore; so with tide and wind against me, and the darkness of night settling down gloomily upon the wide bay, I pulled a strong oar for five miles to the entrance of Kill Van Kull Strait, which separates Staten Island from New Jersey and connects the upper bay with Raritan Bay.

The bright beams from the light-house on Robbin's Reef, which is one mile and a quarter off the entrance of the strait, guided me on my course. The head-sea, in little, splashy waves, began to fill my canoe. The water soon reached the foot-rest; but there was no time to stop to bale out the boat, for a friendly current was near, and if once reached, my little craft would enter smoother waters. The flood which poured into the mouth of Kill Van Kull soon caught my boat, and the head-tide was changed to a favorable current which carried me in its strong arms far into the salt-water strait, and I reached West New Brighton, along the high banks of which I found my haven of rest. Against the sky I traced the outlines of my land-mark, three poplars, standing sentinel-like before the house of the gentleman who had so kindly offered me his hospitality. The canoe was emptied of its shifting liquid ballast and carefully sponged dry. My host and his son carried it into the main hall of the mansion and placed it upon the floor, where the entire household gathered, an admiring group. Proud, indeed, might my dainty craft have been of the appreciation of so lovely a company. Her master fully appreciated the generous board of his kind host, and in present comfort soon forgot past trials and his wet pull across the upper bay of New York harbor.

My work for the next day, October 27th, was the navigation of the interesting strait of the old Dutch settlers and the Raritan River, of New Jersey, as far as New Brunswick. The average width of Kill Van Kull is three-eighths of a mile. From its entrance, at Constable's Point, to the mouth of Newark Bay, which enters it on the Jersey side, it is three miles, and nearly two miles across the bay to Elizabethport. Bergen Point is on the east and Elizabethport on the west entrance of the bay, while on Staten Island, New Brighton, Factoryville, and North Shore, furnish homes for many New York business men.

At Elizabethport the strait narrows to one eighth of a mile, and as the mouth of the Rahway is approached it widens. It now runs through marshes for most of the way, a distance of twelve miles to Raritan Bay, which is an arm of the lower bay of New York harbor. The strait, from Elizabethport to its mouth, is called Arthur Kill; the whole distance through the Kills, from Constable's Point to Raritan Bay, is about seventeen statute miles. At the mouth of Arthur Kill the Raritan River opens to the bay, and the city of Perth Amboy rests on the point of high land between the river and the strait.

Roseville and Tottenville are on the Staten

Island shores of Arthur Kill, the former six miles, the latter ten miles from Elizabethport. The tide runs swiftly through the Kills. Leaving Mr. Campbell's residence at nine A. M., with a tide in my favor as far as Newark Bay, I soon had the tide against me from the other Kill until I passed the Rahway River, when it commenced to ebb towards Raritan Bay. The marshy shores of the Kills were submerged in places by the high tide, but their monotony was relieved by the farms upon the hills back of the flats.

At one o'clock my canoe rounded the heights upon which Perth Amboy is perched, with its snug cottages, the homes of many oystermen whose fleet of boats was anchored in front of the town. Curious yard-like pens constructed of poles rose out of the water, in which boats could find shelter from the rough sea.

The entrance to the Raritan River is wide, and above its mouth it is crossed by a long railroad bridge. The pull up the crooked river (sixteen miles) against a strong ebb-tide, through extensive reedy marshes, was uninteresting. I came upon the entrance of the canal which connects the rivers Raritan and Delaware after six o'clock P. M., which at this season of the year was after dark. Hiding the canoe in a secure place I went to visit an old friend, Professor George Cook, of the New Jersey State Geological Survey, who resides at New Brunswick. . In the morning the professor kindly assisted me, and we climbed the high bank of the canal with the canoe upon our shoulders, putting it into the water below the first two locks. I now commenced an unexciting row of forty-two miles to Bordentown, on the Delaware, where this artificial watercourse ends.

This canal is much travelled by steam tugs towing schooners of two hundred tons, and by barges and canal-boats of all sizes drawing not above seven feet and a half of water. The boats are drawn through the locks by stationary steam-engines, the use of which is discontinued when the business becomes slack; then the boatmen use their mules for the same purpose. To tow an average-sized canal-boat, loaded, requires four mules, while an empty one is easily drawn by two. It proved most expeditious as well as convenient not to trouble the lock-master to open the gates, but to secure his assistance in carrying the canoe along the tow-path to the end of the lock, which service occupied less than five minutes. In this way the canoe was carried around seven locks the first day, and when dusk approached she was sheltered beside a paper shell in the boat-house of Princeton College Club, which is located on the banks of the canal about one mile and a half from the city of Princeton.

In this narrow watercourse these indefatigable collegians, under great disadvantages, drill their crews for the annual intercollegiate struggle for championship. One Noah Reed provided entertainment for man and beast at his country inn half a mile from the boat-house, and thither I repaired for the night.

This day's row of twenty-six miles and a half had been through a hilly country, abounding in rich farm lands which were well cultivated. The next morning an officer of the Princeton Bank awaited my coming on the banks of the sluggish canal. He had taken an early walk from the town to see the canoe. At Baker's Basin the bridge-tender, a one-legged man, pressed me to tarry till he could summon the Methodist minister, who had charged him to notify him of the approach of a paper canoe.

Through all my boat journeys I have remarked that professional men take more interest in canoe journeys than professional oarsmen; and nearly all the canoeists of my acquaintance are ministers of the gospel. It is an innocent way of obtaining relaxation; and opportunities thus offered the weary clergyman of studying nature in her ever-changing but always restful moods, must indeed be grateful after being for months in daily contact with the world, the flesh, and the devil. The tendency of the present age to liberal ideas permits clergymen in large towns and cities to drive fast horses, and spend an hour of each day at a harmless game of billiards, without giving rise to remarks from *his own* congregation, but let the overworked rector of a *country* village seek in his friendly canoe that relief which nature offers to the tired brain, let him go into the wilderness and live close to his Creator by studying his works, and a whole community vex him on his return with " the appearance of the thing." These self-constituted critics, who are generally ignorant of the laws which God has made to secure health and give contentment to his creatures, would poison the sick man's body with drugs and nostrums when he might have the delightful and generally successful services of Dr. Camp Cure without the after dose of a bill. These hard-worked and miserably paid country clergymen, who are rarely, nowadays, treated as the head of the congregation or the shepherd of the flock they are supposed to lead, but rather as victims of the whims of influential members of the church, tell me that to own a canoe is indeed a cross, and that if they spend a vacation in the grand old forests of the Adirondacks, the brethren are sorely exercised over the time wasted in such unusual and unministerial conduct.

Everywhere along the route the peculiar character of the paper canoe attracted many remarks from the bystanders. The first impression given was that I had engaged in this rowing enterprise under the stimulus of a bet; and when the curious were informed that it was a voyage of study, the next question was, "How much are you going to make out of it?" Upon learning that there was neither a bet nor money in it, a shade of disappointment and incredulity rested upon the features of the bystanders, and the canoeist was often rated as a "blockhead" for risking his life without being paid for it.

At Trenton the canal passes through the city, and here it was necessary to carry the boat around two locks. At noon the canoe ended her voyage of forty-two miles by reaching the last lock, on the Delaware River, at Bordentown, New Jersey, where friendly arms received the Maria Theresa and placed her on the trestles which had supported her sister craft, the Mayeta, in the shop of the builder, Mr. J. S. Lamson, situated under the high cliffs along the crests of which an ex-king of Spain, in times gone by, was wont to walk and sadly ponder on his exile from *la belle France*.

The Rev. John H. Brakeley, proprietor as well as principal of the Bordentown Female Seminary, took me to his ancient mansion, where Thomas Paine, of old Revolutionary war times, had lodged. Not the least attraction in the home of my friend was the group of fifty young ladies, who were kind enough to gather upon a high bluff when I left the town, and wave a graceful farewell to the paper canoe as she entered the tidal current of the river Delaware *en route* for the Quaker city.

During my short stay in Bordentown Mr. Isaac Gabel kindly acted as my guide, and we explored the Bonaparte Park, which is on the outskirts of the town. The grounds are beautifully laid out. Some of the old houses of the ex-king's friends and attendants still remain in a fair state of preservation. The elegant residence of Joseph Bonaparte, or the Count de Surveilliers, which was always open to American visitors of all classes, was torn down by Mr. Henry Beckett, an Englishman in the diplomatic service of the British government, who purchased this property some years after the Count returned to Europe, and erected a more elaborate mansion near the old site. The old citizens of Bordentown hold in grateful remembrance the favors showered upon them by Joseph Bonaparte and his family, who seem to have lived a democratic life in the grand old park. The Count returned to France in 1838, and never visited the United States again. New Jersey had welcomed the exiled monarch, and had given him certain legal privileges in property rights which New York had refused him; so he settled upon the lovely shores of the fair Delaware, and lavished his wealth upon the people of the state which had so kindly received him. The citizens of neighboring states becoming somewhat jeal-

ous of the good luck that had befallen New Jersey in her capture of the Spanish king, applied
to the state the cognomen of "New Spain,"
and called the inhabitants thereof "Spaniards."

The Delaware River, the Makeriskitton of the
savage, upon whose noble waters my paper
canoe was now to carry me southward, has its
sources in the western declivity of the Catskill
Mountains, in the state of New York. It is fed
by two tributary streams, the Oquago (or Co-
quago) and the Popacton, which unite their
waters at the boundary line of Pennsylvania, at
the northeast end of the state, from which it
flows southward seventy miles, separating the
Empire and Keystone states. When near Port
Jervis, which town is connected with Rondout,
on the Hudson River, by the Hudson and Delaware Canal, the Delaware turns sharply to the
southwest, and becomes the boundary line between the states of New Jersey and Pennsylvania. Below Easton the river again takes a
southeasterly course, and flowing past Trenton,
Bristol, Bordentown, Burlington, Philadelphia,
Camden, Newcastle, and Delaware City, empties
its waters into Delaware Bay about forty miles
below Philadelphia.

This river has about the same length as the
Hudson — three hundred miles. The tide
reaches one hundred and thirty-two miles from
the sea at Cape May and Cape Henlopen. Phil-

adelphia is the head of navigation for vessels of the heaviest tonnage; Trenton for light-draught steamboats. At Bordentown the river is less than half a mile wide; at Philadelphia it is three-fourths of a mile in width; while at Delaware City it widens to two miles and a half. Delaware Bay is twenty-six miles across in the widest part, which is some miles within the entrance of the Capes.

October 31st was cool and gusty. The river route to Philadelphia is twenty-nine statute miles. The passage was made against a strong head-wind, with swashy waves, which made me again regret that I did not have my canoe-decking made at Troy, instead of at Philadelphia. The highly-cultivated farms and beautiful country-seats along both the Pennsylvania and New Jersey sides of the river spoke highly of the rich character of the soil and the thrift of the inhabitants. These river counties of two states may be called a land of plenty, blessed with bountiful harvests.

Quaker industry and wise economy in managing the agricultural affairs of this section in the early epochs of our country's settlement have borne good fruit. All praise to the memory of William Penn of Pennsylvania and his worthy descendants. The old towns of Bristol on the right, and Burlington on the left bank, embowered in vernal shades, have a most comfortable and home-like appearance.

At five o'clock P. M. I arrived at the city pier opposite the warehouse of Messrs. C. P. Knight & Brother, No. 114 South Delaware Avenue, where, after a struggle with wind and wave for eight hours, the canoe was landed and deposited with the above firm, the gentlemen of which kindly offered to care for it while I tarried in the "City of Brotherly Love."

Among the many interesting spots hallowed by memories of the past in which Philadelphia abounds, and which are rarely sought out by visitors, two especially claim the attention of the naturalist. One is the old home of William Bartram, on the banks of the Schuylkill at Grey's Ferry; the other, the grave of Alexander Wilson, friends and co-laborers in nature's extended field;—the first a botanist, the second the father of American ornithology.

William Bartram, son of the John Bartram who was the founder of the Botanic Garden on the west bank of the Schuylkill, was born at that interesting spot in 1739. All botanists are familiar with the results of his patient labors and his pioneer travels in those early days, through the wilderness of what now constitutes the southeastern states. One who visited him at his home says: "Arrived at the botanist's garden, we approached an old man who, with a rake in his hand, was breaking the clods of earth in a tulip-bed. His hat was old, and flapped over his face; his coarse shirt was seen near his neck, as he wore no cravat nor kerchief; his waistcoat and breeches were both of leather, and his shoes were tied with leather strings. We approached and accosted him. He ceased his work, and entered into conversation with the ease and politeness of nature's nobleman. His countenance was expressive of benignity and happiness. This was the botanist, traveller and philosopher we had come to see."

William Bartram gave important assistance and encouragement to the friendless Scotch pedagogue, Alexander Wilson, while the latter was preparing his American Ornithology for the press. This industrious and peaceable botanist died within the walls of his dearly-loved home a few minutes after he had penned a description of a plant. He died in 1823, in the eighty-fifth year of his age. The old house of John and William Bartram remains nearly the same as when the last Bartram died, but the grounds have been occupied and improved by the present proprietor, whose fine mansion is near the old residence of the two botanists.

Without ample funds to enable him to carry out his bold design, Alexander Wilson labored and suffered in body and mind for several years, until his patient and persistent efforts achieved the success they so richly merited. All but the last volume of his American Ornithology were completed when the overworked naturalist died.

The old Swedes' Church is the most ancient religious edifice in Philadelphia, and is located near the wharves in the vicinity of Christian and Swanson streets, in the old district of South-wark. The Swedes had settlements on the Del-aware before Penn visited America. They built a wooden edifice for worship in 1677, on the spot where the brick "Swedes' Church" now stands, and which was erected in 1700. Thread-ing narrow streets, with the stenographic reporter of the courts, Mr. R. A. West, for my guide, we came into a quiet locality where the ancient landmark reared its steeple, like the finger of faith pointing heavenward. Few indeed must be the fashionable Christians who worship under its unpretentious roof, but there is an air of antiquity surrounding it which interests every visitor who enters its venerable doorway.

The church-yard is very contracted in area, yet there is room for trees to grow within its sacred precincts, and birds sometimes rest there while pursuing their flight from the Schuylkill to the Delaware. Among the crowded graves is a square brick structure, covered with an horizontal slab of white marble, upon which I read:

"THIS MONUMENT COVERS THE REMAINS OF

ALEXANDER WILSON,

AUTHOR OF THE AMERICAN ORNITHOLOGY.

HE WAS BORN IN RENFREWSHIRE, SCOTLAND, ON THE 6 JULY, 1766;

EMIGRATED TO THE UNITED STATES IN THE YEAR 1794;

AND DIED IN PHILADELPHIA, OF THE DYSENTERY,

ON THE 23 AUGUST, 1813, AGED 47.

Ingenio stat sine morte decus."

Philadelphia has been called the "city of homes," and well does she merit that comfortably sounding title, for it is not a misnomer. Unlike some other large American cities, the artisan and laborer can here own a home by becoming a member of a building association and paying the moderate periodical dues. Miles upon miles of these cosy little houses, of five or six rooms each, may be found, the inmates of which are a good and useful class of citizens, adding strength to the city's discipline and government.

The grand park of three thousand acres, one of, if not *the* largest in the world, is near at hand, where the poor as well as the rich can resort at pleasure. I took leave of the beautiful and well laid-out city with a pang of regret not usual with canoeists, who find it best for their comfort and peace of mind to keep with their dainty crafts away from the heterogeneous and not over-civil population which gathers along the water-fronts of a port.

CHAPTER VII.

PHILADELPHIA TO CAPE HENLOPEN.

DESCENT OF DELAWARE RIVER. — MY FIRST CAMP. — BOMBAY
HOOK. — MURDERKILL CREEK. — A STORM IN DELAWARE BAY. —
CAPSIZING OF THE CANOE. — A SWIM FOR LIFE. — THE PER-
SIMMON GROVE. — WILLOW GROVE INN. — THE LIGHTS OF
CAPES MAY AND HENLOPEN.

MONDAY, November 9, was a cold, wet day. Mr. Knight and the old, enthusiastic gunsmith-naturalist of the city, Mr. John Krider, assisted me to embark in my now decked, provisioned, and loaded canoe. The stock of condensed food would easily last me a month, while the blankets and other parts of the outfit were good for the hard usage of four or five months. My friends shouted adieu as the little craft shot out from the pier and rapidly descended the river with the strong ebb-tide which for two hours was in her favor. The anchorage of the iron Monitor fleet at League Island was soon passed, and the great city sank into the gloom of its smoke and the clouds of rainy mist which enveloped it.

This pull was an exceedingly dreary one. The storms of winter were at hand, and even along

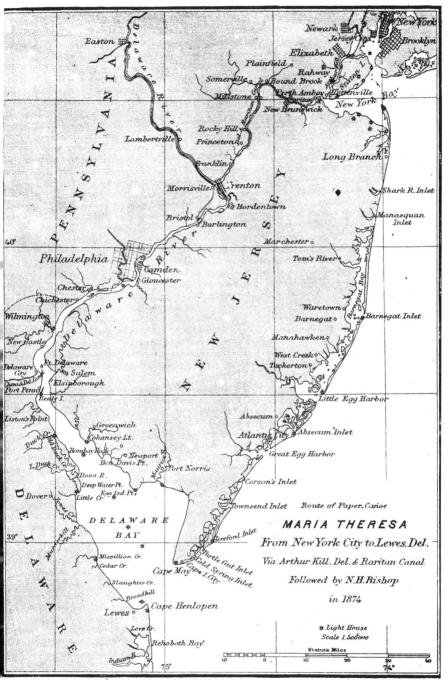

MARIA THERESA

From New York City to Lewes, Del.

Via Arthur Kill, Del. & Raritan Canal

Followed by N.H.Bishop

in 1874

* Light House
Scale 1.500000

Statute Miles

10   0   10   20   30   40

the watercourses between Philadelphia and Nor-folk, Virginia, thin ice would soon be forming in the shallow coves and creeks. It would be necessary to exert all my energies to get south of Hatteras, which is located on the North Carolina coast in a region of storms and local disturbances. The canoe, though heavily laden, behaved well. I now enjoyed the advantages resulting from the possession of the new canvas deck-cover, which, being fastened by buttons along each gunwale of the canoe, securely covered the boat, so that the occasional swash sent aboard by wicked tug-boats and large schooners did not annoy me or wet my precious cargo.

By two o'clock P. M. the rain and wind caused me to seek shelter at Mr. J. C. Beach's cottage, at Markus Hook, some twenty miles below Philadelphia, and on the same side of the river. While Mr. Beach was varnishing the little craft, crowds of people came to *feel* of the canoe, giving it the usual punching with their finger-nails, "to see if it were truly paper." A young Methodist minister with his pretty wife came also to satisfy their curiosity on the *paper* question, but the dominie offered me not a word of encouragement in my undertaking. He shook his head and whispered to his wife: " A wild, wild enterprise indeed." Markus Hook derived its name from Markee, an Indian chief, who sold it to the civilized white man for four barrels of whiskey.

The next morning, in a dense fog, I followed the shores of the river, crossing the Pennsylvania and Delaware boundary line half a mile below the "Hook," and entered Delaware, the little state of three counties. Thirty-five miles below, the water becomes salt. Reaching New Castle, which contained half its present number of inhabitants before Philadelphia was founded, I pulled across to the New Jersey side of the river and skirted the marshy shore past the little Pea Patch Island, upon which rises in sullen dreariness Fort Delaware. West of the island is Delaware City, where the Chesapeake and Delaware Canal, fourteen miles in length, has one of its termini, the other being on a river which empties into Chesapeake Bay. Philadelphia and Baltimore steamboat lines utilize this canal in the passage of their boats from one city to the other.

After crossing Salem Cove, and passing its southern point, Elsinborough, five miles and a half below Fort Delaware, the inhospitable marshes became wide and desolate, warning me to secure a timely shelter for the night. Nearly two miles below Point Elsinborough the high reeds were divided by a little creek, into which I ran my canoe, for upon the muddy bank could be seen a deserted, doorless fish-cabin, into which I moved my blankets and provisions, after cutting with my pocket-knife an ample supply of dry reeds for a bed. Drift-wood, which a friendly tide had deposited around the shanty, furnished the material for my fire, which lighted up the dismal hovel most cheerfully. And thus I kept house in a comfortable manner till morning, being well satisfied with the progress I had made that day in traversing the shores of three states. The booming of the guns of wild-fowl shooters out upon the water roused me before dawn, and I had ample time before the sun arose to prepare breakfast from the remnant of canned ox-tail soup left over from last night's supper.

I was now in Delaware Bay, which was assuming noble proportions. From my camp I crossed to the west shore below Reedy Island, and, filling my water-bottles at a farm-house, kept upon that shore all day. The wind arose, stirring up a rough sea as I approached Bombay Hook, where the bay is eight miles wide. I tried to land upon the salt marshes, over the edges of which the long, low seas were breaking, but failed in several attempts. At last roller after roller, following in quick succession, carried the little craft on their crests to the land, and packed her in a thicket of high reeds.

I quickly disembarked, believing it useless to attempt to go further that day. About an eighth of a mile from the water, rising out of the salt grass and reeds, was a little mound, covered by trees and bushes, into which I conveyed my cargo by the back-load, and then easily drew the light canoe over the level marsh to the camp. A bed of reeds was soon cut, into which the canoe was settled to prevent her from being strained by the occupant at night, for I was determined to test the strength of the boat as sleeping-quarters. Canoes built for one person are generally too light for such occupancy when out of water. The tall fringe of reeds which encircled the boat formed an excellent substitute for chamber walls, giving me all the starry blue heavens for a ceiling, and most effectually screening me from the strong wind which was blowing. As it was early when the boat was driven ashore, I had time to wander down to the brook, which was a mile distant, and replenish my scanty stock of water.

With the canvas deck-cover and rubber blanket to keep off the heavy dews, the first night passed in such contracted lodgings was endurable, if not wholly convenient and agreeable. The river mists were not dispelled the next day until nine o'clock, when I quitted my warm nest in the reeds and rowed down the bay, which seemed to grow broader as I advanced. The bay was still bordered by extensive marshes, with here and there the habitation of man located upon some slight elevation of the surface. Having rowed twenty-six miles, and being off the mouth of Murderkill Creek, a squall struck the canoe and forced it on to an oyster reef, upon the sharp shells of which she was rocked for several minutes by the shallow breakers. Fearing that the paper shell was badly cut, though it was still early in the afternoon, I ascended the creek of ominous name and associations to the landing of an inn kept by Jacob Lavey, where I expected to overhaul my injured craft. To my surprise and great relief of mind there were found only a few superficial scratches upon the horn-like shellacked surface of the paper shell. To apply shellac with a heated iron to the wounds made by the oyster-shells was the work of a few minutes, and my craft was as sound as ever. The gunner's resort, " Bower's Beach Hotel," furnished an excellent supper of oyster fritters, panfish, and fried pork-scrapple. Mine host, before a blazing wood fire, told me of the origin of the name of Murderkill Creek.

" In the early settlement of the country," began the innkeeper, " the white settlers did all they could to civilize the Indians, but the cussed savages wouldn't take to it kindly, but worried the life out of the new-comers. At last a great landed proprietor, who held a big grant of land in these parts, thought he'd settle the troubles. So he planted a brass cannon near the creek, and invited all the Indians of the neighborhood to come and hear the white man's Great Spirit talk. The crafty man got the savages before the

mouth of the cannon, and said, 'Now look into
the hole there, for it is the mouth of the white
man's Great Spirit, which will soon speak in tones
of thunder.' The fellow then touched off the
gun, and knocked half the devils into splinters.
The others were so skeerd at the big voice they
had heard that they were afraid to move, and
were soon all killed by one charge after another
from the cannon: so the creek has been called
Murderkill ever since."

I afterwards discovered that there were other
places on the coast which had the same legend
as the one told me by the innkeeper. Holders
of small farms lived in the vicinity of this tavern,
but the post-office was at Frederica, five miles
inland. Embarking the next day, I felt sure of
ending my cruise on Delaware Bay before night,
as the quiet morning exhibited no signs of rising
winds. The little pilot town of Lewes, near
Cape Delaware, and behind the Breakwater, is a
port of refuge for storm-bound vessels. From
this village I expected to make a portage of six
miles to Love Creek, a tributary of Rehoboth
Sound. The frosty nights were now exerting a
sanitary influence over the malarial districts
which I had entered, and the unacclimated canoeist of northern birth could safely pursue his
journey, and sleep at night in the swamps along
the fresh-water streams if protected from the
dews by a rubber or canvas covering. My hopes

of reaching the open sea that night were to be drowned, and in cold water too; for that day, which opened so calmly and with such smiling promises, was destined to prove a season of trial, and before its evening shadows closed around me, to witness a severe struggle for life in the cold waters of Delaware Bay.

An hour after leaving Murderkill Creek the wind came from the north in strong squalls. My little boat taking the blasts on her quarter, kept herself free of the swashy seas hour after hour. I kept as close to the sandy beach of the great marshes as possible, so as to be near the land in case an accident should happen. Mispillion Creek and a light-house on the north of its mouth were passed, when the wind and seas struck my boat on the port beam, and continually crowded her ashore. The water breaking on the hard, sandy beach of the marshy coast made it too much of a risk to attempt a landing, as the canoe would be smothered in the swashy seas if her headway was checked for a moment. Amidships the canoe was only a few inches out of water, but her great sheer, full bow, and smoothness of hull, with watchful management, kept her from swamping. I had struggled along for fourteen miles since morning, and was fatigued by the strain consequent upon the continued manœuvring of my boat through the rough waves. I reached a point on Slaughter Beach, where the bay has a width of nearly nineteen miles, when the tempest rose to such a pitch that the great raging seas threatened every moment to wash over my canoe, and to force me by their violence close into the beach. To my alarm, as the boat rose and fell on the waves, the heads of sharp-pointed stakes appeared and disappeared in the broken waters. They were the stakes of fishermen to which they attach their nets in the season of trout-fishing. The danger of being impaled on one of these forced me off shore again.

There was no undertow; the seas being driven over shoals were irregular and broken. At last *my* sea came. It rolled up without a crest, square and formidable. I could not calculate where it would break, but I pulled for life away from it towards the beach upon which the sea was breaking with deafening sound. It was only for a moment that I beheld the great brown wave, which bore with it the mud of the shoal, bearing down upon me; for the next, it broke astern, sweeping completely over the canoe from stern to stem, filling it through the opening of the canvas round my body. Then for a while the watery area was almost smooth, so completely had the great wave levelled it. The canoe being water-logged, settled below the surface, the high points of the ends occasionally emerging from the water. Other heavy seas followed the first, one of which striking me as high as my head and shoulders, turned both the canoe and canoeist upside-down.

Kicking myself free of the canvas deck, I struck out from under the shell, and quickly rose to the surface. It was then that the words of an author of a European Canoe Manual came to my mind: " When you capsize, first right the canoe and get astride it over one end, keeping your legs in the water; when you have crawled to the well or cockpit, bale out the boat with your hat." Comforting as these instructions from an experienced canoe traveller seemed when reading them in my hermitage ashore, the present application of them (so important a principle in Captain Jack Bunsby's log of life) was in this emergency an impossibility; for my hat had disappeared with the seat-cushion and one iron outrigger, while the oars were floating to leeward with the canoe.

The boat having turned keel up, her great sheer would have righted her had it not been for the cargo, which settled itself on the canvas deck-cloth, and ballasted the craft in that position. So smooth were her polished sides that it was impossible to hold on to her, for she rolled about like a slippery porpoise in a tideway. Having tested and proved futile the kind suggestions of writers on marine disasters, and feeling very stiff in the icy water, I struck out in an almost exhausted condition for the shore. Now a new experience taught me an interesting lesson. The seas rolled over my head and shoulders in such rapid succession, that I found I could not get my head above water to breathe, while the sharp sand kept in suspension by the agitated water scratched my face, and filled my eyes, nostrils, and ears. While I felt this pressing down and burying tendency of the seas, as they broke upon my head and shoulders, I understood the reason why so many good swimmers are drowned in attempting to reach the shore from a wreck on a shoal, when the wind, though blowing heavily, is in the victim's favor. The land was not over an eighth of a mile away, and from it came the sullen roar of the breakers, pounding their heavy weight upon the sandy shingle. As its booming thunders or its angry, swashing sound increased, I knew I was rapidly nearing it, but, blinded by the boiling waters, I could see nothing.

At such a moment do not stop to make vows as to how you will treat your neighbor in future if once safely landed, but strike out, fight as you never fought before, swallowing as little water as possible, and never relaxing an energy or yielding a hope. The water shoaled; my feet felt the bottom, and I stood up, but a roller laid me flat on my face. Up again and down again, swimming and crawling, I emerged from the sea, bearing, I fear, a closer resemblance to Jo-

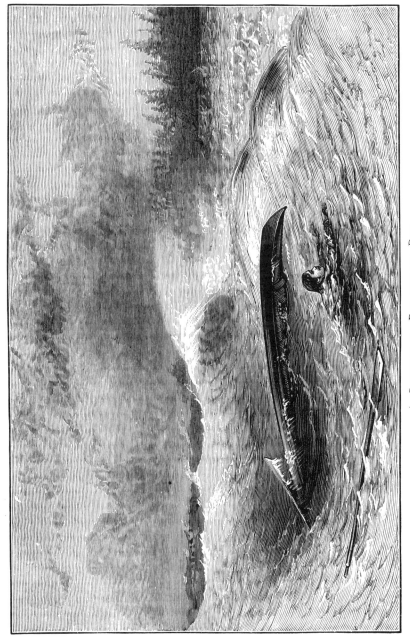

A Capsize in Delaware Bay.

nah (being at last pitched on shore) than to Cabnel's Venus, who was borne gracefully upon the rosy crests of the sky-reflecting waves to the soft bed of sparkling foam awaiting her.

Wearily dragging myself up the hard shingle, I stood and contemplated the little streams of water pouring from my woollen clothes. A new danger awaited me as the cold wind whistled down the barren beach and across the desolate marshes. I danced about to keep warm, and for a moment thought that my canoe voyage had come to an unfortunate termination. Then a buoyant feeling succeeded the moment's depression, and I felt that this was only the first of many trials which were necessary to prepare me for the successful completion of my undertaking. But where was the canoe, with its provisions that were to sustain me, and the charts which were to point out my way through the labyrinth of waters she was yet to traverse? She had drifted near the shore, but would not land. There was no time to consider the propriety of again entering the water. The struggle was a short though severe one, and I dragged my boat ashore.

Everything was wet excepting what was most needed, — a flannel suit, carefully rolled in a water-proof cloth. I knew that I must change my wet clothes for dry ones, or perish. This was no easy task to perform, with hands be-

numbed and limbs paralyzed with the cold. O
shade of Benjamin Franklin, did not one of thy
kinsmen, in his wide experience as a traveller,
foresee this very disaster, and did he not, when
I left the "City of Brotherly Love," force upon
me an antidote, a sort of spiritual fire, which my
New England temperance principles made me
refuse to accept?   "It is old, *very* old," he whispered, as he slipped the flask into my coat-pock-
et, "and it may save your life.   Don't be foolish.
I have kept it well bottled.   It is a pure article,
and cost sixteen dollars per gallon.   *I use it only
for medicine.*"   I found the flask; the *water*
had not injured it.   A small quantity was taken,
when a most favorable change came over my
entire system, mental as well as physical, and I
was able to throw off one suit and put on another in the icy wind, that might, without the
stimulant, have ended my voyage of life.

I had doctored myself homœopathically under
the *old practice*.   Filled with feelings of gratitude to the Great Giver of good, I reflected, as
I carried my wet cargo into the marsh, upon the
wonderful effects of my friend's medicine when
taken *only as medicine*.   Standing upon the cold
beach and gazing into the sea, now lashed by
the wild frenzy of the wind, I determined never
again to do so mean a thing as to say a *bad*
word against *good* brandy.

Having relieved my conscience by this just

resolve, I transported the whole of my wet but still precious cargo to a persimmon grove, on a spot of firm land that rose out of the marsh, where I made a convenient wind-break by stretching rubber blankets between trees. On this knoll I built a fire, obtaining the matches to kindle it from a water-proof safe presented to me by Mr. Epes Sargent, of Boston, some years before, when I was ascending the St. Johns River, Florida.

Before dusk, all things not spoiled by the water were dried and secreted in the tall sedge of the marshes. The elevation which had given me friendly shelter is known as " Hog Island." The few persimmon-trees that grew upon it furnished an ample lunch, for the frosts had mellowed the plum-like fruit, making it sweet and edible. The persimmon (*Diospyrus Virginiana*) is a small tree usually found in the middle and southern states. Coons and other animals feast upon its fruit. The deepening gloom warned me to seek comfortable quarters for the night.

Two miles up the strand was an old gunners' inn, to which I bent my steps along Slaughter Beach, praying that one more day's effort would take me out of this bleak region of ominous names. A pleasant old gentleman, Mr. Charles Todd, kept the tavern, known as Willow Grove Hotel, more for amusement than for profit. I said nothing to him about the peculiar manner in which I had landed on Slaughter Beach; but to his inquiry as to where my boat was, and what kind of a boat it was to live in such a blow, I replied that I found it too wet and cold on the bay to remain there, and too rough to proceed to Cape Henlopen, and there being no alternative, I was obliged to land much against my inclination, and in doing so was drenched to the skin, but had managed to get dry before a fire in the marshes. So the kind old man piled small logs in the great kitchen fireplace, and told me tale upon tale of his life as a school-master out west; of the death of his wife there, and of his desire to return, after long years of absence, to his native Delaware, where he could be comfortable, and have all the clams, oysters, fish, and bay truck generally that a man could wish for.

"Now," he added, "I shall spend my last days here in peace." He furnished an excellent supper of weak-fish or sea trout (*Otolithus regalio*), fried oysters, sweet potatoes, &c.

This locality offers a place of retirement for men of small means and limited ambition. The broad bay is a good sailing and fishing ground, while the great marshes are the resort of many birds. The light, warm soil responds generously to little cultivation. After a day of hunting and fishing, the new-comer can smoke his pipe in peace, to the music of crackling flames in the wide old fireplace. Here he may be *comfortable*, and spend his last days quietly vegetating, with no criticisms on his deterioration, knowing that he is running to seed no faster than his neighbors.

The wind had gone to rest with the sun, and the sharp frost that followed left its congealed breath upon the shallow pools of water nearly half an inch in thickness by morning. From my bed I could see through the window the bright flashes from Cape May and Cape Henlopen lights. Had not misfortune beset me, a four-hours' pull would have landed me at Lewes. There was much to be thankful for, however. Through a merciful Providence it was my privilege to enjoy a soft bed at the Willow Grove Inn, and not a cold one on the sands of Slaughter Beach. So ended my last day on Delaware Bay.

CHAPTER VIII.

FROM CAPE HENLOPEN TO NORFOLK, VIRGINIA.

THE PORTAGE TO LOVE CREEK. — THE DELAWARE WHIPPING-POST. — REHOBOTH AND INDIAN RIVER BAYS. — A PORTAGE TO LITTLE ASSAWAMAN BAY. — ISLE OF WIGHT BAY. — WIN-CHESTER PLANTATION. — CHINCOTEAGUE. — WATCHAPREAGUE INLET. — COBB'S ISLAND. — CHERRYSTONE. — ARRIVAL AT NOR-FOLK. — THE "LANDMARK'S" ENTERPRISE.

MY first thought the next morning was of the lost outrigger, and how I should replace it. My host soon solved the problem for me. I was to drive to the scene of the late disaster in his light, covered wagon, load it with the canoe and cargo, and take the shortest route to Love Creek, six miles from Lewes, stopping on the way at a blacksmith's for a new outrigger. We drove over sandy roads, through forests of pine and oak, to the village of Milton, where a curious crowd gathered round us and facetiously asked if we had " brought the canoe all the way from Troy in that 'ere wagon." The village smith, without removing the paper boat from her snug quarters, made a fair outrigger in an hour's time, when we continued our monotonous ride

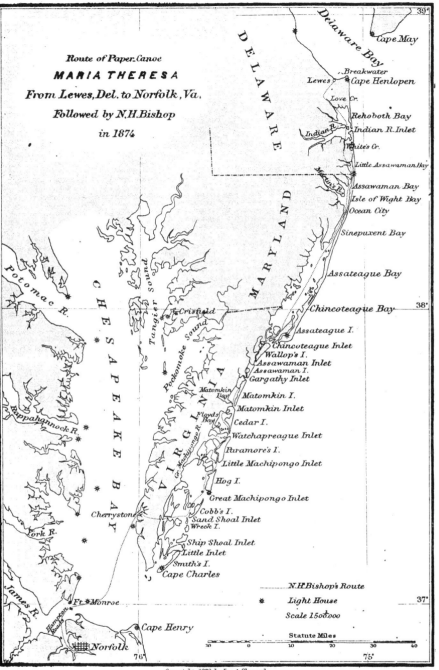

Route of Paper Canoe

MARIA THERESA

From Lewes, Del. to Norfolk, Va.

Followed by N. H. Bishop

in 1874

DELAWARE

Cape May

Delaware Bay

Breakwater
Lewes
Cape Henlopen
Love Cr.
Rehoboth Bay
Indian R.
Indian R. Inlet
White's Cr.
Little Assawaman Bay
Martin's R.
Assawaman Bay
Isle of Wight Bay
Ocean City
Sinepuxent Bay
Assateague Bay
Chincoteague Bay

MARYLAND

Crisfield

CHESAPEAKE BAY

Tangier Sound

Pocomoke Sound

VIRGINIA

Assateague I.
Chincoteague Inlet
Wallop's I.
Assawaman Inlet
Assawaman I.
Gargathy Inlet
Matomkin Bay
Matomkin I.
Matomkin Inlet
Floyds Bay
Cedar I.
Watchapreague Inlet
Gr. Machipongo R.
Paramore's I.
Little Machipongo Inlet
Hog I.
Great Machipongo Inlet
Cherrystone
Cobb's I.
Sand Shoal Inlet
Wreck I.
Ship Shoal Inlet
Little Inlet
Smith's I.
Cape Charles

Potomac R.

Rappahannock R.

York R.

James R.

Ft. Monroe
Hampton Roads
Cape Henry
Norfolk

.... N. H. Bishop's Route
✳ Light House
Scale 1500.000

Statute Miles

10   0   10   20   30   40

39°

38°

37°

76°   75°

Copyright. 1878. by Lee & Shepard

through dreary woods to a clearing upon the banks of a cedar swamp, where in a cottage lived Mr. George Webb, to whom Bob Hazzle, my driver, presented me. Having now reached Love Creek, I deposited my canoe with Mr. Webb, and started off for Lewes to view the town and the ocean.

Across the entrance of Delaware Bay, from Cape Henlopen Light to Cape May Light on the southern end of New Jersey, is a distance of twelve statute miles. Saturday night and Sunday were passed in Lewes, which is situated inside of Cape Henlopen, and behind the celebrated stone breakwater which was constructed by the government. This port of refuge is much frequented by coasters, as many as two or three hundred sails collecting here during a severe gale. The government is building a remarkable pier of *solid* iron spiles, three abreast, which, when completed, will run out seventeen hundred feet into the bay, and reach a depth of twenty-three feet of water. Captain Brown, of the Engineers, was in charge of the work. By the application of a jet of water, forced by an hydraulic pump through a tube down the outside of the spile while it is being screwed into the sand, a puddling of the same is kept up, which relieves the strain upon the screw-flanges, and saves fourteen-fifteenths of the time and labor usually expended by the old method of inserting the screw spile. This invention was a happy thought of Captain Brown.

The government has purchased a piece of land at Lewes for the site of a fort. Some time in the future there will be a railroad terminating on the pier, and coal will be brought directly from the mines to supply the fleets which will gather within the walls of the Breakwater. Here, free from all danger of an ice blockade, this port will become a safe and convenient harbor and coaling-station during the winter time for government and other vessels.

At dusk on Sunday evening the collector of the port, Captain Lyons, and his friends, took me in their carriage back to Love Creek, where Mr. Webb insisted upon making me the recipient of his hospitality for the night. A little crowd of women from the vicinity of the swamp were awaiting my arrival to see the canoe. One ancient dame, catching sight of the alcohol-stove which I took from my vest-pocket, clapped her thin hands and enthusiastically exclaimed, "What a nice thing for a sick-room — the best nuss-lamp I ever seed!" Having satisfied the curiosity of these people, and been much amused by their quaint remarks, I was quietly smuggled into Mr. Webb's "best room," where, if my spirit did not make feathery flights, it was not the fault of the downy bed in whose unfathomable depths I now lost myself.

Before leaving Delaware I feel it an imperative duty to the public to refer to one of her time-honored institutions.

Persons unacquainted with the fact will find it difficult to believe that one state of the great American Republic still holds to the practice of lashing men and women, white and black. Delaware — one of the smallest states of the Union, the citizens of which are proverbially generous and hospitable, a state which has produced a Bayard — is, to her shame we regret to say, the culprit which sins against the spirit of civilization in this nineteenth century, one hundred years after the fathers of the Republic declared equal rights for all men. In treating of so delicate a subject, I desire to do no one injustice; therefore I will let a native of Delaware speak for his community.

"DOVER, DELAWARE, August 2, 1873.

" EDITOR CAMDEN SPY: According to promise, I now write you a little about Delaware. Persons in your vicinity look upon the ' Little Diamond State' as a mere bog, or marsh, and mud and water they suppose are its chief productions ; but, in my opinion, it is one of the finest little states in the Union. Although small, in proportion to the size it produces more grain and fruit than any other state in the country, and they are unexcelled as regards quality and flavor.

Crime is kept in awe by that best of institutions, the *whipping-post and pillory!* These are the bugbear of all the northern newspapers, and they can say nothing too harsh or severe against them. The whipping-post in Kent County is situated in the yard of the jail, and is about six feet in height and three feet in circumference; the prisoner is fastened to it by means of bracelets, or arms, on the wrist; and the sheriff executes the sentence of the law by baring the convict to the waist, and on the bare back lashing him twenty, forty, or sixty times, according to the sentence. But the blood does not run in streams from the prisoner's back, nor is he thrown into a barrel of brine, and salt sprinkled over the lashes. On the contrary, I have seen them laugh, and coolly remark that ' it's good exercise, and gives us an appetite.' But there are others who raise the devil's own row with their yells and horrible cries of pain. The whipping is public, and is witnessed each time by large numbers of people who come from miles around to see the culprit disgraced.

"A public whipping occurred not very long ago, and the day was very stormy, yet there were fully three hundred spectators on the ground to witness this wholesome punishment! A person who has been lashed at the whipping-post cannot vote again in this state; thus, most of the criminals who are whipped leave the state in order to regain their citizenship. The newspapers can blow until they are tired about this ' horrible, barbaric, and unchristian punishment,' but if their own states would adopt this form of punishment, they would find crime continually on the decrease. What is imprisonment for a few months or years? It is soon over with; and then they are again let out upon the community, to beg, borrow, and steal. But to be publicly whipped is an everlasting disgrace, and deters men from committing wrong. Women are whipped in the same manner, and they take it very hard; but, to my recollection, there has not been a female prisoner for some time. I did not intend to comment so long upon the whipping-posts in the state of Delaware.

" The pillory next claims our attention. This is a long piece of board that runs through the whipping-post at the top, and has holes [as per engraving] for the neck and arms to rest in a very constrained position. The prisoner is compelled to stand on his toes for an hour with his neck and arms in the holes, and if he sinks from exhaustion, as it sometimes happens, the neck is instantly broken. Josiah Ward, the villain who escaped punishment for the murder of the man Wady in your county, came into Delaware, broke into a shoe-store, succeeded in stealing one pair of shoes, — was arrested, got sixty lashes at the post, was made to stand in the pillory one

hour, is now serving out a term of two years'
imprisonment, — and *he never got the shoes!*
The pillory is certainly a terrible and cruel punishment, and, while I heartily favor the whipping-
post, I think this savage punishment should be
abolished.

"Since writing the above, I have heard that a
colored woman was convicted of murder in the
second degree last May, and on Saturday the
17th of that month received sixty lashes on her
bare back, and stood in the pillory one hour.

"What do you think of Delaware law, after
what I have written? I have written enough
for the present, so I will close, ever remaining,

"Yours very truly,

P. P."

For twenty years past, Delaware and Maryland farmers have given much attention to peach
culture, which has gradually declined in New
Jersey and states further north. There are said
to be over sixty thousand acres of land on the
peninsula planted with peach-trees, which are
estimated to be worth fifty dollars per acre, or
three million dollars. To harvest this crop requires at least twenty-five thousand men, women,
and children. The planting of an acre of peach-
trees, and its cultivation to maturity, costs from
thirty to forty dollars. The canners take a large
portion of the best peaches, which are shipped
to foreign as well as to domestic markets.

The low lands and river-shores of the peninsula exhale malaria which attacks the inhabitants in a mild form of ague. During the spring, summer, and early fall months, a prudent man will not expose himself to the air until after the sun has risen and dispelled the mists of morning. The same caution should be observed all through the low regions of the south, both as to morning and evening exercise. Chills and fever are the bane of the southern and middle states, as this disease affects the health and elastic vigor of the constitution, and also produces great mental depression. Yet those who suffer, even on every alternate day, from chills, seem to accept the malaria as nothing of much importance; though it is a well-known fact that this form of intermittent fever so reduces the strength, that the system is unable to cope with other and more dangerous diseases for which it paves the way.

Upon a little creek, tributary to St. Martin's River, and near its confluence with the Isle of Wight Bay, a long day's pull from the swamp of Love Creek, was the old plantation home of a friend of my boyhood, Mr. Taylor, who about this time was looking out for the arrival of the paper canoe. It was a question whether I could descend Love Creek three miles, cross Rehoboth and Indian River sounds, ascend White's Creek, make a portage to Little Assawaman Bay, thread the thoroughfare west of Fenwick's Island Light, cross the Isle of Wight Bay, ascend and cross St. Martin's River to Turval's Creek, and reach the home of my friend, all in one day. But I determined to attempt the task. Mr. Webb roused his family at an early hour, and I rowed down Love Creek and crossed the shallow waters of Rehoboth Bay in the early part of the day.

From Cape Henlopen, following the general contour of the coast, to Cape Charles at the northern entrance of Chesapeake Bay, is a distance of one hundred and thirty-six miles; from Cape Charles across the mouth of Chesapeake Bay to Cape Henry is thirteen miles; from Henlopen south, the state of Delaware occupies about twenty miles of the coast; the eastern shore of Maryland holds between thirty and forty miles, while the eastern shore of Virginia, represented by the counties of Accomac and Northampton, covers the peninsula to Cape Charles.

Commencing at Rehoboth Bay, a small boat may follow the interior waters to the Chesapeake Bay. The watercourses of this coast are protected from the rough waves of the ocean by long, narrow, sandy islands, known as beaches, between which the tides enter. These passages from the sea to the interior waters are called inlets, and most of them are navigable for coasting vessels of light draught. These inlets are so influenced by the action of storms, and their shores and locations are so changed by them, that the cattle may graze to-day in tranquil happiness where only a generation ago the old skipper navigated his craft.   During June of the year 1821 a fierce gale opened Sandy Point Inlet with a foot depth of water, but it closed in 1831. Green Point Inlet was cut through the beach during a gale in 1837, and was closed up seven years later.   Old Sinepuxent Inlet, which was forced open by the sea more than sixty years ago, closed in 1831.   These three inlets were within a space of three miles, and were all north of Chincoteague village.   Green Run Inlet, which had a depth of about six feet of water for nearly ten years, also closed after shifting half a mile to the south of its original location.   The tendency of inlets on this coast is to shift to the southward, as do the inlets on the coast of New Jersey.

Oystermen, fishermen, and farmers live along the upland, and in some cases on the island beaches.   From these bays, timber, firewood, grain, and oysters are shipped to northern ports. The people are everywhere kind and hospitable to strangers.   A mild climate, cheap and easily worked soils, wild-fowl shooting, fine oysters and fishing privileges, offer inducements to Northerners and Europeans to settle in this country; the mild form of ague which exists in most of its localities being the only objection. While debating this point with a native, he attacked my argument by saying:

"Law sakes! don't folks die of *something*, any way? If you don't have fever 'n' ague round Massachusetts, you've got an awful lot of things we hain't got here — a tarnashun sight wuss ones, too; sich as cumsempsun, brown-critters, mental spinageetis, lung-disease, and all sorts of brown-kill disorders. Besides, you have such awful cold winters that a farmer has to stay holed four months out of the year, while we folks in the south can work most of the time out of doors. I'll be dog-goned if I hadn't ruther live here in poverty than die up north a-rolling in riches. Now, stranger, as to what you said about sickness, why we aren't no circumstance to you fellows up north. Why, your hull country is chuckfull of pizenous remedies. When I was a-coasting along Yankeedom and went ashore, I found all the rocks along the road were jist kivered with quack-medicine notices, and all the farmers hired out the outsides of their barns to advertise doctor's stuff on."

In no portion of America do the people seem to feel the burden of earning a livelihood more lightly. They get a great deal of social enjoyment out of life at very little cost, and place much less value on the "mighty dollar" than do their brother farmers of the northern section of the states. The interesting inquiry of "Who was his father?" commences at Philadelphia, and its importance intensifies as you travel southward. Old family associations have great weight among all classes.

It was six miles from the mouth of Love Creek across the little sound to Burton's marshy island at the entrance of Indian River Sound. Indian River supplies its bay with much of its fresh water, and the small inlet in the beach of the same name with the salt water of the ocean. Large flocks of geese and ducks were seen upon the quiet waters of the sound. Pursuing my southward course across Indian River Sound three miles, I entered a small creek with a wide mouth, which flows north from the cedar swamp, known as White's Creek, which I ascended until the stream became so narrow that it seemed almost lost in the wilderness, when suddenly an opening in the forest showed me a clearing with the little buildings of a farm scattered around. It was the home of a Methodist exhorter, Mr. Silas J. Betts. I told him how anxious I was to make a quick portage to the nearest southern water, Little Assawaman Bay, not much more than three miles distant by road.

After calmly examining my boat, he said: "It is now half-past eleven o'clock. Wife has dinner about ready. I'll hurry her up a little, and while she is putting it on the table we will get the cart ready." The cart was soon loaded with pine needles as a bed for the canoe. We lashed her into a firm position with cords, and went in to dinner.

In a short time after, we were rattling over a level, wooded country diversified here and there by a little farm. The shallow bay, the east side of which was separated from the ocean by sandy hills, was bounded by marshes. We drove close to the water and put the Maria Theresa once more into her true element. A friendly shake of the hand as I paid the conscientious man his charge of one dollar for his services, with many thanks for his hospitality, for which he would accept nothing—and the canoe was off, threading the narrow and very shallow channel-way of this grassy-bottomed bay.

The tall tower of Fenwick's Island Light, located on the boundary line of Delaware and Maryland, was now my landmark. It rises out of the low land that forms a barrier against which the sea breaks. The people on the coast pronounce Fenwick "Phœnix." Phœnix Island, they say, was once a part of the mainland, but a woman, wishing to keep her cattle from straying, gave a man a shirt for digging a narrow ditch between Little and Great Assawaman bays. The tide ebbed and flowed so strongly through this new channel-way that it was worn to more than a hundred feet in width, and has at high tide a depth in places of from ten to fifteen feet of water. The opening of this new thoroughfare so diminished the flow of water through the Little Assawaman Inlet to the sea, that it became closed. The water was almost fresh here, as the nearest inlet which admits salt water at high tide is at Chincoteague Island, some fifty miles distant.

Passing to the west of the light-house through this passage, I thought of what a woman could do, and almost expected to hear from the rippling waters the "Song of the Shirt," which would have been in this case a much more cheerful one than Hood's. I now entered Great Assawaman Bay, the waters of which lay like a mirror before me; and nearly five miles away, to the southwestern end, the tall forests of the Isle of Wight loomed up against the setting sun. Ducks rose in flocks from the quiet waters as my canoe glided into their close vicinity. If I could have taken less cargo, I should have carried a light gun; but this being impossible, a pocket revolver was my only fire-arm: so the ducks and other wild-fowl along my route had reason to hold the paper canoe in grateful remembrance.

Upon reaching the shores of the Isle of Wight I entered the mouth of St. Martin's River, which is, at its confluence with Isle of Wight Bay, more than two miles wide. I did not then possess the fine Coast Chart No. 28, or the General Chart of the Coast, No. 4, with the topography of the land clearly delineated, and showing every man's farm-buildings, fields, landings, &c., so plainly located as to make it easy for even a novice to navigate these bays. Now, being chartless so far as these waters were concerned, I peered about in the deepening twilight for my friend's plantation buildings, which I knew were not far off; but the gloomy forests of pine upon the upland opened not the desired vista I so longed to find.

Crossing the wide river, I came upon a long point of salt-marsh, which I hoped might be Keyser's Point, for I knew that to the west of this point I should find Turval's Creek. While rowing along the marsh I came upon two duck-shooters in their punt, but so enveloped were they in the mist that it was impossible to do more than define their forms. I, however, ventured a question as to my locality, when, to my utter astonishment, there came back to me in clear accents my own name. Never before had it sounded so sweet to my ears. It was the voice of my friend, who with a companion was occupied in removing from the water the flock of decoys which they had been guarding since sunrise. Joyful was the unexpected meeting.

We rowed around Keyser's Point, and up Turval's Creek, a couple of miles to the plantation landing. Here, upon the old estate in the little family burial-ground, slept, "each in his narrow cell," the children of four generations. Our conversation before the blazing wood-fire that night related to the ground travelled over during the day, a course of about thirty-five miles. Mr. Taylor's father mentioned that a friend, during one week in the previous September, had taken upon his hook, while fishing from the marshes of Rehoboth Bay, five hundred rock-fish, some of which weighed twenty pounds. The oysters in Rehoboth and Indian River bays had died out, probably from the decrease in the amount of salt water now entering them. A delightful week was spent with my friends at Winchester Plantation, when the falling of the mercury warned me to hurry southward.

On Wednesday, November 25, I descended the plantation creek and rowed out of St. Martin's River into the Bay. My course southward led me past "the Hommack," an Indian mound of oyster-shells, which rises about seven feet above the marsh on the west side of the entrance to Sinepuxent bay, and where the mainland approaches to within eight hundred feet of the beach. This point, which divides the Isle of Wight Bay from Sinepuxent, is the terminus of the Wicomico and Pocomoke Railroad, which has been extended from Berlin eastwardly seven miles. A short ferry conveys the passengers

across the water to a narrow island beach, which
is considered by Bayard Taylor, the author, the
finest beach he has ever visited.   This new
watering-place is called Ocean City; and my
friend, B. Jones Taylor, was treasurer of the
company which was engaged in making the
much-desired improvements.   The shallow bays
in the vicinity of Ocean City offer safe and pleasant sailing-grounds.   The summer fishing consists chiefly of white perch, striped bass, sheep's-
head, weak-fish, and drum.   In the fall, bluefish
are caught.   All of these, with oysters, soft
crabs, and diamond-backed terrapin, offer tempt-
ing dishes to the epicure.   This recently isolated
shore is now within direct railroad communication with Philadelphia and New York, and can
be reached in nine hours from the former, and
in twelve hours from the latter city.

From the Hommack to South Point is included
the length of Sinepuxent Bay, according to Coast
Survey authority.   From South Point to below
the middle of Chincoteague Island the bay is
put down as "Assateague," though the oystermen
do not call it by that name.   The celebrated
oyster-beds of the people of Chincoteague commence about twenty miles south of the Hommack.   There are two kinds of oysters shipped
from Chincoteague Inlet to New York and
other markets.   One is the long native plant;
the other, that transplanted from Chesapeake

Bay: this bivalve is rounded in form, and the most prized of the two. The average width of Sinepuxent was only a mile. When I turned westwardly around South Point, and entered Assateague Bay, the watery expanse widened, between the marshes on the west and the sandy-beach island on the east, to over four miles.

The debouchure of Newport Creek is to the west of South Point. The marshes here are very wide. I ascended it in the afternoon to visit Dr. F. J. Purnell, whose attempts to introduce the pinnated grouse and California partridges on his plantation had attracted the attention of Mr. Charles Hallock, editor of "Forest and Stream"; and I had promised him, if possible, to investigate the matter. This South Point of Sinepuxent Neck is a place of historical interest, it being now asserted that it is the burial-place of Edward Whalley, the regicide.

Early in 1875, Mr. Robert P. Robins found in a bundle of old family documents a paper containing interesting statements written by his great-great-grandfather, Thomas Robins, 3d, of South Point, Worcester County, Maryland, and dated July 8, 1769. We gather from this reliable source that Edward Whalley left Connecticut and arrived in Virginia in 16—, and was there met by a portion of his family. From Virginia he travelled to the " province of Maryland, and settled first at ye mouth of ye Pokemoke River; and finding yt too publick a place he came to Sinepuxent, a neck of land open to ye Atlantic Ocean, where Colonel Stephen was surveying and bought a tract of land from him and called it Genezar; it contained two thousand two hundred acres, south end of Sinepuxent; and made a settlement on ye southern extremity, and called it South Point; to ye which place he brought his family about 1687, in ye name of Edward Middleton. His own name he made not publick until after this date, after ye revolution in England, (in ye year of our Lord 1688,) when he let his name be seen in publick papers, and had ye lands patented in his own name."

The writer of the above quotation was the great-grandson of Edward Whalley (alias Edward Middleton), the celebrated regicide.

Four miles from South Point I struck the marshes which skirted Dr. Purnell's large plantation, and pushing the canoe up a narrow branch of the creek, I waded through the partially submerged herbage to the firm ground, where the doctor was awaiting me. His house was close at hand, within the hospitable walls of which I passed the night. Dr. Purnell has an estate of one thousand five hundred acres, lying along the banks of Newport Creek. Since the civil war it has been worked by tenants. Much of it is woodland and salt-marshes. Five years before my visit, a Philadelphian sent the doctor a few pairs of prairie-chickens, and a covey of both the valley and the mountain partridge. I am now using popular terms. The grouse were from a western state; the partridges had been obtained from California. The partridges were kept caged for several weeks and were then set at liberty. They soon disappeared in the woods, with the exception of a single pair, which returned daily to the kitchen-door of a farm tenant to obtain food. These two birds nested in the garden close to the house, and reared a fine brood of young; but the whole covey wandered away, and were afterwards heard from but once. They had crossed to the opposite side of Newport Creek, and were probably shot by gunners.

The prairie-chickens adapted themselves to their new home in a satisfactory manner, and became very tame. Their nests, well filled with eggs, were found along the rail-fences of the fields in the close vicinity of the marshes, for which level tracts they seemed to have strong attachment. They multiplied rapidly, and visited the cattle-pens and barn-yards of the plantation.

The Maryland legislature passed a law to protect all grouse introduced into the state; but a new danger threatened these unfortunate birds. A crew of New Jersey terrapin-hunters entered Chincoteague Inlet, and searched the ditches and little creeks of the salt-marshes for the " diamond-backs." While thus engaged, the gentle grouse, feeding quietly in the vicinity, attracted their attention, and they at once bagged most of them. A tenant on the estate informed me that he had seen eighteen birds in a cornfield a few days before — the remnant of the stock.

The Ruffled Grouse (*Bonasa umbellus*), so abundant in New Jersey, is not a resident of the peninsula.   Dr. Purnell's first experiment with the Pinnated Grouse (*Cupidonia cupido*) has encouraged others to bring the ruffled grouse to the eastern shore of Maryland. That unapproachable songster of the south, the American Mocking-bird (*Mimus polyglottus*), is becoming scarce in this region, from the inroads made by bird-catchers who ship the young to northern cities. This delightful chorister is only an accidental visitor in the New England states. Indeed, as far south as Ocean County, New Jersey, I saw but one of these birds, in a residence of nine years on my cranberry plantations; though I have heard that their nests are occasionally found about Cape May, at the extreme southern end of New Jersey.

My time being limited, I could enjoy the doctor's hospitality for but one night. The next morning the whole family, with tenants both black and white, assisted me to embark. By dusk I had crossed the division line of two states, and had entered Virginia near the head of Chincoteague Island, a locality of peculiar interest to the student of American character. The ebb-tide had left but little water around the rough pier abreast of the town, and heaps of oyster-shells rose from the mud flats and threatened the safety of my canoe. I looked up through the darkness to the light pier-head above me, and called for assistance. Two men leaned over to inquire, "What's the row now, stranger?" To which I replied, " I wish to land a light boat on your pier; and as it is made of paper, it should be carefully handled." For a moment the oys-termen observed a silence, and then, without one word of explanation, disappeared. I heard their heavy boots tramping up the quay towards the tavern. Soon a low murmur arose on the night air, then hoarse shouts, and there came thunder-ing down the wharf an army of men and boys. " Pass her up, stranger!" they cried. " Here, give us your bow and starn painters, and jest step overboard yourself, and we'll hist her up." Some of the motley crew caught me by the shoulders, others " histed away," and the canoe and its captain were laid roughly upon the ground.

There was a rush to *feel* of the paper shell. Many were convinced that there was no humbug about it; so, with a great shout, some of the men tossed it upon their shoulders, while the rest seized upon the miscellaneous cargo, and a rush was made for the hotel, leaving me to follow at

discretion and alone.   The procession burst open
the doors of the tavern, and poured through
the entrance to a court-yard, where they laid
the boat upon a long table under a shed, and
thought they had earned " drinks."   This was the
spontaneous way in which the Chincoteague people welcomed me.   " If you don't drink, stranger,
up your way, what on airth keeps your buddies
and soulds together? " queried a tall oysterman.
A lady had kindly presented me with a peck of fine
apples that very morning; so, in lieu of " drinks,"
I distributed the fruit among them.   They joked
and questioned me, and all were merry save one
bilious-looking individual, not dressed, like the
others, in an oysterman's garb, but wearing, to
use a term of the place, " store clothes."

After the crowd had settled in the bar-room,
at cards, &c., this doubting Thomas remained
beside the boat, carefully examining her.   Soon
he was scraping her hull below the gunwale,
where the muddy water of the bay had left a
thin coat of sediment which was now dry.   The
man's countenance lighted up as he pulled the
bartender aside and said, " Look ahere; didn't
I tell you that boat looked as if she was made to
carry on a deck of a vessel, and to be a-shoved off
into the water at night jest abreast of a town to
make fools of folks, and git them to believe that
that fellow had a-rowed *all* the way ahere?
Now see, here is *dust, dry dust,* on her hull.

She ahain't ben in the water mor'n ten minutes, I sware." It required but a moment's investigation of my Chincoteague audience to discover that the dust was mud from the tide, and the doubter brought down the ridicule of his more discriminating neighbors upon him, and slunk away amid their jeers.

Of all this community of watermen but one could be found that night who had threaded the interior watercourses as far as Cape Charles, and he was the youngest of the lot. Taking out my note-book, I jotted down his amusing directions. " Look out for Cat Creek below Four Mouths," he said; "you'll catch it round there." "Yes," broke in several voices, " Cat Creek's an awful place unless you run through on a full ebb-tide. Oyster boats always has a time a-shoving through Cat Creek," &c.

After the council with my Chincoteague friends had ended, the route to be travelled the next day was in my mental vision " as clear as mud." The inhabitants of this island are not all oystermen, for many find occupation and profit in raising ponies upon the beach of Assateague, where the wild, coarse grass furnishes them a livelihood. These hardy little animals are called " Marsh Tackies," and are found at intervals along the beaches down to the sea-islands of the Carolinas. They hold at Chincoteague an annual fair, to which all the " pony-penners," as they

are called, bring their surplus animals to sell.
The average price is about ninety dollars for a
good beast, though some have sold for two hundred and fifty dollars. All these horses are sold
in a semi-wild and unbroken state.

The following morning Mr. J. L. Caulk, ex-
collector of the oyster port, and about fifty persons, escorted me to the landing, and sent me
away with a hearty "Good luck to ye."

It was three miles and three quarters to the
southern end of the island, which has an inlet
from the ocean upon each side of that end — the
northern one being Assateague, the southern one
Chincoteague Inlet. Fortunately, I crossed the
latter in smooth water to Ballast Narrows in
the marshes, and soon reached Four Mouths,
where I found *five* mouths of thoroughfares, and
became perplexed, for had not the pilots of
Chincoteague called this interesting display of
mouths "Four Mouths"? I clung to the authority
of local knowledge, however, and was soon in a
labyrinth of creeks which ended in the marshes
near the beach.

Returning over the course, I once more faced
the four, or *five* mouths rather, and taking a new
departure by entering the next mouth to the one
I had so unsatisfactorily explored, soon entered
Rogue's Bay, across which could be seen the
entrance to Cat Creek, where I was to experience the difficulties predicted by my Chinco-

teague friends.   Cat Creek furnished at half tide sufficient water for my canoe, and not the slightest difficulty was experienced in getting through it.   The oystermen had in their minds their own sloop-rigged oyster-boats when they discoursed to me about the hard passage of Cat Creek. They had not considered the fact that my craft drew only five inches of water.

Cat Creek took me quite down to the beach, where, through an inlet, the dark-blue ocean, sparkling in its white caps, came pleasantly into view.   Another inlet was to be crossed, and again I was favored with smooth water.   This was Assawaman Inlet, which divided the beach into two islands — Wallops on the north, and Assawaman on the south.

It seemed a singular fact that the two Assawaman bays are forty-five miles to the north of an inlet of the same name.   In following the creeks through the marshes between Assawaman Island and the mainland, I crossed another shoal bay, and another inlet opened in the beach, through which the ocean was again seen.   This last was Gargathy Inlet.   Before reaching it, as night was coming on, I turned up a thoroughfare and rowed some distance to the mainland, where I found lodgings with a hospitable farmer, Mr. Martin R. Kelly.   At daybreak I crossed Gargathy Inlet.

It was now Saturday, November 28; and being encouraged by the successful crossing of the inlets in my tiny craft, I pushed on to try the less inviting one at the end of Matomkin Island. Fine weather favored me, and I pushed across the strong tide that swept through this inlet without shipping a sea. Assawaman and Gargathy are constantly shifting their channels. At times there will be six feet of water, and again they will shoal to two feet. Matomkin, also, is not to be relied on. Every northeaster will shift a buoy placed in the channels of these three inlets, so they are not buoyed.

Watchapreague Inlet, to the south of the three last named, is less changeable in character, and is also a much more dangerous inlet to cross in rough weather. From Matomkin Inlet the interior thoroughfares were followed inside of Cedar Island, when darkness forced me to seek shelter with Captain William F. Burton, whose comfortable home was on the shore of the mainland, about five miles from Watchapreague Inlet. Here I was kindly invited to spend Sunday. Captain Burton told me much of interest, and among other things mentioned the fact that during one August, a few years before my visit, a large lobster was taken on a fish-hook in Watchapreague Inlet, and that a smaller one was captured in the same manner during the summer of 1874.

Monday was a gusty day. My canoe scraped its keel upon the shoals as I dodged the broken oyster reefs, called here "oyster rocks," while on the passage down to Watchapreague Inlet. The tide was very low, but the water deepened as the beach was approached. A northeaster was blowing freshly, and I was looking for a lee under the beach, when suddenly the canoe shot around a sandy point, and was tugging for life in the rough waters of the inlet. The tide was running in from the sea with the force of a rapid, and the short, quick puffs of wind tossed the waves wildly. It was useless to attempt to turn the canoe back to the beach in such rough water, but, intent on keeping the boat above the caps, I gave her all the momentum that muscular power could exert, as she was headed for the southern point of the beach, across the dangerous inlet.

Though it was only half a mile across, the passage of Watchapreague taxed me severely. Waves washed over my canoe, but the gallant little craft after each rebuff rose like a bird to the surface of the water, answering the slightest touch of my oar better than the best-trained steed. After entering the south-side swash, the wind struck me on the back, and seas came tumbling over and around the boat, fairly forcing me on to the beach. As we flew along, the tumultuous waters made my head swim; so, to prevent mental confusion, I kept my eyes only upon the oars, which, strange to say, never betrayed me into a false stroke.

As a heavy blast beat down the raging sea for a moment, I looked over my shoulder and beheld the low, sandy dunes of the southern shore of the inlet close at hand, and with a severe jolt the canoe grounded high on the strand. I leaped out and drew my precious craft away from the tide, breathing a prayer of thankfulness for my escape from danger, and mentally vowing that the canoe should cross all other treacherous inlets in a fisherman's sloop. I went into camp in a hollow of the beach, where the sand-hills protected me from the piercing wind. All that afternoon I watched from my burrow in the ground the raging of the elements, and towards evening was pleased to note a general subsidence of wind and sea.

The canoe was again put into the water and the thoroughfare followed southward for a mile or two, when the short day ended, leaving me beside a marshy island, which was fringed with an oyster-bed of sharp-beaked bivalves. Stepping overboard in the mud and water, the oars and paddle were laid upon the shell reef to protect the canoe, which was dragged on to the marsh. It grew colder as the wind died out. The marsh was wet, and no fire-wood could be found. The canvas cover was removed, the cargo was piled up on a platform of oars and shells to secure it from the next tide, and then I slowly and laboriously packed myself away in the narrow shell for the night. The canvas deck-cover was buttoned in its place, a rubber blanket covered the cockpit, and I tried to sleep and dream that I was not a sardine, nor securely confined in some inhospitable vault. It was impossible to turn over without unbuttoning one side of the deck-cover and going through contortions that would have done credit to a first-class acrobat. For the first time in my life I found it necessary to get *out* of bed in order to turn over *in* it.

At midnight, mallards (*Anas boschas*) came close to the marsh. The soft *whagh* of the drake, which is not in this species blessed with the loud quack of the female bird, sufficiently established the identity of the duck. Then muskrats, and the oyster-eating coon, came round, no doubt scenting my provisions. Brisk raps from my knuckles on the inside shell of the canoe astonished these animals and aroused their curiosity, for they annoyed me until daybreak.

When I emerged from my narrow bed, the frosty air struck my cheeks, and the cold, wet marsh chilled my feet. It was the delay at Watchapreague Inlet that had lodged me on this inhospitable marsh; so, trying to exercise my poor stock of patience, I completed my toilet, shaking in my wet shoes. The icy water, into which I stepped ankle-deep in order to launch my canoe, reminded me that this wintry morning was in fact the first day of December, and that

stormy Hatteras, south of which was to be found
a milder climate, was still a long way off.

The brisk row along Paramore's Island (called
Palmer's by the natives) to the wide, bay-like
entrance of Little Machipongo Inlet, restored
warmth to my benumbed limbs. This wide
doorway of the ocean permitted me to cross its
west portal in peace, for the day was calm.
From Little to Great Machipongo Inlet the
beach is called Hog Island. The inside thoroughfare is bounded on the west by Rogue's
Island, out of the flats of which rose a solitary
house. At the southern end of Hog Island
there is a small store on a creek, and near the
beach a light-house, while a little inland is located, within a forest of pines, a small settlement.

At noon, Great Machipongo Inlet was crossed
without danger, and Cobb's Island was skirted
several miles to Sand Shoal Inlet, near which
the hotel of the three Cobb brothers rose
cheerfully out of the dreary waste of sands and
marshes. The father of the present proprietors
came to this island more than thirty years ago,
and took possession of this domain, which had
been thrown up by the action of the ocean's
waves. He refused an offer of one hundred
thousand dollars for the island. The locality is
one of the best on this coast for wild-fowl shooting. Sand Shoal Inlet, at the southern end of

Cobb's Island, has a depth of twelve feet of water on its bar at low tide.

In company with the regular row-boat ferry I crossed, the next day, the broad bay to the mainland eight miles distant, where the canoe was put upon a cart and taken across the peninsula five miles to Cherrystone, the only point near Cape Charles at which a Norfolk steamer stopped for passengers. It was fully forty miles across Chesapeake Bay from Cherrystone Landing to Norfolk, and it was imperative to make the portage from this place instead of from Cape Charles, which, though more than fifteen miles further south, and nearer to my starting-point on the other side, did not possess facilities for transportation. The slow one-horse conveyance arrived at Cherrystone half an hour *after* the steamer N. P. Banks had left the landing, though I heard that the kind-hearted captain, being told I was coming, waited and whistled for me till his patience was exhausted.

The only house at the head of the pier was owned by Mr. J. P. Powers, and fortunately offered hotel accommodations. Here I remained until the next trip of the boat, December 4. Arriving in Norfolk at dusk of the same day, I stored my canoe in the warehouse of the Old Dominion Steamship Company, and quietly retired to an hotel which promised an early meal in the morning, congratulating myself the while that I had avoided the usual show of curiosity tendered to canoeists at city piers, and above all had escaped the inevitable reporter. Alas! my thankfulness came too soon; for when about to retire, my name was called, and a veritable reporter from the Norfolk Landmark cut off my retreat.

"Only a few words," he pleadingly whispered. "I've been hunting for you all over the city since seven o'clock, and it is near midnight now."

He gently took my arm and politely furnished me with a chair. Then placing his own directly before me, he insinuatingly worked upon me until he derived a knowledge of the log of the Paper Canoe, when leaning back in his chair he leisurely surveyed me and exclaimed:

"Mr. Bishop, you are a man of *snap*. We like men of snap; we admire men of snap; in fact, I may say we *cotton* to men of snap, and I am proud to make your acquaintance. Now if you will stop over a day we will have the whole city out to see your boat."

This *kind* offer I firmly refused, and we were about to part, when he said in a softly rebuking manner:

"You thought, Mr. Bishop, you would give us the slip—did you not? I assure you that would be quite impossible. Eternal Vigilance is our motto. No, you could not escape us. Good evening, sir, and the 'Landmark's' welcome to you."

Six hours later, as I entered the restaurant of the hotel with my eyes half open, a newsboy bawled out in the darkness: "'Ere's the 'Landmark.' Full account of the Paper Canoe," &c. And before the sun was up I had read a column and a half of "The Arrival of the Solitary Voyager in Norfolk." So much for the zeal of Mr. Perkins of the "Landmark," a worthy example of American newspaper enterprise. Dreading further attentions, I now prepared to beat a hasty retreat from the city.

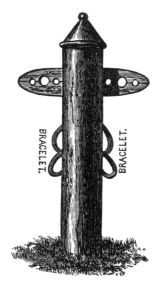

DELAWARE WHIPPING-POST AND PILLORY

CHAPTER IX.

FROM NORFOLK TO CAPE HATTERAS.

THE ELIZABETH RIVER. — THE CANAL. — NORTH LANDING RIVER.
— CURRITUCK SOUND. — ROANOKE ISLAND. — VISIT TO BODY
ISLAND LIGHT-HOUSE. — A ROMANCE OF HISTORY. — PAMPLICO
SOUND. — THE PAPER CANOE ARRIVES AT CAPE HATTERAS.

ON Saturday morning, December 5, I left the
pier of the Old Dominion Steamship Company, at Norfolk, Virginia, and, rowing across the
water towards Portsmouth, commenced ascending Elizabeth River, which is here wide and
affected by tidal change. The old navy yard,
with its dismantled hulks lying at anchor in the
stream, occupies both banks of the river. About
six miles from Norfolk the entrance to the Dismal Swamp Canal is reached, on the left bank
of the river. This old canal runs through the
Great Dismal Swamp, and affords passage for
steamers and light-draught vessels to Elizabeth
City, on the Pasquotank River, which empties
into Albemarle Sound to the southward. The
great cypress and juniper timber is penetrated by
this canal, and schooners are towed into the

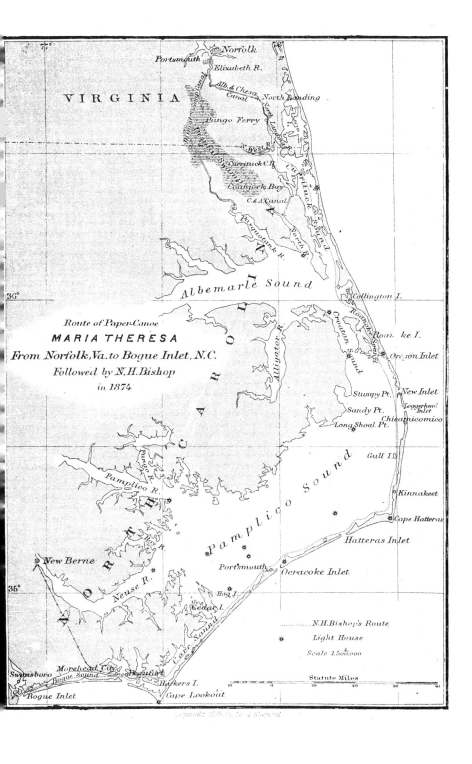

VIRGINIA

Norfolk
Portsmouth
Elizabeth R.
Alb. & Chesa. Canal
North Landing
North Landing R.
Pungo Ferry
N. West R.
Currituck C.H.
Coanjock Bay
C. & A. Canal
Pasquotank R.
North R.
Currituck Sound

36°

Albemarle Sound

Collington I.

Route of Paper-Canoe
MARIA THERESA
From Norfolk, Va. to Bogue Inlet, N.C.
Followed by N. H. Bishop
in 1874

Alligator R.
Croatan Sound
Roanoke Sound
Roanoke I.
Oregon Inlet
Stumpy Pt.
New Inlet
Sandy Pt.
Loggerhead Inlet
Chicamicomico
Long Shoal Pt.

NORTH CAROLINA

Gull I.

Pamplico R.
Pungo R.

Kinnakeet

Pamplico Sound

Cape Hatteras

New Berne

Hatteras Inlet

35°
Neuse R.
Portsmouth
Ocracoke Inlet

Hog I.

Cedar I.

.... N. H. Bishop's Route

✴ Light House

Scale 1.500.000

Core Sound

Statute Miles

Swansboro
Morehead City
Beaufort
Bogue Sound
Harkers I.
Cape Lookout
Bogue Inlet

10   0   10   20   30   40

swamp to landings where their cargoes are de-
livered.

In the interior of the Dismal Swamp is Drum-
mond's Lake, named after its discoverer.   It is
seven miles long by five miles wide, and is the
feeder of the canal.   A branch canal connects it
with the main canal; and small vessels may
traverse the lake in search of timber and shingles.
Voyagers tell me that during heavy gales of
wind a terrible sea is set in motion upon this
shoal sheet of water, making it dangerous to
navigate.   Bears are found in the fastnesses of
the swamp.   The Dismal Swamp Canal was dug
in the old days of the wheelbarrow and spade.

The Albemarle and Chesapeake Canal, the entrance to which is sixteen miles from Norfolk,
on the right or east bank of the Elizabeth River,
and generally known as the "new canal," was
commenced about the year 1856, and finished in
1859.   It is eight miles and a half in length,
and connects the Elizabeth and North Landing
rivers.   This canal was dug by dredging-machines.   It is kept in a much better state for
navigation, so far as the depth of water is concerned, than the old canal, which from inatten-
tion is gradually shoaling in places; consequently
the regular steam-packets which ply between
Elizabeth City and Norfolk, as well as steamers
whose destinations are further north, have given
up the use of the Dismal Swamp Canal, and

now go round through Albemarle Sound up the
North River, thence by a six-mile cut into Currituck Sound, up North Landing River, and
through the new canal to the Elizabeth River
and into Chesapeake Bay. The shores of the
Elizabeth are low and are fringed by sedgy
marshes, while forests of second-growth pine
present a green background to the eye. A few
miles above Norfolk the cultivation of land
ceases, and the canoeist traverses a wilderness.

About noon I arrived at the locks of the Albemarle and Chesapeake Canal. The telegraph
operator greeted me with the news that the company's agent in Norfolk had telegraphed to the
lock-master to pass the paper canoe through with
the freedom of the canal — the first honor of the
kind that had fallen to my lot. The tide rises
and falls at the locks in the river about three feet
and a half. When I passed through, the difference in the level between the ends of the locks
did not reach two feet. The old lock-master
urged me to give up the journey at once, as I
never could " get through the Sounds with that
little boat." When I told him I was on my
second thousand miles of canoe navigation since
leaving Quebec, he drew a long breath and
gave a low groan.

When once through the canal-gates, you are
in a heavy cypress swamp. The dredgings
thrown upon the banks have raised the edge of

the swamp to seven feet above the water. Little
pines grow along these shores, and among them
the small birds, now on their southern migrations,
sported and sang. Whenever a steamer or tug-
boat passed me, it crowded the canoe close to
the bank; but these vessels travel along the
canal at so slow a rate, that no trouble is experienced by the canoeist from the disturbance
caused by their revolving screws. Freedmen,
poling flats loaded with shingles or frame stuff,
roared out their merry songs as they passed.
The canal entered the North Landing River
without any lockage; just beyond was North
Landing, from which the river takes its name.
A store and evidences of a settlement meet the
eye at a little distance. The river is tortuous,
and soon leaves the swamp behind. The pine
forest is succeeded by marshes on both sides of
the slow-flowing current.

Three miles from North Landing a single
miniature house is seen; then for nearly five
miles along the river not a trace of the presence
of man is to be met, until Pungo Ferry and Landing loom up out of the low marshes on the east
side of the river. This ferry, with a store three-
quarters of a mile from the landing, and a farm
of nearly two hundred acres, is the property of
Mr. Charles N. Dudley, a southern gentleman,
who offers every inducement in his power to
northern men to settle in his vicinity. Many of

the property-holders in the uplands are willing to sell portions of their estates to induce northern men to come among them.

It was almost dark when I reached the storehouse at Pungo Ferry; and as Sunday is a sacred day with me, I determined to camp there until Monday. A deformed negro held a lease of the ferry, and pulled a flat back and forth across the river by means of a chain and windlass. He was very civil, and placed his quarters at my disposal until I should be ready to start southward to Currituck Sound. We lifted the canoe and pushed it through an open window into the little store-room, where it rested upon an unoccupied counter. The negro went up to the loft above, and threw down two large bundles of flags for a bed, upon which I spread my blankets. An old stove in a corner was soon aglow with burning light wood. While I was cooking my supper, the little propeller Cygnet, which runs between Norfolk and Van Slyck's Landing, at Currituck Narrows, touched at Pungo Ferry, and put off an old woman who had been on a two years' visit to her relatives. She kindly accosted the dwarfed black with, "Charles, have you got a match for my pipe?"

"Yes, missus," civilly responded the negro, handing her a light.

"Well, this *is good!*" soliloquized the ancient dame, as she seated herself on a box and puffed away at the short-stemmed pipe. "Ah, good indeed to get away from city folks, with their stuck-up manners and queer ways, a-fault-finding when you stick your knife in your mouth in place of your fork, and a-feeding you on *China* tea in place of dear old yaupon. Charles, you can't reckon how I longs to get a cup of good yaupon."

As the reader is about entering a country where the laboring classes draw largely upon nature for their supply of "the cup that cheers but not inebriates," I will describe the shrub which produces it.

This substitute for the tea of China is a holly (*ilex*), and is called by the natives "yaupon" (*I. cassine, Linn.*). It is a handsome shrub, growing a few feet in height, with alternate, per-ennial, shining leaves, and bearing small scarlet berries. It is found in the vicinity of salt water, in the light soils of Virginia and the Carolinas. The leaves and twigs are dried by the women, and when ready for market are sold at one dollar per bushel. It is not to be compared in excel-lence with the tea of China, nor does it approach in taste or good qualities the well-known *yerba-maté*, another species of holly, which is found in Paraguay, and is the common drink of the people of South America.

The old woman having gone on her way, and we being again alone in the rude little shanty, the good-natured freedman told me his history, ending with, —

"O that was a glorious day for me,
When Massa Lincoln set me free."

He had too much ambition, he said, deformed as he was, to be supported as a pauper by the public. "I can make just about twelve dollars a month by dis here ferry," he exclaimed. "I don't want for nuffin'; I'se got no wife — no woman will hab me. I want to support myself and live an honest man."

About seven o'clock he left me to waddle up the road nearly a mile to a little house.

"I an' another cullo'd man live in partnership," he said. He could not account for the fact that I had no fear of sleeping alone in the shanty on the marshes. He went home for the company of his partner, as he "didn't like to sleep alone noways."

Though the cold wind entered through broken window-lights and under the rudely constructed door, I slept comfortably until morning. Before Charles had returned, my breakfast was cooked and eaten.

With the sunshine of the morning came a new visitor. I had made the acquaintance of the late slave; now I received a call from the late master. My visitor was a pleasant, gentlemanly personage, the owner of the surrounding

acres.   His large white house could be seen
from the landing, a quarter of a mile up the
road.

"I learned that a stranger from the north was
camped here, and was expecting that he would
come up and take breakfast with me," was his
kindly way of introducing himself.

I told him I was comfortably established in
dry quarters, and did not feel justified in forcing myself upon his hospitality while I had so
many good things of this life in my provision-
basket.

Mr. Dudley would take no excuse, but conducted me to his house, where I remained that
day, attending the religious services in a little
church in the vicinity.   My kind host introduced
me to his neighbors, several of whom returned
with us to dinner.   I found the people about
Pungo Ferry, like those I had met along the
sounds of the eastern shore of Maryland and
Virginia, very piously inclined,—the same kind-
hearted, hospitable people.

My host entertained me the next day, which
was rainy, with his life in the Confederate army,
in which he served as a lieutenant.   He was a
prisoner at Johnson's Island for twenty-two
months.   He bore no malice towards northern
men who came south to join with the natives in
working for the true interests of the country.
The people of the south had become weary of

political sufferings inflicted by a floating population from the north; they needed actual settlers,
not politicians. This sentiment I found everywhere expressed. On Tuesday I bade farewell
to my new friends, and rowed down the North
Landing River towards Currituck Sound.

· The North Carolina line is only a few miles
south of the ferry. The river enters the head
of the sound six or eight miles below Pungo
Ferry. A stiff northerly breeze was blowing,
and as the river widened, on reaching the head
of the sound, to a mile or more, and bays were
to be crossed from point to point, it required
the exercise of considerable patience and muscular exertion to keep the sea from boarding
the little craft amidship. As I was endeavoring
to weather a point, the swivel of one of the outriggers parted at its junction with the row-lock,
and it became necessary to get under the south
point of the marshes for shelter.

The lee side offered a smooth bay. It was
but a few minutes' work to unload and haul the
canoe into the tall rushes, which afforded ample
protection against the cold wind. It was three
hours before the wind went down, when the
canoe was launched, and, propelled by the double
paddle, (always kept in reserve against accidents
to oars and row-locks,) I continued over the
waters of Currituck Sound.

Swans could now be seen in flocks of twenties

and fifties. They were exceedingly wary, not permitting the canoe to approach within rifle range. Clouds of ducks, and some Canada geese, as well as brant, kept up a continuous flutter as they rose from the surface of the water. Away to the southeast extended the glimmering bosom of the sound, with a few islands relieving its monotony. The three or four houses and two small storehouses at the landing of Currituck Court House, which, with the brick court-house, comprise the whole village, are situated on the west bank; and opposite, eight miles to the eastward, is the narrow beach island that serves as a barrier to the ingress of the ocean.

At sunset I started the last flock of white swans, and grounded in the shoal waters at the landing. There is no regular hotel here, but a kind lady, Mrs. Simmons, accommodates the necessities of the occasional traveller. The canoe was soon locked up in the landing-house. Fortunately a blacksmith was found outside the village, who promised to repair the broken row-lock early upon the following morning. Before a pleasant wood fire giving out its heat from a grand old fireplace, with an agreeable visitor, — the physician of the place, — the tediousness of the three-hours' camp on the marshes was soon forgotten, while the country and its resources were fully discussed until a late hour.

Dr. Baxter had experimented in grape culture,

and gave me many interesting details in regard to the native wine. In 1714, Lawson described six varieties of native grapes found in North Carolina. Our three finest varieties of native grapes were taken from North Carolina. They are the Scuppernong, the Catawba, and the Isabella. The Scuppernong was found upon the banks of the stream bearing that name, the mouth of which is near the eastern end of Albemarle Sound. The Catawba was originally obtained on the Catawba River, near its head-waters in Buncombe County. The Long Island stock of the Isabella grape was brought to New York by Mrs. Isabella Gibbs: hence the derivation of the name.

Of the six varieties of North Carolina grapes, five were found in Tyrrel County by Amadas and Barlow. Tradition relates that these travellers carried one small vine to Roanoke Island, which still lives and covers an immense area of ground. There are five varieties of the grape growing wild on the shores of Albemarle Sound, all of which are called Scuppernong,—the legitimate Scuppernong being a white grape, sweet and large, and producing a wine said to resemble somewhat in its luscious flavor the Malmsey made on Mount Ida, in Candia.

The repairing of the outrigger detained me until nearly noon of the next day, when the canoe was got under way; but upon rowing off

the mouth of Coanjock Bay, only four miles from
Currituck Court House, a strong tempest arose
from the south, and observing an old gentleman standing upon Bell Island Point, near his
cottage, beckoning me to come ashore, I obeyed,
and took refuge with my new acquaintance, Captain Peter L. Tatum, proprietor of Bell Island.

"The war has left us without servants," said
the captain, as he presented me to his wife, "so
we make the best of it, and if you will accept
our hospitality we will make you comfortable."

Captain Tatum drew my attention to the flocks
of swans which dotted the waters in the offing,
and said: "It is hard work to get hold of a swan,
though they are a large bird, and abundant in
Currituck Sound. You must use a good rifle
to bring one down. After a strong norther has
been blowing, and the birds have worked well
into the bight of the bay, near Goose Castle Point,
if the wind shifts to the south suddenly, gunners
approach from the outside, and the birds becoming cramped in the cove are shot as they rise
against the wind."

More than forty years ago old Currituck Inlet
closed, and the oysters on the natural beds, which
extended up North Landing River to Green
Point, were killed by the freshening of the
water. Now winds influence the tides which
enter at Oregon Inlet, about fifty-five miles
south of the Court House. The difference be-

tween the highest and lowest tide at Currituck
Court House is three feet. The sound is filled
with sandy shoals, with here and there spots of
mud. ˙ The shells of the defunct oysters are
everywhere found mixed with the debris of the
bottom of the sound. This is a favorite locality
with northern sportsmen. The best " gunning
points," as is the case in Chesapeake Bay, are
owned by private parties, and cannot be used
by the public.

Thursday, the 10th of December, was cold,
and proved as tempestuous as the previous day;
but the wind had changed to the north, and I
embarked amid a swashy beam-sea, with the
hope of reaching Van Slyck's Landing at Currituck Narrows. The norther, however, proved
too much for my safety. My course would be
easterly until I had passed the mouth of Coanjock Bay and Goose Castle Point, then following
the trend of the west shore southerly down the
sound; but the wind raised such a rough sea
that I was obliged to turn southward into Coanjock Bay, ascend it five miles, and seek for a
crossing-place overland to the sound again,
which I found near the entrance of the lock-
less canal that is used by steamers to pass from
North Landing River to North River and Albemarle Sound.

A fire was soon built, upon which I placed
long, light poles taken from the drift-wood, and

burning them in pieces of the required lengths, (no axe being at hand,) I was prepared to make the portage.   Laying these pieces of wood on the ground, I drew my canoe over them to the shore of Currituck Sound; then, by making up back-loads of the cargo, transported everything to the point of embarkation, which was just inside the mouth of a little creek.

The row to Currituck Narrows was not diffi-cult, as the north wind was a fair one.   Along the west shore of the sound there were many little houses upon the high banks, and a wind-mill supplied the place of a water-power for grinding corn.   The improvements made by Mr. Van Slyck, of New York, were in cheering con-trast to what had been seen since leaving Nor-folk.   Here a comfortable hotel welcomes the northern sportsmen, few of whom, for lack of accommodations and travelling conveniences, go much south of this locality, in this state, to shoot wild-fowl.   Currituck Sound has an average width of four miles.   Its length is about thirty-five miles.   At the Narrows, a group of marshy islands divides it into two sections, the northern one being the longest.

The keen, cold air of the next day made row-ing a pleasant exercise.   After passing through the tortuous channel, I should have crossed to the beach and followed it; but this part of the bay is very shallow, and deeper water was found on the west side. It was an enjoyable morning, for gunners were passed, secreted behind their " blinds," or pens, of pine brush, which looked like little groves of conifera growing out of the shoal water. Geese were honking and ducks were quacking, while the deep booming of guns was heard every few minutes. Decoy-birds were anchored in many places near the marshes. Every sportsman gave me a cheering word as the canoe glided over the smooth water, while here and there the violet-backed swallow darted about over the marshes as though it were summer.

When opposite Dew's Quarter Island, several men hailed me from a newly constructed shanty. When the oldest man in the company, who had never seen a shell like the paper canoe, had examined it, he shook his head ominously; and when I told him Nag's Head must be reached that day, he grew excited, exclaiming, " Then be off now! now! Git across the bay under Bald Beach as soon as ye can, and hug the shore, *hug* it well clean down to Collington's, and git across the sound afore the wind rises. Sich a boat as that aren't fit for these here waters."

Taking this kindly meant advice, I pulled to the east side, where there was now a good depth of water for the canoe. On this high beach the hills were well covered with yellow pines, many of which were noble old trees. On a narrow point of the shore was the comfortable house of Hodges Gallup, the Baptist minister, a generous old gentleman, who seemed to be loved by all the watermen along the sound. He was described as being "full of fun and hospitality." His domain extended for several miles along the beach, and, with deer quietly browsing in his grand old woods, formed a pretty picture.

The beach shore now became more thickly settled, while out in the water, a few rods from each little house, arose the duck-blind, with the gunner and his boat inside, anxiously watching for birds, while their decoys floated quietly on the surface of the water. A few miles below Mr. Gallup's estate the canoe entered upon the broad waters of Albemarle Sound, and at dusk I approached Roanoke Island. The large buildings of the hotels of Nag's Head on the beach rose up as boldly to the eye as a fortification. The little sound between Roanoke Island and the beach was traversed at dusk as far as the first long pier of Nag's Head, upon which with great difficulty I landed, and was soon joined by the keeper of the now deserted summer wateringplace, Mr. C. D. Rutter, who helped me to carry my property into a room of the old hotel.

Nag's Head Beach is a most desolate locality, with its high sand-hills, composed of fine sand, the forms of which are constantly changing with the action of the dry, hard, varying winds. A new and very large hotel was located south of the first one, and was inhabited by the family of Captain Jasper Toler, who furnished me with lodgings. A few fishermen have their homes on this dreary beach, but the village, with its one store, is a forlorn place.

The bright flashes of Body Island Light, ten miles distant, on the north side of Oregon Inlet, showed me my next abiding-place.

The beach from Nag's Head to Oregon Inlet is destitute of trees, and the wind sweeps across it, from the ocean to the sound, with great violence, forcing the shallow waters to retire, and leaving the bottom dry as far out as three miles.

The next day was very windy, and the long, finger-like, sandy shoals, which extended one or two miles out into the sound, were covered with only from three to eight inches of water. I could not hug the beach for protection, but was forced to keep far out in the sound. Frequently it became necessary to get overboard and wade, pushing my boat before me. Then a deep channel between the shoals would be crossed; so, by *walking and rowing* in Roanoke Sound, with the wind blowing the water over the canoe and drenching its captain, the roundabout twelve miles' passage to Oregon Inlet was at last accomplished, and a most trying one it was.

Body Island Light House was erected in 1872, on the north side of Oregon Inlet, to take the place of the old tower on the south shore. It is in latitude 35° 48′, and longitude 75° 33′. Captain William F. Hatzel, a loyal North Carolinian, is the principal keeper, and a most efficient one he is.

The temperature was falling rapidly when I crawled into the high rushes of the wet marsh near the light-house to seek shelter from the strong wind that was blowing. As this treeless beach was destitute of fire-wood, or natural shelter of any kind, necessity compelled me to have recourse to other means for procuring them. I carried in my pocket a talisman which must open any light-keeper's door; from Maine to the Rio Grande, from Southern California to Alaska, even to the vicinity of the Arctic Circle, wherever the Light-house Establishment of the United States has planted a tower or erected a light. While shivering in wet clothes on this desolate beach, most thankfully did I remember that kind and thoughtful friend, who through his potent influence had supplied me with this open sesame to light-keepers.

There resides in Washington, when not engaged elsewhere in the important duties of the Commission of Fisheries, a genial gentleman, an ardent naturalist, a great scientist. To him the young naturalists of America turn for information and advice, and to the humblest applicant Professor Spencer F. Baird never turns a deaf ear.

How this distinguished author can attend to so
many and such varied duties with his laborious
investigations, and can so successfully keep up a
large correspondence with perhaps one thousand
scientific associations of nearly every nation of
the universe, is a difficult thing to imagine; but
the popular and much beloved Assistant Secretary of the Smithsonian Institution, seemingly
ubiquitous in his busy life, does all this and much
more.   America may well feel proud of this man
of noble nature, shedding light and truth wheresoever he moves, encouraging alike old and
young with his kindly sympathy; — now taking
his precious moments to answer with his own
busy hand the question in the letter of some boy
naturalist about beasts, birds, reptiles, or fishes,
with which epistles his desk is always covered;
now stimulating to further effort the old man of
science as he struggles with the cares of this
world, striving, sometimes vainly, save for this
ever ready aid, to work out patiently theories
which are soon to blaze forth as substantial facts.
The young generation of naturalists, which is
soon to fill the place of their predecessors, have
in this man the type of all they need ever strive
to attain.   How many, alas, will fall far short
of it!

Since boyhood the counsels of this friend had
guided me on many a journey of exploration.
He had not deserted me even in this experiment,

which my friends called "your wildest and most
foolish undertaking." He had obtained from the
Light House Board a general letter to the light-
keepers of the United States, signed by the
naval secretary, Mr. Walker, in which the keepers were authorized to grant me shelter, &c.,
when necessary. I did not have occasion to use
this letter more than twice during my journey.
Having secreted my canoe in the coarse grass
of the lowland, I trudged, with my letter in hand,
over the sands to the house of the light-keeper,
Captain Hatzel, who received me cordially; and
after recording in his log-book the circumstances
and date of my arrival, conducted me into a
comfortable room, which was warmed by a
cheerful fire, and lighted up by the smiles of his
most orderly wife. Everything showed discipline and neatness, both in the house and the
light-tower. The whitest of cloths was spread
upon the table, and covered with a well-cooked
meal; then the father, mother, and two sons,
with the stranger within their gates, thanked the
Giver of good gifts for his mercies.

Joining the night-watch of the chief light-
keeper, I also joined in the good man's enthusiasm for his wonderful "fixed white light," the
bright beams of which poured out upon the surrounding waters a flood of brilliancy, gladdening
hearts far out at sea, even though twenty miles
away, and plainly saying, "This is Body Island

Beach: keep off! " How grand it was to walk
out on this gallery in the sky! Looking eastward, a limitless expanse of ocean; gazing westward, the waters of the great sound, the shores
of which were low marshes miles away. Below
me could be heard the soft cackle of the snow-
goose (*Anser hyperboreus*), which had left its
nesting-place on the barren grounds of arctic
America, and was now feeding contentedly in its
winter home in the shallow salt-ponds; while the
gentle shur–r–r– of the waves softly broke on
the strand. Above, the star-lit heavens, whose
tender beauty seemed almost within my grasp.

Perched thus upon a single shaft, on a narrow
strip of sand far out in the great water, the many
thoughts born of solitude crowded my mind,
when my reverie was abruptly broken by an
exclamation from Captain Hatzel, who threw
open the door, and exclaimed, with beaming
eyes peering into the darkness as he spoke, "I
see it! Yes, it *is!* Hatteras Light, thirty-five
miles away. This night, December 13th, is the
first time I have caught its flash. Tell it to the
Hatteras keeper when you visit the cape."

From Captain Hatzel I gleaned some facts of
deep interest in regard to the inhabitants of the
sound. Some of them, he told me, had Indian
blood in their veins; and to prove the truth of his
assertion he handed me a well-worn copy of the
" History of North Carolina," by Dr. Francis L.

Hawks, D. D.   From this I obtained facts which might serve for the intricate mazes of a romance.

It had been a pet scheme with Sir Walter Raleigh to colonize the coast of North Carolina, then known as Virginia, and though several expeditions had been sent out for that object, each had failed of successful issue. One of these expeditions sent by Sir Walter to Roanoke Island consisted of one hundred and twenty-one persons, of whom seventeen were women and six children. Of all these souls only two men returned to the old country, the fate of the remainder being unknown, and shrouded in the gloom which always attends mystery. England did not, however, leave her children to perish on a barren shore in the new land without at least an effort to succor them.

On March 20, in the year 1590, there sailed from Plymouth three ships, the Hopewell, John Evangelist, and Little John, taking in tow two shallops which were afterwards lost at sea. In those days the largest vessels of a fleet did not exceed one hundred to one hundred and forty tons burden. This expedition was under the charge of Admiral John White, governor of the colony of Sir Walter Raleigh on Roanoke Island, and who had left the feeble band on the island in 1587. In thirty-six days and eight hours these small vessels arrived off " Hatorask " — Hatteras Beach. The fleet dropped anchor three leagues off the beach, and sent a well-manned boat through an inlet to Pamplico Sound.

There existed in those days passages from the ocean through the beaches into the sounds, which have since been filled up by the action of the sea. Old Roanoke Inlet, now closed, which was about four miles north of the modern Oregon Inlet, is supposed to be the one used by Sir Walter Raleigh's expeditions. It is only four miles from the site of this closed inlet to Shallowbag Bay, on Roanoke Island. At the southern entrance of the bay, near Ballast Point, some vessel evidently grounded and threw overboard her stone ballast; hence the name of the point. Captain Hatzel has examined this stone, and gives his opinion, as an old pilot, that it is foreign in character. He never met with similar stones, and believes that this ballast was deposited at Shallowbag Bay by some of the vessels of Sir Walter's expeditions.

As the boat's crew above mentioned rowed northward to Roanoke Island — made famous two hundred and seventy-two years later by the National and Confederate struggles — they sounded their trumpets and sang familiar songs, which they hoped might be borne to their countrymen on the shore; but the marshes and upland wilderness returned no answering voice.

At daybreak the explorers landed upon Roanoke Island, which is twelve miles long by two and a half wide, and found the spot where Admiral White had left the colony in 1587. Eagerly searching for any tokens of the lost ones, they soon traced in the light soil of the island the imprint of the moccasin of the savage, but looked in vain for any footprint of civilized man. What had become of their countrymen?

At last some one spied a conspicuous tree, far up on a sandy bank, blazed and carved. There were but three letters cut upon it, C. R. O., but these simple symbols possessed a world of meaning. Three years before, when the sad farewells were being spoken, and the ships were ready to set sail for England, this feeble band, left to struggle in the wilds of the new land with sad forebodings of their possible fate, had agreed upon a signal, and had promised Admiral White that if driven to starvation upon the island, they would plant their colony fifty miles inland, near a tribe of friendly Indians. Indeed, before the ships sailed for England, they were making preparations for this move. Admiral White requested them to carve upon a tree the name of the locality to which they should remove, and if distress had overtaken them they were to add a *cross* over the lettering. Anxiously gathering round this interesting relic of the lost Englishmen, the rude chirography was eagerly scanned, but no vestige of a cross was found.

Much relieved in mind, the little company

continued their investigations, when, farther on, almost in their very pathway, there rose a noble tree, pointing its top heavenward, as though to remind them in whose care their lost ones had been. Approaching this giant, who had stood a silent sentinel through winter storms and summer skies, they found he bore upon his body a message for them. Stripped of its bark, five feet upward from the ground there appeared upon the bare surface in bold lettering the word so full of hope—*Croatan;* and now also, as in the last case, without the graven cross. Cheered by these signs, and believing that the lost colonists had carried out their early intentions, and were now located among the friendly tribe of Croatans, wheresoever their country might be, the boat's company decided to go at once to the ships, and return the next day in search of the lost colony.

One of the ships, in moving its position from the unprotected anchorage-ground, parted its cable and left an anchor on the bottom — the second that had been lost. The wind drove the ships towards the beach, when a third anchor was lowered; but it held the little fleet so close in to the breakers, that the sailors were forced to slip their cable and work into a channel-way, where, in deeper water, they held their ground.

In debating the propriety of holding on and

attempting to wear out the gale, the scarcity of their provisions, and the possession of but one cask of water, and only one anchor for the fleet to ride at, decided them to go southward in quest of some favorable landing, where water could be found. The council held out the hope of capturing Spanish vessels in the vicinity of the West Indies; and it was agreed that, if successful, they should return, richly laden with spoils, to seek their exiled countrymen. One of these vessels returned to England, while the Admiral laid his course for Trinidad; and this was the last attempt made to find the colonists.

More than a century after Admiral White had abandoned his colony, Lawson, in writing about the Hatteras Indians, says: "They said that several of their ancestors were white people, and could talk in a book as we do; the truth of which is confirmed by grey eyes being frequently found among them, and no others. They value themselves extremely for their affinity to the English, and are ready to do them all friendly offices. It is probable that the settlement miscarried for want of supplies from England, or through the treachery of the natives; for we may reasonably suppose that the English were forced to cohabit with them for relief and conversation, and that in process of time they conformed themselves to the manners of their Indian relations."

Dr. Hawks thinks, "that, driven by starvation, such as survived the famine were merged into the tribes of friendly Indians at Croatan, and, alas! lost ere long every vestige of Christianity and civilization; and those who came to shed light on the darkness of paganism, in the mysterious providence of God ended by relapsing themselves into the heathenism they came to remove. It is a sad picture of poor human nature."

It needed not the fierce gusts of wind that howled about the tall tower, causing it to vibrate until water would be spilled out of a pail resting upon the floor of the lantern, blowing one day from one quarter of the compass, and changing the next to another, to warn me that I was near the Cape of Storms.

Refusing to continue longer with my new friends, the canoe was put into the water on the 16th, and Captain Hatzel's two sons proceeded in advance with a strong boat to break a channel-way through the thin ice which had formed in the quiet coves. We were soon out in the sound, where the boys left me, and I rowed out of the southern end of Roanoke and entered upon the wide area of Pamplico Sound. To avoid shoals, it being calm, I kept about three miles from the beach in three feet of water, until beyond Duck Island, when the trees on Roanoke Island slowly sank below the horizon; then gradually drawing

in to the beach, the two clumps of trees of north
and south Chicamicomico came into view. A
life-saving station had recently been erected
north of the first grove, and there is another
fourteen miles further south. The two Chicamicomico settlements of scattered houses are
each nearly a mile in length, and are separated
by a high, bald sand-beach of about the same
length, which was once heavily wooded; but the
wind has blown the sand into the forest and
destroyed it. A wind-mill in each village raised
its weird arms to the breeze.

Three miles further down is Kitty Midget's
Hammock, where a few red cedars and some
remains of live-oaks tell of the extensive forest
that once covered the beach. Here Captain
Abraham Hooper lives, and occupies himself in
fishing with nets in the ocean for blue-fish, which
are salted down and sent to the inland towns for
a market. I had drawn my boat into the sedge
to secure a night's shelter, when the old captain
on his rounds captured me. The change from a
bed in the damp sedge to the inside seat of the
largest fireplace I had ever beheld, was indeed
a pleasant one. ' Its inviting front covered almost
one side of the room. While the fire flashed up
the wide chimney, I sat inside the fireplace with
the three children of my host, and enjoyed the
genial glow which arose from the fragments of
the wreck of a vessel which had pounded her-

self to death upon the strand near Kitty Midget's Hammock. How curiously those white-haired children watched the man who had come so far in a paper boat! "Why did not the paper boat soak to pieces?" they asked. Each explanation seemed but to puzzle them the more; and I found myself in much the same condition of mind when trying to make some discoveries concerning Kitty Midget. She must, however, have lived somewhere on Clark's Beach long before the present proprietor was born. We spent the next day fishing with nets in the surf for blue-fish, it being about the last day of their stay in that vicinity. They go south as far as Cape Hatteras, and then disappear in deep water; while the great flocks of gulls, that accompany them to gather the remnants of fish they scatter in their savage meals, rise in the air and fly rapidly away in search of other dainties.

On Thursday I set out for Cape Hatteras. The old sailor's song, that —

> "Hatteras has a blow in store
> For those who pass her howling door,"

has far more truth than poetry in it. Before proceeding far the wind blew a tempest, when a young fisherman in his sailboat bore down upon me, and begged me to come on board. We attempted to tow the canoe astern, but she filled with water, which obliged us to take her on board. As we flew along before the wind, dashing over the shoals with mad-cap temerity, I discovered that my new acquaintance, Burnett, was a most daring as well as reckless sailor. He told me how he had capsized his father's schooner by carrying sail too long. "This 'ere slow way of doing things" he detested. His recital was characteristic of the man.

"You see, sir, we was bound for Newbern up the Neuse River, and as we were well into the sound with all sail set, and travelling along lively, daddy says, 'Lorenzo, I reckon a little yaupon wouldn't hurt me, so I'll go below and start a fire under the kittle.' 'Do as you likes, daddy,' sez I. So down below he goes, and I takes command of the schooner. A big black squall soon come over Cape Hatteras from the Gulf Stream, and it did look like a screecher. Now, I thought, old woman, I'll make your sides ache; so I pinted her at it, and afore I could luff her up in the wind, the squall kreened her on to her beam-ends. You'd a laughed to have split yourself, mister, if you could have seen daddy a-crawling out of the companion-way while the water was a-running down stairs like a crick. Says he, ruther hurriedly, 'Sonny, what's up?' 'It isn't what's *up*, daddy; but what's *down*,' sez I; 'it sort o' looks as if we had capsized.' 'Sure 'nuff,' answered dad, as the ballast shifted and the schooner rolled over keel uppermost. We floundered about like porpoises, but managed to get astride her backbone, when dad looked kind of scornfully at me, and burst out with, 'Sonny, do you call yourself a keerful sailor?' 'Keerful enough, dad,' sez I, 'for a *smart* one. It's more credit to a man to *drive* his vessel like a sailor, than to be crawling and bobbing along like a diamond-backed terrapin.' Now, stranger, if you'll believe me, that keerful old father of mine would never let me take the helum again, so I sticks to my aunt at the cape."

I found that the boat in which we were sailing was a dug-out, made from two immense cypress logs. Larger boats than this are made of three logs, and smaller ones are dug out of one.

Burnett told me that frame boats were so easily pounded to pieces on the shoals, that dug-outs were preferred — being very durable. We soon passed the hamlet of North Kinnakeet, then Scarsborough with its low houses, then South Kinnakeet with its two wind-mills, and after these arose a sterile, bald beach·with Hatteras light-tower piercing the sky, and west of it Hatteras woods and marshes. We approached the low shore and ascended a little creek, where we left our boats, and repaired to the cottage of Burnett's aunt.

After the barren shores I had passed, this little house, imbedded in living green, was like a bright star in a dark night. It was hidden away in a heavy thicket of live-oaks and cedars, and surrounded by yaupons, the bright red berries of which glistened against the light green leaves. An old woman stood in the doorway with a kindly greeting for her "wild boy," rejoicing the while that he had "got back to his old aunty once more."

"Yes, aunty," said my friend Lorenzo, "I am back again like a bad penny, but not empty-handed; for as soon as our season's catch of blue-fish is sold, old aunty will have sixty or seventy dollars."

"He has a good heart, if he is so head-strong," whispered the motherly woman, as she wiped a tear from her eyes, and gazed with pride upon the manly-looking young fellow, and — invited us in to tea — YAUPON.

BODY ISLAND LIGHT-HOUSE.

CHAPTER X.

FROM CAPE HATTERAS TO CAPE FEAR, NORTH CAROLINA.

CAPE HATTERAS LIGHT. — HABITS OF BIRDS. — STORM AT HAT-
TERAS INLET. — MILES OF WRECKS. — THE YACHT JULIA
SEARCHING FOR THE PAPER CANOE. — CHASED BY PORPOISES.
— MARSH TACKIES. — OCRACOKE INLET. — A GRAVE-YARD BE-
ING SWALLOWED UP BY THE SEA. — CORE SOUND. — THREE
WEDDINGS AT HUNTING QUARTERS. — MOREHEAD CITY. —
NEWBERN. — SWANSBORO. — A PEA-NUT PLANTATION. — THE
ROUTE TO CAPE FEAR.

CAPE HATTERAS is the apex of a tri-
angle. It is the easternmost part of the
state of North Carolina, and it extends farther
into the ocean than any Atlantic cape of the
United States. It presents a low, broad, sandy
point to the sea, and for several miles beyond it,
in the ocean, are the dangerous Diamond Shoals,
the dread of the mariner.

The Gulf Stream, with its river-like current
of water flowing northward from the Gulf of
Mexico, in its oscillations from east to west frequently approaches to within eighteen or twenty
miles of the cape, filling a large area of atmosphere with its warmth, and causing frequent
local disturbances. The weather never remains

Route of Paper Canoe
MARIA THERESA
From Bogue Inlet, N.C. to Bull's Bay, S.C.
Followed by N.H. Bishop.
in 1875

Bogue Inlet
Bear Inlet
New River Inlet
Stump Inlet
New Topsail Inlet
Old Topsail Inlet
Rich Inlet
Barren Inlet
Masonboro Inlet
New Inlet
Cape Fear R.
Cape Fear
Lockwood's Folly Inlet
Shallotte Inlet
Little River Inlet
Murrell's Inlet
Conwayborough
Waccamaw River
Pee Dee R.
Black R.
Georgetown
Winyah Bay
Mosquito Cr.
N. Santee R.
S. Santee R.
Alligator Cr.
C. Roman
Bull's Bay

Swansboro

NORTH CAROLINA

SOUTH CAROLINA

Wilmington
Brinkley's
Flemington
Waccamaw Lake

N.H. Bishop's Route
Light House
Scale 1:56'0000

Statute Miles

Copyright, 1878. by Le & Shepard

long in a settled state. As most vessels try to make Hatteras Light, to ascertain their true position, &c., and because it juts out so far into the Atlantic, the locality has become the scene of many wrecks, and the beach, from the cape down to Hatteras Inlet, fourteen miles, is strewn with the fragments of vessels.

The coast runs north and south above, and east and west south of the cape. The old light-house had been replaced by the finest light-tower I had ever examined, which was completed in 1870. It is one hundred and ninety feet in height, and shows a white, revolving light.

Body Island Light, though forty feet less in elevation, is frequently seen by the Hatteras light-keeper, while the splendid Hatteras Light had been seen but once by Captain Hatzel, of Body Island. One nautical mile south of Hatteras Light is a small beacon light-tower, which is of great service to the coasting-vessels that pass it in following the eighteen-feet curve of the cape two miles from the land inside of Diamond Shoals.

While speaking of light-houses, it may be interesting to naturalists who live far inland to know that while (as they are well aware) thousands of birds are killed annually during their flights by striking against telegraphic wires, many wild-fowls are also destroyed by dashing against the lanterns of the light-towers during

the night. While at Body Island Beach, Captain
Hatzel remarked to me that, during the first
winter after the new light-tower was completed,
the snow-geese, which winter on the island, would
frequently at night strike the thick glass panes
of the chamber, and fall senseless upon the floor
of the gallery. The second season they did not
in a single instance repeat the mistake, but had
seemingly become educated to the character of
the danger.

I have seen one lantern damaged to the
amount of five hundred dollars, by a goose
breaking a pane of glass and striking heavily
upon the costly lens which surrounds the lamp.
Light-keepers sometimes sit upon the gallery,
and, looking along the pathway of light which
shoots into the outer darkness over their heads,
will see a few dark specks approaching them in
this beam of radiance. These specks are birds,
confused by the bright rays, and ready to fall an
easy prey to the eager keeper, who, quickly levelling his double-barrelled gun, brings it to bear
upon the opaque, moving cloud, and with the
discharge of the weapon there goes whirling
through space to the earth below his next morning's breakfast of wild-fowl.

I found Mr. W. R. Jennett and his first assistant light-keeper, Mr. A. W. Simpson, intelligent
gentlemen. The assistant has devoted his time,
when off duty, to the study of the habits of

food-fishes of the sound, and has furnished the United States Commission of Fisheries with several papers on that interesting subject.

Here also was Mr. George Onslow, of the United States Signal Service, who had completed his work of constructing a telegraph line from Norfolk along the beach southward to this point, its present terminus. With a fine telescope he could frequently identify vessels a few miles from the cape, and telegraph their position to New York. He had lately saved a vessel by telegraphing to Norfolk its dangerous location on Hatteras beach, where it had grounded. By this timely notice a wrecking-steamer had arrived and hauled the schooner off in good condition.

A low range of hills commences at Cape Hatteras, in the rear of the light-house, and extends nearly to Hatteras Inlet. This range is heavily wooded with live-oaks, yellow pines, yaupons, cedars, and bayonet-plants. The fishermen and wreckers live in rudely constructed houses, sheltered by this thicket, which is dense enough to protect them from the strong winds that blow from the ocean and the sound.

I walked twelve miles through this pretty, green retreat, and spent Sunday with Mr. Homer W. Styron, who keeps a small store about two miles from the inlet. He is a self-taught astronomer, and used an ingeniously constructed telescope of his own manufacture for studying the heavens.

I found at the post-office in his store a letter from a yachting party which had left Newbern, North Carolina, to capture the paper canoe and to force upon its captain the hospitality of the people of that city, on the Neuse River, one hundred miles from the cape. Judge I. E. West, the owner of the yacht "Julia," and his friends, had been cruising since the eleventh day of the month from Ocracoke Inlet to Roanoke Island in search of me. Judge West, in his letter, expressed a strong desire to have me take my Christmas dinner with his family. This generous treatment from a stranger was fully appreciated, and I determined to push on to Morehead City, from which place it would be convenient to reach Newbern by rail without changing my established route southward, as I would be compelled to do if the regular water route of the Neuse River from Pamplico Sound were followed.

On this Saturday night, spent at Hatteras Inlet, there broke upon us one of the fiercest tempests I ever witnessed, even in the tropics. My pedestrian tramp down the shore had scarcely ended when it commenced in reality. For miles along the beach thousands of acres of land were soon submerged by the sea and by the torrents of water which fell from the clouds. While for a moment the night was dark as Erebus, again the vivid flash of lightning exposed to view the swaying forests and the gloomy sound. The sea pounded on the beach as if asking for admission to old Pamplico. It seemed to say, I demand a new inlet; and, as though trying to carry out its desire, sent great waves rolling up the shingle and over into the hollows among the hills, washing down the low sand dunes as if they also were in collusion with it to remove this frail barrier, this narrow strip of low land which separated the Atlantic from the wide interior sheet of water.

The phosphorescent sea, covered with its tens of millions of animalcula, each one a miniature light-house, changed in color from inky blackness to silver sheen. Will the ocean take to itself this frail foothold? — we queried. Will it ingulf us in its insatiable maw, as the whale did Jonah? There was no subsidence, no pause in the storm. It howled, bellowed, and screeched like a legion of demons, so that the crashing of falling trees, and the twisting of the sturdy live-oak's toughest limbs, could hardly be heard in the din. Yet during this wild night my storm-hardened companion sat with his pretty wife by the open fireplace, as unmoved as though we were in the shelter of a mountain side, while he calmly discoursed of storms, shipwrecks, and terrible struggles for life that this lonely coast had witnessed, which sent thrills of horror to my heart.

While traversing the beach during the afternoon, as wreck after wreck, the gravestones of departed ships, projected their timbers from the sands, I had made a calculation of the number of vessels which had left their hulls to rot on Hatteras beach since the ships of Sir Walter Raleigh had anchored above the cape, and it resulted in making *one continuous* line of vessels, wreck touching wreck, along the coast for many, many miles. Hundreds of miles of the Atlantic coast beaches would have been walled in by the wrecks could they have come on to the strand at one time, and all the dwellers along the coast, outside of the towns, would have been placed in independent circumstances by wrecking their cargoes.

During this wild night, while the paper canoe was safely stowed in the rushes of the marsh at the cape, and its owner was enjoying the warmth of the young astronomer's fire at the inlet, less than twenty miles from us, on the dangerous edge of Ocracoke shoals, the searching party of the yacht Julia were in momentary expectation of going to the bottom of the sound. For hours the gallant craft hung to her anchors, which were heavily backed by all the iron ballast that could be attached to the cables. Wave after wave swept over her, and not a man could put his head above the hatches. Then, as she rolled in the sea, her cabin-windows went under, and streams of water were forced through the ports into the confined space which was occupied by the little party. For a time they were in imminent danger, for the vessel dragged anchor to the edge of the shoal, and with a heavy thud the yacht struck on the bottom. All hopes of ever returning to Newbern were lost, when the changing tide swung the boat off into deeper water, where she rode out the storm in safety.

Before morning the wind shifted, and by nine o'clock I retraced my steps to the cape, and on Tuesday rowed down to Hatteras Inlet, which was reached a little past noon. Before attempting to cross this dangerous tidal gate-way of the ocean I hugged the shore close to its edge, and paused to make myself familiar with the sand-hills of the opposite side, a mile away, which were to serve as the guiding-beacons in the passage. How often had I, lying awake at night, thought of and dreaded the crossing of this ill-omened inlet! It had given me much mental suffering. Now it was before me. Here on my right was the great sound, on my left the narrow beach island, and out through the portal of the open inlet surged and moaned under a leaden sky that old ocean which now seemed to frown at me, and to say: "Wait, my boy, until the inlet's waves deliver you to me, and I will put you among my other victims for your temerity."

As I gazed across the current I remarked that it did not seem very rough, though a strong ebb was running out to the sea, and if crossed immediately, before the wind arose, there could be no unreasonable risk. My canvas deck-cover was carefully pulled close about my waist, and a rigid inspection of oars and row-locks was made; then, with a desire to reserve my strength for any great demand that might be made upon it a little later, I rowed with a steady stroke out into Hatteras Inlet. There was no help nearer than Styron's, two miles away on the upper shore, while the beach I was approaching on the other side was uninhabited for nearly sixteen miles, to the village at its southern end, near Ocracoke Inlet. Upon entering the swash I thought of the sharks which the Hatteras fishermen had told me frequently seized their oars, snapping the thin blades in pieces, assuring me, at the same time, that mine would prove very attractive, being so white and glimmering in the water, and offering the same glittering fascination as a silver-spoon bait does to a blue-fish. These cheerful suggestions caused a peculiar creeping sensation to come over me, but I tried to quiet myself with the belief that the sharks had followed the blue-fish into deeper water, to escape cold weather.

The canoe crossed the upper ebb, and entered an area where the ebb from the opposite side of the inlet struck the first one. While crossing the union of the two currents, a wind came in at the opening through the beach, and though not a strong one, it created a great agitation of the water. The dangerous experience at Watcha-preague Inlet had taught me that when in such a sea one must pull with all his strength, and that the increased momentum would give greater buoyancy to the shell; for while under this treatment she bounced from one irregular wave to another with a climbing action which greatly relieved my anxiety. The danger seemed to be decreasing, and I stole a furtive glance over my shoulder at the low dunes of the beach shore which I was approaching, to see how far into the inlet the tide had dragged me. The white water to leeward warned me of a shoal, and forced me to pull hard for the sound to escape being drawn into the breakers. This danger was hardly passed, when suddenly the waters around me seethed and foamed, and the short waves parted and closed, as great creatures rose from the deep into the air several feet, and then fell heavily into the sea. My tiny shell rocked and pitched about wildly as these animals appeared and disappeared, leaping from the waves all around me, diving under the boat and reappearing on the opposite side. They lashed the current with their strong tails, and snorted or blowed most dismally. For an instant surprise and alarm took such possession of me that not a muscle of my arms obeyed my will, and the canoe commenced to drift in the driving stream towards the open sea. This confusion was only momentary, for as soon as I discovered that my companions were porpoises and only old acquaintances, I determined to avoid them as soon as possible.

With a quick glance at my stern range, a sand-hill on the shore of the inlet, and another look over my shoulder for the sand dunes of the other side, I exerted every muscle to reach the beach; but my frisky friends were in no mood to leave me, but continued their fun with increased energy as reinforcements came up from all directions. The faster I rowed the more they multiplied, ploughing the sea in erratic courses. They were from five to seven feet in length, and must have weighed from two hundred to four hundred pounds each. Though their attentions were kindly meant, their brusqueness on such an unsteady footing was unpardonable. I most feared the strong, shooting movements of their tails in the sudden dives under my canoe, for one sportive touch of such a *caudality* would have rolled me over, and furnished material for a tale the very anticipation of which was unpleasant.

The aquatic gambols of the porpoises lasted but a few minutes after they had called in all

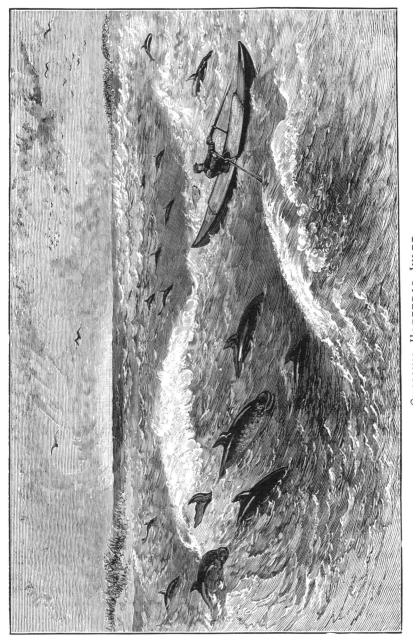

CROSSING HATTERAS INLET.

their neighbors, and had chased me into three feet depth of water.   They then spouted a nasal farewell, which sounded more catarrhal than guitaral, and left me for the more profitable occupation of fishing in the tide-way of the inlet, while I rowed into a shallow cove, out of the ebb, to rest, and to recover from the effects of my fright.

As I pulled along the beach the tide receded so rapidly that the canoe was constantly grounding, and wading became necessary, for I could not get within several feet of the shore.   When five miles from Hatteras Inlet I espied an empty grass cabin, which the fishermen used in February while catching shad; and, as a southerly wind was now blowing from the sea, and rain was falling, it offered a night's shelter for the traveller. This Robinson Crusoe looking structure was located upon the low land near the sound, while bleak, sharp-pointed, treeless and grassless sand-hills, blown into shape by the winds, arose in the background, and cut off a view of the ocean, which, judging from the low, melancholy moaning coming over the dunes, was in a sad mood.

The canoe was hauled into the bushes and tied securely for fear a deceptive tide might bear it away.   The provisions, blankets, &c., were moved into the grass hut, which needed repairing.   The holes in the south wall were soon thatched, and a bed easily prepared from the rushes of the marsh. It mattered not that they were wet, for a piece of painted canvas was spread over them, and the inviting couch finished.

As fresh water can usually be obtained on all these low beaches by digging two or three feet into the sand, I looked for a large clam-shell, and my search being rewarded, I was soon engaged in digging a well near the cabin.

Upon looking up from my work a curious sight met my gaze. In some mysterious way every sharp-pointed sand-hill had been covered by a black object, which swayed about and nodded up and down in a strange manner. As I watched the development of this startling phenomenon, the nodding, black objects grew in size until the head, body, and four legs of a horse were clearly cut against the sky. A little later every crest was surmounted by the comical figure of a marsh-tacky. Then a few sheep came out of the hollows among the hills and browsed on the coarse grass near the cabin, as though they felt the loneliness of their situation so far removed from mankind. With the marsh-ponies, the sheep, the wild-fowls of the sound, and the sighing sea for companions, the night passed away.

The bright moonlight roused me at five o'clock in the morning, and I pushed off again in shoal water on an ebb-tide, experiencing much difficulty in dragging the canoe over shallow places until deep water was entered, when the row to Ocracoke became an agreeable one. The landing-place at Ocracoke, not far from the lighthouse, was reached at noon, and the people gathered to see the paper boat, having been notified of my proximity by fishermen.

The women here can pull a pretty good stroke, and frequently assist their husbands in the fisheries. These old dames ridiculed the idea of having a boat so small and light as the canoe. One old lady laid aside her pipe and snuff-paddle (snuff-rubbing is a time-honored institution in the south), and roughly grasping the bow of the craft, lifted it high in the air, then, glancing at the fine model, she lowered it slowly to the ground, exclaiming, " I reckon I wouldn't risk my life acrossing a creek in her."

These people told me that the yacht Julia had stopped there to make inquiries for me, and had departed for Newbern.

It was more than a mile from the landing to Ocracoke Inlet, and a mile and three quarters across it to the beach. A straight course from the landing to the village of Portsmouth, on the lower side of the inlet, was a distance of five miles, and not one of the hardy watermen, who thumped the sides of my boat with their hard fists to ascertain its strength, believed that I could cross the sound to the other village without rolling over. One kind-hearted oysterman offered to carry myself and boat to Portsmouth; but as the day was calm, I rowed away on the five-mile stretch amid doleful prognostications, such as: "That feller will make a coffin for his-self out of that yere gimcrack of an egg-shell. It's all a man's life is wurth to go in her," &c.

While approaching the low Portsmouth shore of the sound, flocks of Canada geese flew within pistol-shot of my head. A man in a dug-out canoe told me that the gunners of the village had reared from the egg a flock of wild geese which now aggregated some seven or eight hundred birds, and that these now flying about were used to decoy their wild relatives.

Near the beach a sandy hill had been the place of sepulture for the inhabitants of other generations, but for years past the tidal current had been cutting the shore away until coffin after coffin with its contents had been washed into the sound. Captain Isaac S. Jennings, of Ocean County, New Jersey, had described this spot to me as follows:

"I landed at Portsmouth and examined this curious burial-ground. Here by the water were the remains of the fathers, mothers, brothers, and sisters of the people of the village so near at hand; yet these dismal relics of their ancestors were allowed to be stolen away piecemeal by the encroaching ocean. While I gazed sadly upon the strata of coffins protruding from the banks, shining objects like jewels seemed to be sparkling from between the cracks of their fractured sides; and as I tore away the rotten wood, rows of toads were discovered sitting in solemn council, their bright eyes peering from among the debris of bones and decomposed substances."

Portsmouth Island is nearly eight miles long. Whalebone Inlet is at its lower end, but is too shallow to be of any service to commerce. Hatteras and Ocracoke inlets admit sea-going vessels. It is thirty-eight miles from Whalebone Inlet to Cape Lookout, which projects like a wedge into the sea nearly three miles from the mainland, and there is not another passage through the narrow beach in all that distance that is of any use to the mariner. Following the trend of the coast for eleven miles from the point of Cape Lookout, there is an inlet, but, from the character of its channel and its shallowness, it is not of much value.

Leaving Portsmouth, the canoe entered Core Sound, which grew narrower as the shoals inside of Whalebone Inlet were crossed, partly by rowing and partly by wading on the sand-flats. As night came on, a barren stretch of beach on my left hand was followed until I espied the only house within a distance of sixteen miles along the sea. It was occupied by a coasting skipper, whose fine little schooner was anchored a long distance from the land on account of the shoalness of the water. Dreary sand-hills protected the cottage from the bleak winds of the ocean.

While yet a long distance from the skipper's home, a black object could be seen crawling up the sides of a mound of white sand, and after it reached the apex it remained in one position, while I rowed, and waded, and pulled my canoe towards the shore. When the goal was reached, and the boat was landed high up among the scrub growth, I shouldered my blankets and charts, and plodded through the soft soil towards the dark object, which I now recognized to be a man on a lookout post. He did not move from his position until I reached the hillock, when he suddenly slid down the bank and landed at my feet, with a cheery —

"Well, now, I thought it was you. Sez I to myself, That's him, sure, when I seed you four miles away. Fust thinks I, It's only a log, or a piece of wrak-stuff afloating. Pretty soon up comes your head and shoulders into sight; then sez I, It's a man, sure, but where is his boat? for you see, I couldn't see your boat, it was so low down in the water. Then I reckoned it was a man afloating on a log, but arter a while the boat loomed up too, and I says, I'll be dog-goned if that isn't him. I went up to Newbern, some time ago, in the schooner, and the people there said there was a man coming down the coast a-rowing a paper boat on a *bet*. The *boat* weighed only fifty-eight pounds, and the *man* had a heft of only eighty pounds. When pa and me went up to the city agin, the folks said the man was close on to us, and this time they said the man and his boat together weighed only eighty pounds. Now I should think you weighed more than that yourself, letting alone the boat."

Having assured the young man that I was indeed myself, and that the Newbern people had played upon his credulity, we walked on to the house, where the family of Captain James Mason kindly welcomed me to a glowing wood-fire and hearty supper. Though I had never heard of their existence till I entered Core Sound, the kindness of these people was like that of old friends.

Half a mile below Captain Mason's home, a short time before my visit, a new breach had been made by the ocean through the beach. About twenty years before a similar breach had occurred in the same locality, and was known during its short life as "Pillintary Inlet." The next day I crossed the sound, which is here four miles in width, and coasted along to the oyster-men's village of Hunting Quarters, on the mainland. The houses were very small, but the hearts of the poor folks were very large. They came to the water's edge and carried the canoe into the only store in the neighborhood. Its proprietor, Mr. William H. Stewart, insisted upon my sharing his bachelor's quarters in an unfinished room of the storehouse. My young host was hardly out of his teens. In his boyish way he kindly remarked:

"I am here all alone. Father told me, before he died, never to let a stranger pass my door but to make him share my lodgings, humble though they are; and now, any way, you're just in time for the fun, for we are to have three weddings to-night, and all the boys and girls of the neighborhood will be at Hunting Quarters."

I entered a mild protest against joining in the festivities, on the plea of not having received an invitation; at which the handsome youth laughed heartily.

"Invitation!" he exclaimed; "why, no one ever gives out invitations in Hunting Quarters. When there is to be a 'jollification' of any sort, everybody goes to the house without being asked. You see we are all neighbors here. Up at Newbern and at Beaufort, and other *great* cities, people have their ways, but here all are friends."

So we went to the little house in the piny forest, where two hearts were to be made one. The only room on the first floor was crowded with people. The minister had not arrived, and the crowd was gazing at the young groom and his pretty bride-elect as they sat in two chairs in the middle of the company, with their arms around each other, never speaking a word to any one. The heavy weight of people began to settle the floor, and as two joists gave way I struggled to escape through an open window, thinking we would be precipitated into the cellar below. But the good-natured company took no notice of the snapping timbers, only ejaculating, "She'll soon touch bottom;" and to my inquiries about the inconvenience of being pitched through to the cellar, a rustic youth, with great merriment depicted upon his countenance, replied:

"Sullers, captain, why, there ain't a suller to a buildin' within thirty miles of the Quarters. We never uses sullers hereabouts."

By my side was a young fisherman, who had got home from a cruise, and was overflowing with affection towards every girl present. "O, gals," he would cry, "you don't know how nice I feels to get back to you once more!" Throwing his arms around a bright-eyed girl, who vainly tried to escape him, he said, "O, weary mariner, here is thy rest! No more shall he wander from thee."

This sentimental strain was interrupted by an old lady, who reached her arm over my shoulder to administer a rebuke. "Sam, ye're a fool!" she cried; "ye're beside yourself to-night, and afore this paper-canoe captain, too. Ef I was a gal I'd drap yere society, wid yere familiar ways right in company."

The blow and the admonition fell harmlessly upon the head and the heart of the sailor, who replied, "Aunty, I knows my advantages in Hunting Quarters — *wimen is plenty, and men is few.*"

The crowd roared with laughter at this truism, but were quieted by the shout of a boy that the preacher was a-coming; whereupon the reverend gentleman elbowed his way through the guests to the quiet couple, and requested them to stand up. A few hurried words by the clergyman, a few bashful replies from the young people, and the two were made one. The crowd rushed outside of the house, where a general scramble took place among the boys for their girls. Then a procession was formed, headed by the clergyman, which marched along the sandy road to another house in the woods, where the second marriage was to be celebrated.

It was amusing to see the young men dash away from the procession, to run to the village store for candy at twenty-five cents per pound, containing as much *terra alba* (white clay) as sugar. With well-filled pockets they would run back to the procession and fill the girls' aprons with the sweets, soon repeating the process, and showering upon the fair ones cakes, raisins, nuts, and oranges. The only young man who seemed to find no favor in any woman's eyes invested more capital in sweetmeats than the others; and though every girl in the procession gave him a sharp word or a kick as he passed, yet none refused his candies as he tossed them at the maidens, or stuffed them into the pockets of their dresses.

The second ceremony was performed in about three minutes, and the preacher feeling faint from his long ride through the woods, declared he must have some supper. So, while he was being served, the girls chatted together, the old ladies helped each other to snuff with little wooden paddles, which were left protruding from one corner of their mouths after they had taken "a dip," as they called it. The boys, after learning that the preacher had postponed the third marriage for an hour, with a wild shout scampered off to Stewart's store for more candies. I took advantage of the interim to inquire how it was that the young ladies and gentlemen were upon such terms of pleasant intimacy.

" Well, captain," replied the person interrogated, " you sees we is all growed up together, and brotherly love and sisterly affection is our teaching. The brethren love the sisteren; and they say that love begets love, so the sisteren loves the brethren. It's parfecly nateral. That's the hull story, captain. How is it up your way? "

At last the preacher declared himself satisfied with all he had eaten, and that enough was as good as a feast; so the young people fell into line, and we trudged to the third house, where, with the same dispatch, the third couple were united. Then the fiddler scraped the strings of his instrument, and a double-shuffle dance commenced. The girls stamped and moved their feet about in the same manner as the men. Soon four or five of the young ladies left the dancing-party, and seated themselves in a corner, pouting discontentedly. My companion explained to me that the deserters were a little stuck-up, having made two or three visits on a schooner to the city (Newbern), where they had other ways of dancing, and where the folks didn't think it pretty for a girl to strike her heels upon the floor, &c.

How long they danced I know not, for the prospect of a long row on the morrow sent me to rest in the storehouse, from which I was called by a kind old couple sending for me to take tea with them at half an hour after midnight. Unwilling to wound the sensitive feelings of these hospitable people, I answered the summons *in propria persona*, and found it was the mother of bride No. 1, to whom I was indebted for the invitation. A well-filled table took up the space in the centre of the room, where a few hours before the timbers creaked beneath the weight of the curious crowd; and there, sitting on one side in the same affectionate manner I have described, were the bride and groom, apparently unmoved by the change of scene, while the bride's mother rocked in her chair, moaning, " O John, if you'd taken the other gal, I might have stood it, but this yere one has been my comfort."

At dawn the canoe was put into Core Sound, and I followed the western shore, cheered by the bright sun of our Saviour's natal day. At noon the mouth of the thoroughfare between Harker's Island and the mainland was unintentionally passed, and I rowed along by the side of the island next Fort Macon, which is inside of the angle made by Cape Lookout.

Finding it impossible to reach Newbern *via* Morehead City that day, the canoe was beached upon the end of Harker's Island, where I breakfasted at the fashionable hour of two P. M., with men, women, and children around me. My mode of cooking the condensed food and liquid beef, so quickly prepared for the palate, and the remarkable boat of *paper*, all filled the islanders with wonder. They were at first a little shy, looking upon the apparition — which seemed in some wonderful way to have dropped upon their beach — with the light of .curiosity in their eyes.

Then, as I explained the many uses to which

paper was put, even to the paying off of great national debts, my audience became very friendly, and offered to get me up a Christmas dinner in their cabins among the groves of trees near the strand, if I would tarry with them until night. But time was precious; so, with thanks on my part for their kind offers, we parted, they helping me launch my little boat, and waving a cheerful adieu as I headed the canoe for Beaufort, which was quietly passed in the middle of the afternoon.

Three miles further on, the railroad pier of Morehead City, in Bogue Sound, was reached, and a crowd of people carried the canoe into the hotel. A telegram was soon received from the superintendent of the railroad at Newbern, inviting me to a free ride to the city in the first train of the following morning.

The reader who has followed me since I left the chilly regions of the St. Lawrence must not have his patience taxed by too much detail, lest he should weary of my story and desert my company. Were it not for this fear, it would give me pleasure to tell how a week was passed in Newbern; how the people came even from interior towns to see the paper canoe; how some, doubting my veracity, slyly stuck the blades of their pocket-knives through the thin sides of the canoe, forgetting that it had yet to traverse many dangerous inlets, and that its owner preferred a tight, dry boat to one punc-

tured by knives. Even old men became enthusiastic, and when I was absent from my little
craft, an uncontrollable ambition seized them,
and they got into the frail shell as it rested upon
the floor of a hall, and threatened its destruction. It seemed impossible to make one gentleman of Newbern understand that when the
boat was in the water she was resting upon all
her bearings, but when out of water only upon
a thin strip of wood.

"By George," said this stout gentleman in a
whisper to a friend, "I told my wife I would get
into that boat if I smashed it."

"And what did the lady say, old fellow?"
asked the friend.

"O," he replied, "she said, ' Now don't make
a fool of yourself, Fatness, or your ambition may
get you into the papers,'" and the speaker fairly
shook with laughter.

While at Newbern, Judge West and his brother
organized a grand hunt, and the railroad company sent us down the road eighteen miles to a
wild district, where deer, coons, and wild-fowl
were plentiful, and where we hunted all night for
coons and ducks, and all day for deer. Under
these genial influences the practical study of
geography for the first time seemed dull, and I
became aware that, under the efforts of the citizens of Newbern to remind me of the charms

of civilized society, I was, as a travelling geographer, fast becoming demoralized.

Could I, after the many pleasures I was daily enjoying, settle down to a steady pull and one meal a day with a lunch of dry crackers; or sleep on the floor of fishermen's cabins, with fleas and other little annoyances attendant thereon? Having realized my position, I tore myself away from my many new friends and retraced my steps to Morehead City, leaving it on Tuesday, January 5th, and rowing down the little sound called Bogue towards Cape Fear.

As night came on I discovered on the shore a grass cabin, which was on the plantation of Dr. Emmett, and had been left tenantless by some fisherman. This served for shelter during the night, though the struggles and squealings of a drove of hogs attempting to enter through the rickety door did not contribute much to my repose.

The watercourses now became more intricate, growing narrower as I rowed southward. The open waters of the sound were left behind, and I entered a labyrinth of creeks and small sheets of water, which form a network in the marshes between the sandy beach-islands and the mainland all the way to Cape Fear River. The Core Sound sheet of the United States Coast Survey ended at Cape Lookout, there being no charts of the route to Masonboro. I was therefore now travelling upon *local* knowledge, which proves usually a very uncertain guide.

In a cold rain the canoe reached the little village of Swansboro, where the chief personage of the place of two hundred inhabitants, Mr. McLain, removed me from my temporary camping-place in an old house near the turpentine distilleries into his own comfortable quarters.

There are twenty mullet fisheries within ten miles of Swansboro, which employ from fifteen to eighteen men each. The pickled and dried roe of this fish is shipped to Wilmington and to Cincinnati. Wild-fowls abound, and the shooting is excellent. The fishermen say flocks of ducks seven miles in length have been seen on the waters of Bogue Sound. Canvas-backs are called " raft-ducks " here, and they sell from twelve to twenty cents each. Wild geese bring forty cents, and brant thirty.

The marsh-ponies feed upon the beaches, in a half wild state, with the deer and cattle, cross the marshes and swim the streams from the mainland to the beaches in the spring, and graze there until winter, when they collect in little herds, and instinctively return to the piny woods of the uplands. Messrs. Weeks and Taylor had shot, while on a four-days' hunt up the White Oak River, twenty deer. Captain H. D. Heady, of Swansboro, informed me that the ducks and geese he killed in one winter supplied him with one hundred pounds of selected feathers. Captain Heady's description of Bogue Inlet was not encouraging for the future prosperity of this coast, and the same may be said of all the inlets between it and Cape Fear.

Rainy weather kept me within doors until Friday, the 7th of January, when I rowed down White Oak River to Bogue Inlet, and turned into the beach thoroughfare, which led me three miles and a half to Bear Inlet. My course now lay through creeks among the marshes to the Stand-Back, near the mainland, where the tides between the two inlets head. Across this shoal spot I traversed tortuous watercourses with mud flats, from which beds of sharp raccoon oysters projected and scraped the keel of my boat.

The sea was now approached from the mainland to Brown's Inlet, where the tide ran like a mill-race, swinging my canoe in great circles as I crossed it to the lower side. Here I took the widest thoroughfare, and left the beach only to retrace my steps to follow one nearer the strand, which conducted me to the end of the natural system of watercourses, where I found a ditch, dug seventy years before, which connected the last system of waters with another series of creeks that emptied their waters into New River Inlet.

Emerging from the marshes, my course led me away from New River Inlet, across open sheets of water to the mainland, where Dr. Ward's cotton plantation occupied a large and cultivated area in the wilderness. It was nearly two miles from his estate down to the inlet. The intervening flats among the island marshes of New River were covered with natural beds of oysters, upon which the canoe scraped as I crossed to the narrow entrance of Stump Sound. Upon rounding a point of land I found, snugly ensconced in a grove, the cot of an oysterman, Captain Risley Lewis, who, after informing me that his was the last habitation to be found in that vicinity, pressed me to be his guest.

The next day proved one of trial to patience and muscle. The narrow watercourses, which like a spider's web penetrate the marshes with numerous small sheets of water, made travelling a most difficult task. At times I was lost, again my canoe was lodged upon oyster-beds in the shallow ponds of water, the mud bottoms of which would not bear my weight if I attempted to get overboard to lighten the little craft.

Alligator Lake, two miles in width, was crossed without seeing an alligator. Saurians are first met with, as the traveller proceeds south, in the vicinity of Alligator Creek and the Neuse River, in the latitude of Pamplico Sound. During the cold weather they hide themselves in the soft, muddy bottoms of creeks and lagoons. All the negroes, and many of the white people of the south, assert, that when captured in his winter bed, this huge reptile's stomach contains the hard knot of a pine-tree; but for what purpose he swallows it they are at a loss to explain.

In twelve miles of tortuous windings there appeared but one sign of human life — a little cabin on a ridge of upland among the fringe of marshes that bordered on Alligator Lake. It was cheering to a lonely canoeist to see this house, and the clearing around it with the season's crop of corn in stacks dotting the field. All this region is called Stump Sound; but that sheet of water is a well-defined, narrow, lake-like watercourse, which was entered not long after I debouched from Alligator Lake. Stump Inlet having closed up eighteen months before my visit, the sound and its tributaries received tidal water from New Topsail Inlet.

It was a cold and rainy evening when I sought shelter in an old boat-house, at a landing on Topsail Sound, soon after leaving Stump Sound. While preparing for the night's camp, the son of the proprietor of the plantation discovered the, to him, unheard-of spectacle of a paper boat upon the gravelly strand. Filled with curiosity and delight, he dragged me, paddle in hand, through an avenue of trees to a hill upon which a large house was located. This was the boy's home. Leaving me on the broad steps of the veranda, he rushed into the hall, shouting to

the family, " Here's a sailor who has come from
the north in a PAPER boat."

This piece of intelligence roused the good
people to merriment. " Impossible! " " A boat
made of paper ! " " Nonsense ! "

The boy, however, would not be put down.
" But it *is* made of paper, I tell you; for I
pinched it and stuck my nails into it," he replied earnestly.

" You are crazy, my boy," some one responded; " a paper boat never could go through
these sounds, the coon oysters would cut it in
pieces. Now tell us, is the sailor made of
paper, like his boat? "

" Indeed, mother, what I tell you is true; and,
O, I forgot! here's the sailor on the steps, where
I left him." In an instant the whole family were
out upon the veranda. Seeing my embarrass-
ment, they tried, like well-bred people, to check
their merriment, while I explained to them the
way in which the boy had captured me, and
proposed at once returning to my camp. To
this, however, they would not listen; and the
charming wife of the planter extended her hand
to me, as she said, " No, sir, you will not go back
to the wet landing to camp. This is our home,
and though marauding armies during the late
war have taken from us our wealth, you must
share with us the little we have left." This lady
with her two daughters, who inherited her beauty

and grace of manner, did all in their power to make me comfortable.

Sunday was the coldest day of the season; but the family, whose hospitality I enjoyed, rode seven miles through the woods, some on horseback, some in the carriage, to the little church in a heavy pine forest. The next day proved stormy, and the driving sleet froze upon the trees and bound their limbs and boughs together with an icy veneer. My host, Mr. McMillan, kindly urged me to tarry. During my stay with him I ascertained that he devoted his attention to raising ground-peas, or peanuts. Along the coast of this part of North Carolina this nut is the chief product, and is raised in immense quantities. The latter state alone raises annually over one hundred thousand bushels; while Virginia and Tennessee produce, some years, a crop of seven hundred thousand bushels.

Wednesday opened with partially clearing weather, and the icy covering of the trees yielded to the softening influences of a southern wind. The family went to the landing to see me off, and the kind ladies stowed many delicacies, made with their own hands, in the bow of the boat. After rowing a half-mile, I took a lingering look at the shore, where those who four days ago were strangers, now waved an adieu as friends. They had been stript of their wealth, though the kind old planter had never raised his hand against the government of his fathers. This family, like thousands of people in the south, had suffered for the rash deeds of others. While the political views of this gentleman differed from those of the stranger from Massachusetts, it formed no barrier to their social intercourse, and did not make him forget to exhibit the warm feelings of hospitality which so largely influence the Southerner. I went to him, as a traveller in search of truth, upon an honest errand. Under such circumstances a Northerner does not require a letter of introduction to nine out of ten of the citizens of the fifteen ex-slave states, which cover an area of eight hundred and eighty thousand square miles, and where fourteen millions of people desire to be permitted to enjoy the same privileges as the Constitution of the United States guarantees to all the states north of Mason and Dixon's line.

From Sloop Landing, on my new friends' plantation, to New Topsail Inlet I had a brisk row of five miles. Vessels drawing eight feet of water can reach this landing from the open sea upon a full tide. The sea was rolling in at this ocean door as my canoe crossed it to the next marsh thoroughfare, which connected it with Old Topsail Inlet, where the same monotonous surroundings of sand-hills and marshes are to be found.

The next tidal opening was Rich Inlet, which

had a strong ebb running through it to the sea. From it I threaded the thoroughfares up to the mainland, reaching at dusk the "Emma Nickson Plantation." The creeks were growing more shallow, and near the bulkhead, or middle-ground, where tides from two inlets met, there was so little water and so many oyster reefs, that, without a chart, the route grew more and more perplexing in character. It was a distance of thirty miles to Cape Fear, and twenty miles to New Inlet, which was one of the mouths of Cape Fear River. From the plantation to New Inlet, the shallow interior sheets of water with their marshes were called Middle, Mason-boro, and Myrtle sounds. The canoe could have traversed these waters to the end of Myr-tle Sound, which is separated from Cape Fear River by a strip of land only one mile and a half wide, across which a portage can be made to the river. Barren and Masonboro are the only inlets which supply the three little sounds above mentioned with water, after Rich Inlet is passed.

The coast from Cape Fear southward eighty miles, to Georgetown, South Carolina, has several small inlets through the beach, but there are no interior waters parallel with the coast in all that distance, which can be of any service to the canoeist for a coast route. It therefore became necessary for me to follow the next watercourse that could be utilized for reaching Winyah Bay, which is the first entrance to the system of continuous watercourses south of Cape Fear.

The trees of the Nickson Plantation hid the house of the proprietor from view; but upon beaching my canoe, a drove of hogs greeted me with friendly grunts, as if the hospitality of their master infected the drove; and, as it grew dark, they trotted across the field, conducting me up to the very doors of the planter's home, where Captain Mosely, late of the Confederate army, gave me a soldier's hearty welcome.

" The war is over," he said, " and any northern *gentleman* is welcome to what we have left." Until midnight, this keen-eyed, intelligent officer entertained me with a flow of anecdotes of the war times, his hair-breadth escapes, &c.; the conversation being only interrupted when he paused to pile wood upon the fire, the chimney-place meantime glowing like a furnace. He told me that Captain Maffitt, of the late Confederate navy, lived at Masonboro, on the sound; and that had I called upon him, he could have furnished, as an old officer of the Coast Survey, much valuable geographical information. This pleasant conversation was at last interrupted by the wife of my host, who warned us in her courteous way of the lateness of the hour. With a good-night to my host, and a sad farewell to the sea, I prepared myself for the morrow's journey.

CHAPTER XI.

FROM CAPE FEAR TO CHARLESTON, SOUTH CAROLINA.

A PORTAGE TO LAKE WACCAMAW. — THE SUBMERGED SWAMPS. — NIGHT AT A TURPENTINE DISTILLERY. — A DISMAL WILDERNESS. — OWLS AND MISTLETOE. — CRACKERS AND NEGROES. — ACROSS THE SOUTH CAROLINA LINE. — A CRACKER'S IDEA OF HOSPITALITY. — POT BLUFF. — PEEDEE RIVER. — GEORGETOWN. — WINYAH BAY. — THE RICE PLANTATIONS OF THE SANTEE RIVERS. — A NIGHT WITH THE SANTEE NEGROES. — ARRIVAL AT CHARLESTON.

TO reach my next point of embarkation a portage was necessary. Wilmington was twelve miles distant, and I reached the railroad station of that city with my canoe packed in a bed of corn-husks, on a one-horse dray, in time to take the evening train to Flemington, on Lake Waccamaw. The polite general freight-agent, Mr. A. Pope, allowed my canoe to be transported in the passenger baggage-car, where, as it had no covering, I was obliged to steady it during the ride of thirty-two miles, to protect it from the friction caused by the motion of the train.

Mr. Pope quietly telegraphed to the few families at the lake, "Take care of the paper canoe;" so when my destination was reached, kind voices greeted me through the darkness and offered me the hospitalities of Mrs. Brothers' home-like inn at the Flemington Station.   After Mr. Carroll had conveyed the boat to his storehouse, we all sat down to tea as sociably as though we were old friends.

On the morrow we carried the Maria Theresa on our shoulders to the little lake, out of which the long and crooked river with its dark cypress waters flowed to the sea.   A son of Mr. Short, a landed proprietor who holds some sixty thousand acres of the swamp lands of the Waccamaw, escorted me in his yacht, with a party of ladies and gentlemen, five miles across the lake to my point of departure.   It was now noon, and our little party picnicked under the lofty trees which rise from the low shores of Lake Waccamaw.

A little later we said our adieu, and the paper canoe shot into the whirling current which rushes out of the lake through a narrow aperture into a great and dismal swamp.   Before leaving the party, Mr. Carroll had handed me a letter addressed to Mr. Hall, who was in charge of a turpentine distillery on my route.   " It is *twenty* miles by the river to my friend Hall's," he said, " but in a straight line the place is just *four* miles from here."   Such is the character of the Waccamaw, this most crooked of rivers.

I had never been on so rapid and continuous a current.   As it whirled me along the narrow watercourse I was compelled to abandon my oars and use the paddle in order to have my face to the bow, as the abrupt turns of the stream seemed to wall me in on every side. Down the tortuous, black, rolling current went the paper canoe, with a giant forest covering the great swamp and screening me from the light of day. The swamps were submerged, and as the water poured out of the thickets into the river it would shoot across the land from one bend to another, presenting in places the mystifying spectacle of water running up stream, but not up an inclined plain. Festoons of gray Spanish moss hung from the weird limbs of monster trees, giving a funeral aspect to the gloomy forest, while the owls hooted as though it were night. The creamy, wax-like berries of the mistletoe gave a Druidical aspect to the woods, for this parasite grew upon the branches of many trees.

One spot only of firm land rose from the water in sixteen miles of paddling from the lake, and passing it, I went flying on with the turbulent stream four miles further, to where rafts of logs blocked the river, and the sandy banks, covered with the upland forest of pines, encroached upon the lowlands. This was Old Dock, with its turpentine distillery smoking and sending out resinous vapors.

Young Mr. Hall read my letter and invited

me to his temporary home, which, though roughly built of unplaned boards, possessed two comfortable rooms, and a large fireplace, in which light-wood, the terebinthine heart of the pine-tree, was cheerfully blazing.

I had made the twenty miles in three hours, but the credit of this quick time must be given to the rapid current. My host did not seem well pleased with the solitude imposed upon him. His employers had sent him from Wilmington, to hold and protect " their turpentine farm," which was a wilderness of trees covering four thousand acres, and was valued, with its distillery, at five thousand dollars. An old negro, who attended the still and cooked the meals, was his only companion.

We had finished our frugal repast, when a man, shouting in the darkness, approached the house on horseback. This individual, though very tipsy, represented Law and Order in that district, as I was informed when " Jim Gore," a justice of the peace, saluted me in a boisterous manner. Seating himself by the fire, he earnestly inquired for the bottle. His stomach, he said, was as dry as a lime-kiln, and, though water answers to slake lime, he demanded something stronger to slake the fire that burned within him. He was very suspicious of me when Hall told him of my canoe journey. After eying me from head to toe in as steady a manner as he was capable of, he broke forth with: "Now, stranger, this won't do. What are ye a-travelling in this sort of way for, in a paper dug-out?"

I pleaded a strong desire to study geography, but the wise fellow replied:

"Geography! geography! Why, the fellers who rite geography never travel; they stay at home and spin their yarns 'bout things they never sees." Then, glancing at his poor butternut coat and pantaloons, he felt my blue woollen suit, and continued, in a slow, husky voice: "Stranger, them clothes cost *something;* they be *store*-clothes. That paper dug-out *cost money*, I tell ye; and it *costs* something to travel the hull length of the land. No, stranger; if ye be not on a bet, then somebody's a-paying ye *well* for it."

For an hour I entertained this roughest of law dignitaries with an account of my long row, its trials and its pleasures. He became interested in the story, and finally related to me his own aspirations, and the difficulties attending his efforts to make the piny-woods people respect the laws and good government. He then described the river route through the swamps to the sea, and, putting his arm around me in the most affectionate manner, he mournfully said:

"O stranger, my heart is with ye; but O, how ye will have to take it when ye go past those awful wretches to-morrow; how they will give it to ye! They most knocked me off my raft, last time I went to Georgetown. Beware of them; I warn ye in time. Dern the hussies."

Squire Jim so emphasized the danger that I became somewhat alarmed, for, more than anything else, I dreaded an outbreak with rough women. And then, too, my new acquaintance informed me that there were four or five of these wretches, of the worst kind, located several miles down the stream. As I was about to inquire into the habits of these ugly old crones, Mr. Hall, wishing to give Squire James a hint, remarked that Mr. B—— might at any time retire to the next room, where half the bed was at his disposal.

"*Half the bed!*" roared the squire; "here are *three* of us, and where's *my half?*"

"Why, squire," hesitatingly responded my host, "Mr. B—— is *my guest*, and having but *one* bed, he must have *half* of it — no less."

"Then what's to become of me?" thundered his Majesty of the law.

Having been informed that a shake-down would have been ready had he given notice of his visit, and that at some future time, when not so crowded, he could be entertained like a gentleman, he drew himself up, wrapped in the mantle of dignity, and replied:

"None of that soft talk, my friend. This man is a traveller; let him take travellers' luck — three in a bed to-night. I'm bound to sleep with him to-night. Hall, where's the bottle?"

I now retired to the back room, and, without undressing, planted myself on the side of the bed next the wall. Sleep was, however, an unattainable luxury, with the squire's voice in the next room, as he told how the country was going to the dogs, because "niggers and white folks wouldn't respect the laws. It took half a man's time to *larn* it to 'em, and much thanks he ever got by setting everybody to rights." He wound up by lecturing Hall for being so temperate, his diligent search in all directions for bottles or jugs being rewarded by finding them filled with unsatisfactory emptiness.

He then tumbled into the centre of the bed, crowding me close against the wall. Poor Hall, having the outside left to him, spent the night in exercising his brain and muscles in vain attempts to keep in his bed; for when his Majesty of the law put his arms akimbo, the traveller went to the wall, and the host to the floor. Thus passed my first night in the great swamps of the Waccamaw River.

The negro cook gave us an early breakfast of bacon, sweet potatoes, and corn bread. The squire again looked round for the bottle, and again found nothing but emptiness. He helped me to carry my canoe along the unsteady footing of the dark swamp to the lower side of the raft of logs, and warmly pressed my hand as he whispered: " My dear B——, I shall think of you until you get past those dreadful ' wretches.' Keep an eye on your little boat, or they'll devil you."

Propelled by my double paddle, the canoe seemed to fly through the great forest that rose with its tall trunks and weird, moss-draped arms, out of the water. The owls were still hooting. Indeed, the dolorous voice of this bird of darkness sounded through the heavy woods at intervals throughout the day. I seemed to have left the real world behind me, and to have entered upon a landless region of sky, trees, and water.

" Beware of the cut-offs," said Hall, before I left. " Only the Crackers and shingle-makers know them. If followed, they would save you many a mile, but every opening through the swamp is not a cut-off. Keep to the main stream, though it be more crooked and longer. If you take to the cut-offs, you may get into passages that will lead you off into the swamps and into interior bayous, from which you will never emerge. Men have starved to death in such places."

So I followed the winding stream, which turned back upon itself, running north and south, and east and west, as if trying to box the compass by following the sun in its revolution. After paddling down one bend, I could toss a stick through the trees into the stream where the canoe had cleaved its waters a quarter of a mile behind me.

The thought of what I should do in this landless region if my frail shell, in its rapid flight to the sea, happened to be pierced by a snag, was, to say the least, not a comforting one. On what could I stand to repair it? To climb a tree seemed, in such a case, the only resource; and then what anxious waiting there would be for some cypress-shingle maker, in his dug-out canoe, to come to the rescue, and take the traveller from his dangerous lodgings between heaven and earth; or it might be that no one would pass that way, and the weary waiting would be even unto death.

But sounds now reached my ears that made me feel that I was not quite alone in this desolate swamp. The gray squirrels scolded among the tree-tops; robins, the brown thrush, and a large black woodpecker with his bright red head, each reminded me of Him without whose notice not a sparrow falleth to the ground.

Ten miles of this black current were passed over, when the first signs of civilization appeared, in the shape of a sombre-looking, two-storied house, located upon a point of the mainland which entered the swamp on the left shore of the river. At this point the river widened to five

or six rods, and at intervals land appeared a few
inches above the water. Wherever the pine
land touched the river a pig-pen of rails offered
shelter and a gathering-place for the hogs,
which are turned loose by the white Cracker
to feed upon the roots and mast of the wilderness.

Reeve's Ferry, on the right bank, with a little
store and turpentine-still, twenty miles from Old
Dock, was the next sign of the presence of man
in this swamp. The river now became broad as
I approached Piraway Ferry, which is two miles
below Piraway Farm. Remembering the warnings of the squire as to the "awful wretches in
the big pine woods," I kept a sharp lookout for
the old women who were to give me so much
trouble, but the raftsmen on the river explained
that though Jim Gore had told me the truth, I
had misunderstood his pronunciation of the word
reaches, or river bends, which are called in
this vicinity *wretches*. The reaches referred to
by Mr. Gore were so long and straight as to
afford open passages for wind to blow up them,
and these fierce gusts of head winds give the
raftsmen much trouble while poling their rafts
against them.

My fears of ill treatment were now at rest, for
my tiny craft, with her sharp-pointed bow, was
well adapted for such work. Landing at the
ferry where a small scow or flat-boat was resting

upon the firm land, the ferryman, Mr. Daniel Dunkin, would not permit me to camp out of doors while his log-cabin was only one mile away on the pine-covered uplands. He told me that the boundary-line between North and South Carolina crossed this swamp three and a half miles below Piraway Ferry, and that the first town on the river Waccamaw, in South Carolina, Conwayborough, was a distance of ninety miles by river and only thirty miles by land. There was but one bridge over the river, from its head to Conwayborough, and it was built by Mr. James Wortham, twenty years before, for his plantation. This bridge was twenty miles below Piraway, and from it by land to a settlement on Little River, which empties into the Atlantic, was a distance of only five miles. A short canal would connect this river and its lumber regions with Little River and the sea.

For the first time in my experience as a traveller I had entered a country where the miles were *short*. When fifteen years old I made my first journey alone and on foot from the vicinity of Boston to the White Mountains of New Hampshire. This boyish pedestrian trip occupied about twenty-one days, and covered some three hundred miles of hard tramping. New England gives honest measure on the finger-posts along her highways. The traveller learns by well-earned experience the length of *her* miles; but in the wilderness of the south there is no standard of five thousand two hundred and eighty feet to a statute mile, and the watermen along the sea-coast are ignorant of the fact that one-sixtieth of a degree of latitude (about six thousand and eighty feet) is the geographical and nautical mile of the cartographer, as well as the " knot" of the sailor.

At Piraway Ferry no two of the raftsmen and lumbermen, ignorant or educated, would give the same distance, either upon the lengths of surveyed roads or unmeasured rivers. " It is one hundred and sixty-five miles by river from Piraway Ferry to Conwayborough," said one who had travelled the route for years. The most moderate estimate made was that of ninety miles by river. The reader, therefore, must not accuse me of over-stating distances while absent from the seaboard, as my friends of the Coast Survey Bureau have not yet penetrated into these interior regions with their theodolites, plane-tables, and telametre-rods. To the canoeist, who is ambitious to score up *miles* instead of collecting geographical notes, these wild rivers afford an excellent opportunity to satisfy his aims.

From sixty to eighty miles can be rowed in ten hours as easily as forty miles can be gone over upon a river of slow current in the nor-thern states. There is, I am sorry to say, a class of American travellers who " *do* " all the capitals of Europe in the same business-like way, and if they have anything to say in regard to every-day life in the countries through which they pass, they forget to thank the compiler of the guide-book for the information they possess.

There was but one room in the cabin of my new acquaintance, who represented that class of piny-woods people called in the south — because they subsist largely upon corn, — Corn Crackers, or Crackers. These Crackers are the " poor white folks " of the planter, and " de white trash " of the old slave, who now as a freedman is beginning to feel the responsibility of his position.

These Crackers are a very kind-hearted people, but few of them can read or write. The children of the negro, filled with curiosity and a new-born pride, whenever opportunity permits, attend the schools in large numbers; but the very indolent white man seems to be destitute of all ambition, and his children, in many places in the south, following close in the father's footsteps, grow up in an almost unimaginable ignorance.

The news of the arrival of the little Maria Theresa at Piraway Ferry spread with astonishing rapidity through the woods, and on Sunday, after " de shoutings," as the negroes call their meetings, were over, the blacks came in numbers to see " dat Yankee-man's paper canno."

These simple people eyed me from head to foot with a grave sort of curiosity, their great mouths open, displaying pearly teeth of which a white man might well be proud. "You is a good man, capt'n — we knows dat," they said; and when I asked why, the answer showed their childlike faith. "'Cause you couldn't hab come all dis way in a *paper* boat if de Lord hadn't helped you. *He* dono help only good folks."

The Cracker also came with his children to view the wonder, while the raftsmen were so struck with the advantages of my double paddle, which originated with the inhabitants of the Arctic regions, that they laid it upon a board and drew its outlines with chalk. They vowed they would introduce it upon the river.

These Crackers declared it would take more than " de shoutings," or any other religious service, to improve the moral condition of the blacks. They openly accused the colored preachers of disturbing the nocturnal rest of their hens and turkeys; and as to hog-stealing and cow-killing, " Why, we won't have any crit- ters left ef this carpet-bag government lasts much longer! " they feelingly exclaimed.

" We does nothing to nobody. We lets the niggers alone; but niggers will steal — they can't help it, the poor devils; it's in 'em. Now, ef they eats us out of house and home, what can a poor man do? They puts 'em up for justices of peace, and sends 'em to the legislature, when they can't read more'n us; and they do say it's 'cause we fit in the Confederate sarvice that they razes the nigger over our heads. Now, does the folkes up north like to see white people tyrannized over by niggers? Jes tell 'em when you go back, stranger, that we's got soulds like yours up north, and we's got feelings too, by thunder! jes like other white men. This was a white man's country once — now it's all niggers and dogs. Why, them niggers in the legislature has spit-boxes lined with gold to spit in! What's this country a-coming to? We wish the niggers no harm if they lets our hogs and chickens alone."

After this tirade it was amusing to see how friendly the whites and blacks were. The Crackers conversed with these children of Ham, who had been stealing their hams for so long a time, in the most kindly way, realizing, perhaps, that they had various peculiar traits of their own, and must, after all, endure their neighbors.

A traveller should place facts before his readers, and leave to them the drawing of the moral. Northern men and women who go to the southern states and reside for even the short space of a year or two, invariably change their life-long views and principles regarding the negro as a moral and social creature. When these people return to their homes in Maine or Massachusetts (as did the representatives of the Granges of the northern states after they had visited South Carolina in 1875) a new light, derived from contact

with *facts*, dawns upon them, while their surprised and untravelled neighbors say: "*So you
have become Southern in your views.* I never
would have thought that of *you*."

The railroad has become one of the great me-
diums of enlightenment to mankind, and joins in
a social fraternity the disunited elements of a
country.   God grant that the resources of the
great South may soon be developed by the capital and free labor of the North.   Our sister states
of the South, exhausted by the struggles of the
late war which resulted in consolidating more
firmly than ever the great Union, are now ready
to receive every honest effort to develop their
wealth or cultivate their territory.   Let every
national patriot give up narrowness of views and
sectional selfishness and become acquainted with
(not the politicians) the people of the New
South, and a harmony of feeling will soon possess the hearts of all true lovers of a government
of the people.

The swamp tributaries were swelling the river
into a very rapid torrent as I paddled away from
the ferry on Monday, January 18.   A warmer
latitude having been reached, I could dispense
with one blanket, and this I had presented to my
kind host, who had refused to accept payment
for his hospitality.   He was very proud of his
present, and said, feelingly, " No one shall touch
this but me."   His good wife had baked some

of a rich and very nice variety of sweet-potatoes, unlike those we get in New Jersey or the other Middle States—which potatoes she kindly added to my stores. They are not dry or mealy when cooked, but seem saturated with honey. The poor woman's gift now occupied the space formerly taken up by the blanket I had given her husband.

From this day, as latitude after latitude was crossed on my way southward, I distributed every article I could spare, among these poor, kind-hearted people. Mr. Macgregor went in his Rob Roy canoe over the rivers of Europe, " diffusing cheerfulness and distributing Evangelical tracts." I had no room for tracts, and if I had followed the example of my well-intentioned predecessor in canoeing, it would have served the cause of truth or creed but little. The Crackers could not read, and but few of the grown negroes had been taught letters. They did not want books, but tobacco. Men and women hailed me from the banks as I glided along in my canoe, with, " Say, captain, hab you eny 'bacca or snuff for dis chile?" Poor humanity! The Cracker and the freedman fill alike their places according to the light they possess. Do we, who have been taught from our youth sacred things, do more than this? Do we love our neighbor as ourself?

For twenty miles (local authority) I journeyed

down the stream, without seeing a human being or a dwelling-place, to Stanley's house and the bridge; from which I urged the canoe thirty-five miles further, passing an old field on a bluff, when darkness settled on the swamps, and a heavy mist rose from the waters and enveloped the forests in its folds. With not a trace of land above water I groped about, running into what appeared to be openings in the submerged land, only to find my canoe tangled in thickets. It was useless to go further, and I prepared to ascend to the forks of a giant tree, with a light rope, to be used for lashing my body into a safe position, when a long, low cry engaged my attention.

"Waugh! ho! ho! ho! peig—peig—pe-ig—pe-ig," came through the still, thick air. It was not an owl, nor a catamount that cried thus; nor was it the bark of a fox. It was the voice of a Cracker calling in his hogs from the forest. This sound was indeed pleasant to my ears, for I knew the upland was near, and that a warm fire awaited my benumbed limbs in the cabin of this unknown man. Pushing the canoe towards the sound, and feeling the submerged border of the swamp with my paddle, I struck the upland where it touched the water, and disembarking, felt my way along a well-trodden path to a little clearing. Here a drove of hogs were crowding around their owner, who was

scattering kernels of corn about him as he vo-
ciferated, "pe-ig — pe-ig — pe-ig — pig — pig —
pig." We stood face to face, yet neither could
see the face of the other in the darkness. I told
my tale, and asked where I could find a sheltered
spot to camp.

"Stranger," slowly replied the Cracker, "my
cabin 's close at hand. Come home with me.
It's a bad night for a man to lay out in; and the
niggers would steal your traps if they knew you
had anything worth taking. Come with me."

In the tall pines near at hand was a cabin of
peeled rails, the chinks between them being
stuffed with moss. A roof of cypress shingles
kept the rain out. The log chimney, which was
plastered with mud, was built outside of the
walls and against an end of the rustic-looking
structure. The wide-mouthed fireplace sent
forth a blaze of light as we entered the poor
man's home. I saw in the nicely swept floor,
the clean bed-spreads, and the general neatness
of the place, the character of Wilson Edge's
wife.

"Hog and hominy 's our food here in the piny
woods," said Mr. Edge, as his wife invited us to
the little table; "and we've a few eggs now and
then to eat with sweet potatoes, but it's up-hill
work to keep the niggers from killing every fowl
and animal we have. The carpet-bag politicians
promised them every one, for his vote, forty acres

of land and a mule. They sed as how the northern government was a-going to give it to um; but the poor devils never got any thanks even for their votes. They had been stuffed with all sorts of notions by the carpet-baggers, and I don't blame um for putting on airs and trying to rule us. It's human natur, that's all. We don't blame the niggers half so much as those who puts it in their heads to do so; but it's hard times we've had, we poor woods folks. They took our children for the cussed war, to fight fur niggers and rich people as owned um.

"We never could find out what all the fuss was about; but when Jeff Davis made a law to exempt every man from the army who owned fifteen niggers, then our blood riz right up, and we sez to our neighbors, 'This ere thing's a-getting to be a rich man's quarrel and a poor man's fight.' After all they dragged off my boy to Chambersburg, Pennsylvania, and killed him a fighting for what? Why, for rich nigger owners. Our young men hid in the swamps, but they were hunted up and forced into the army. Niggers has been our ruin. Ef a white man takes a case before a nigger justice, he gives the nigger everything, and the white man has to stand one side. Now, would you folks up north like to have a nigger justice who can't read nor count ten figgurs?"

I tried to comfort the poor man, by assuring

him that outside of the political enemies of our peace, the masses in the north were honestly inclined towards the south now that slavery was at an end; and that wrong could not long prevail, with the cheerful prospect of a new administration, and the removal of all unconstitutional forces that preyed upon the south.

The two beds in the single room of the cabin were occupied by the family; while I slept upon the floor by the fire, with my blankets for a couch and a roll of homespun for a pillow, which the women called "*heading.*" They often said, "Let me give you some heading for your bed." We waited until eight o'clock the next day for the mists to rise from the swamps. My daily trouble was now upon me. How could I remunerate a southerner for his cost of keeping me, when not, in the true sense of the word, an invited guest to his hospitality?

Wilson Edge sat by the fire, while his wife and little ones were preparing to accompany me to see the paper boat. "Mr. Edge," I stammered, "you have treated me with great kindness, your wife has been put to some inconvenience, as I came in so unexpected a manner, and you will really oblige me if you will accept a little money for all this; though money cannot pay for your hospitality. Grant my wish, and you will send me away with a light heart." The poor Cracker lowered his head and slowly

ran his fingers through his coal black hair.   For
a moment he seemed studying a reply, and then
he spoke as though HE represented the whole
generous heart of the south.

"*Stranger*," he slowly articulated, "*Stranger,
I have known white men to be niggers enough
to take a stranger's money for lodgings and
vittles, but I am not that man.*"

We found the canoe as it had been left the
night before, and I was soon pulling down the
river.   The great wilderness was traversed thirty
miles to the county town of Conwayborough,
where the negroes roared with laughter at the
working of the double paddle, as I shot past the
landing-place where cotton and naval stores
were piled, waiting to be lightered nine miles to
Pot Bluff, — so called from the fact of a pot
being lost from a vessel near it, — which place
is reached by vessels from New York drawing
twelve feet of water.   Though still a long distance from the ocean, I was beginning to feel its
tidal influences.   At Pot Bluff, the landing and
comfortable home of its owner, Mr. Z. W. Du-
senberry, presented a pleasant relief after the
monotony of the great pine forests.   This enterprising business man made my short stay a very
pleasant one.

Wednesday, January 20th, was cold for this
latitude, and ice formed in thin sheets in the
water-pails.   Twenty-two miles below Pot Bluff,

Bull Creek enters the Waccamaw from the Peedee River. At the mouth of this connecting
watercourse is Tip Top, the first rice plantation
of the Waccamaw. The Peedee and its sister
stream run an almost parallel course from Bull
Creek to Winyah Bay, making their debouchure
close to the city of Georgetown. Steam saw-
mills and rice plantations take the place of the
forests from a few miles below Tip Top to the
vicinity of Georgetown.

Mr. M. L. Blakely, of New York, one of the
largest shingle manufacturers of the south, occupied as his headquarters the Bates Hill Plantation, on the Peedee. This gentleman had invited
me, through the medium of the post-office, to
visit him in the rice-growing regions of South
Carolina. To reach his home I took the short
" cut-off " which Bull Creek offered, and entered
upon the strongest of head-currents. The thick,
yellow, muddy torrent of the Peedee rushed
through Bull Creek with such volume, that I
wondered if it left much water on the other side,
to give character to the river, as it followed its
own channel to Winyah Bay.

One and a half miles of vigorous paddling
brought me to a branch of the watercourse,
which is much narrower than the main one, and
is consequently called Little Bull Creek. This
also comes from the Peedee River, and its source
is nearer to the Bates Hill plantation than the

main Bull Creek. To urge the canoe up this narrow stream three miles and a half to the parent river Peedee, was a most trying ordeal. At times the boat would not move a hundred feet in five minutes, and often, as my strength seemed failing me, I caught the friendly branches of trees, and held on to keep the canoe from being whirled down the current towards the Waccamaw. After long and persistent efforts had exhausted my strength, I was about to seek for a resting-place in the swamp, when a view of the broad Peedee opened before me, and with vigorous strokes of the paddle the canoe slowly approached the mighty current. A moment more and it was within its grasp, and went flying down the turbulent stream at the rate of ten miles an hour.

A loud halloo greeted me from the swamp, where a party of negro shingle-makers were at work. They manned their boat, a long cypress dug-out, and followed me. Their employer, who proved to be the gentleman whose abiding-place I was now rapidly approaching, sat in the stern. We landed together before the old plantation-house, which had been occupied a few years before by members of the wealthy and powerful rice-planting aristocracy of the Peedee, but was now the temporary home of a northern man, who was busily employed in guiding the labors of his four hundred freedmen in the swamps of North and South Carolina.

The paper canoe had now entered the regions of the rice-planter. Along the low banks of the Peedee were diked marshes where, before the civil war, each estate produced from five thousand to forty thousand bushels of rice annually, and the lords of rice were more powerful than those of cotton, though cotton was king. The rich lands here produced as high as fifty-five bushels of rice to the acre, under forced slave labor; now the free blacks cannot wrest from nature more than twenty-five or thirty bushels.

Fine old mansions lined the river's banks, but the families had been so reduced by the ravages of war, that I saw refined ladies, who had been educated in the schools of Edinburgh, Scotland, overseeing the negroes as they worked in the yards of the rice-mills. The undaunted spirit of these southern ladies, as they worked in their homes now so desolate, roused my admiration.

A light, graceful figure, enveloped in an old shawl, and mounted on an old horse, flitted about one plantation like a restless spirit.

"That lady's father," said a gentleman to me, "owned three plantations, worth three millions of dollars, before the war. There is a rice-mill on one of the plantations which cost thirty thousand dollars. She now fights against misfortune, and will not give up. The Confederate war would not have lasted six months if it had not been for our women. They drove thousands of us young men into the fight; and now, having lost all, they go bravely to work, even taking the places of their old servants in their grand old homes. It's hard for them, though, I assure you."

On Tuesday, January 25th, I paddled down the Peedee, stopping at the plantations of Dr. Weston and Colonel Benjamin Allston. The latter gentleman was a son of one of the governors of South Carolina. He kindly gave me a letter of introduction to Commodore Richard Lowndes, who lived near the coast. From the Peedee I passed through a cut in the marshes into the broad Waccamaw, and descended it to Winyah Bay.

Georgetown is located between the mouths of the Peedee and Sampit rivers. Cautiously approaching the city, I landed at Mr. David Risley's steam saw-mills, and that gentleman kindly secreted my boat in a back counting-room, while I went up town to visit the post-office. By some, to me, unaccountable means, the people had heard of the arrival of the paper boat, and three elaborately dressed negro women accosted me with, "Please show wees tree ladies de little paper boat."

Before I had reached my destination, the post-office, a body of men met me, on their way to the steam-mill. The crowd forced me back to the canoe, and asked so many questions that I was sorely taxed to find answers for these gentlemen. There were three editors in the crowd: two were white men, one a negro. The young men, who claimed the position of representatives of the spirit of the place and of the times, published "The Comet," while the negro, as though influenced by a spirit of sarcasm, conducted "The Planet." The third newspaper represented at the canoe reception was the "Georgetown Times," which courteously noticed the little boat that had come so far. The "Planet" prudently kept in the dark, and said nothing, but "The Comet," representing the culture of the young men of the city, published the following notice of my arrival:

"Tom Collins has at last arrived in his wonderful paper boat. He has it hitched to Mr. Risley's new saw-mill, where every one can have a view. He intends shooting off his sixpounder before weighing anchor in the morning. Hurrah for Collins."

I left Mr. Risley's comfortable home before noon the next day, and followed the shores of Winyah Bay towards the sea. Near Battery White, on the right shore, in the pine forests, was the birth-place of Marion, the brave patriot of the American revolution, whose bugle's call summoned the youth of those days to arms.

When near the inlet, the rice-plantation marshes skirted the shore for some distance. Out of these wet lands flowed a little stream, called Mosquito Creek, which once connected the North Santee River with Winyah Bay, and served as a boundary to South Island. The creek was very crooked, and the ebb-tide strong. When more than halfway to Santee River I was forced to leave the stream, as it had become closed by tidal deposits and rank vegetation.

The ditches of rice plantations emptied their drainage of the lowlands into Mosquito Creek. Following a wide ditch to the right, through fields of rich alluvial soil, which had been wrested by severe toil from nature, the boat soon reached the rice-mill of Commodore Richard Lowndes. A little further on, and situated in a noble grove of live-oaks, which were draped in the weird festoons of Spanish moss, on the upland arose the stately home of the planter, who still kept his plantation in cultivation, though on a scale of less magnitude than formerly. It was, indeed, a pleasant evening that I passed in the company of the refined members of the old commodore's household, and with a pang of regret the next day I paddled along the main canal of the lowlands, casting backward glances at the old house, with its grand old trees. The canal ended at North Santee Bay.

While I was preparing to ascend the river a

tempest arose, which kept me a weary prisoner among the reeds of the rice marsh. The hollow reeds made poor fuel for cooking, and when the dark, stormy night shut down upon me, the damp soil grew damper as the tide arose, until it threatened to overflow the land. For hours I lay in my narrow canoe waiting for the tidal flood to do its worst, but it receded, and left me without any means of building a fire, as the reeds were wet by the storm. The next afternoon, being tired of this sort of prison-life, and cramped for lack of exercise, I launched the canoe into the rough water, and crossing to Crow Island found a lee under its shores, which permitted me to ascend the river to the mouth of Atchison Creek, through which I passed, two miles, to the South Santee River.

All these rivers are bordered by rice plantations, many of them having been abandoned to the care of the freedmen. I saw no white men upon them. Buildings and dikes are falling into ruins, and the river freshets frequently inundate the land. Many of the owners of these once valuable estates are too much reduced in wealth to attempt their proper cultivation. It is in any case difficult to get the freedmen to work through an entire season, even when well paid for their services, and they flock to the towns whenever opportunity permits.

The North and South Santee rivers empty into

the Atlantic, but their entrances are so shallow that Georgetown Entrance is the inlet through which most of the produce of the country — pitch, tar, turpentine, rice, and lumber — finds exit to the sea. As I left the canal, which, with the creek, makes a complete thoroughfare for lighters and small coasters from one Santee River to the other, a renewal of the tempest made me seek shelter in an old cabin in a negro settlement, each house of which was built upon piles driven into the marshes. The old negro overseer of the plantation hinted to me that his " hands were berry spicious of ebbry stranger," and advised me to row to some other locality. I told him I was from the north, and would not hurt even one of the fleas which in multitudes infested his negroes' quarters; but the old fellow shook his head, and would not be responsible for me if I staid there all night. A tall darkey, who had listened to the conversation, broke in with, " Now, uncle, ye knows dat if dis gemmum is from de norf he is one of wees, and ye must *du* fur him jis *dis* time." But " Uncle Overseer " kept repeating, " Some niggers here is mity spicious. Du not no who white man is anyhow." " Well, uncle," replied the tall black, " ef dis man is a Yankee-mans, Ise will see him *froo*."

Then he questioned me, while the fleas, having telegraphed to each other that a stranger had arrived, made sad havoc of me and my patience.

246 VOYAGE OF THE PAPER CANOE.

"My name's Jacob Gilleu; what's yourn?" I
gave it. "Whar's your home?" came next. "I
am a citizen of the United States," I replied.
"De 'Nited States — whar's dat? neber hurd
him afore," said Jacob Gilleu. Having informed him it was the land which General Grant
governed, he exclaimed: "O, you's a *Grant* man;
all rite den; you is one of wees — all de same as
wees. Den look a-here, boss. I send you to one
good place on Alligator Creek, whar Seba Gillings libs. He black man, but he treat you jes
like white man."

Jacob helped me launch my boat through the
soft mud, which nearly stalled us; and following
his directions I paddled across the South Santee
and coasted down to Alligator Creek, where extensive marshes, covered by tall reeds, hid the
landscape from my view. About half a mile
from the mouth of the creek, which watercourse
was on my direct route to Bull's Bay, a large
tide-gate was found at the mouth of a canal.
This being wide open, I pushed up the canal to
a low point of land which rose like an island out
of the rushes. Here was a negro hamlet of a
dozen houses, or shanties, and the ruins of a
rice-mill. The majority of the negroes were
absent working within the diked enclosures of
this large estate, which before the war had produced forty thousand bushels of rice annually.
Now the place was leased by a former slave,

and but little work was accomplished under the present management.

Seba Gillings, a powerfully built negro, came to the dike upon which I had landed the canoe. I quickly told him my story, and how I had been forced to leave the last negro quarters. I used Jacob Gilleu's name as authority for seeking shelter with him from the damps of the half-submerged lands. The dignified black man bade me "fear nuffing, stay here all de night, long's you please; treat you like white man. I'se mity poor, but gib you de berry best I hab." He locked my boat in a rickety old storehouse, and gave me to understand "dat niggers will steal de berry breff from a man's mouff."

He took me to his home, and soon showed me how he managed "de niggers." His wife sat silently by the fire. He ordered her to "pound de rice;" and she threw a quantity of unhulled rice into a wooden mortar three feet high planted in the ground in front of the shanty. Then, with an enormous pestle, the black woman pounded the grains until the hulls were removed, when, seating herself upon the floor of the dark, smoky cabin, she winnowed the rice with her breath, while her long, slim fingers caught and removed all the specks of dirt from the mass. It was cooked as the Chinese cook it — not to a glutinous mass, as we of the north prepare it — but each grain was dry and entire. Then eggs and

bacon were prepared; not by the woman, but by
the son, a lad of fourteen years.

All these movements were superintended by
old Seba, who sat looking as dark and as solemn
and as learned as an associate judge on the
bench of a New Jersey county court. On the
blackest of tables, minus a cloth, the well-cooked
food was placed for the stranger. As soon as
my meal was finished, every member of the family made a dash for the fragments, and the board
was cleared in a wonderfully short space of time.

Then we gathered round the great, black-
mouthed fireplace, and while the bright coals of
live-oak spread a streak of light through the
darkness, black men and black women stole into
the room until everything from floor to ceiling,
from door to chimney-place, seemed to be growing blacker and blacker, and I felt as black as
my surroundings. The scant clothing of the
men only half covered their shiny, ebony skins.
The whole company preserved a dignified silence, which was occasionally broken by deep
sighs coming from the women in reply to a half-
whispered " All de way from de norf in a *paper
canno* — bless de Lord! bless de Lord! "

This dull monotony was broken by the entrance of a young negro who, having made a
passage in a sloop to Charleston through Bull's
Bay, was looked upon as a great traveller, and
to him were referred disputes upon nautical mat-

ters. He had not yet seen the boat, but he proceeded to tell the negroes present all about it.
He first bowed to me with a " How'dy, how'dy,
cap'n," and then struck an attitude in the middle
of the floor. Upon this natural orator Seba Gillings' dignity had no effect — was he not a travelled man?

His exordium was: " How fur you cum, sar? "
I replied, about fourteen hundred miles. "Fourteen hundred miles! " he roared; " duz you
knows how much dat is, honnies? it's jes *one
tousand* four hundred miles." All the women
groaned out, " Bless de Lord! bless de Lord! "
and clapped their shrivelled hands in ecstasy.

The little black tried to run his fingers through
his short, woolly hair as he continued: " What is
dis yere world a-coming to? Now, yous ere
folks, did ye's eber hear de likes o' dis — a
paper boat? "   To which the crones replied,
clapping their hands, " Bless de Lord! bless de
Lord! Only the Yankee-mens up norf can
make de *paper* boats. Bless de Lord! "

" And what," continued the orator; " and what
will the Yankee-mens do next? Dey duz ebery
ting. Can dey bring a man back agen? Can
dey bring a man back to bref? " " No! no! "
howled the women; " only de Lord can bring a
man back agen — no Yankee-mens can do dat.
Bless de Lord! bless de Lord! " "And what sent
dis Yankee-man *one tousand* four hundred miles

in his *paper* boat?" "De Lord! de Lord! bless de Lord!" shouted the now highly excited women, violently striking the palms of their hands together.

"And why," went on this categorical negro, "did de *Lord* send him down souf in de *paper* boat?" "Kase he couldn't hab cum in de *paper* boat ef de Lord hadn't a-sent him. O, bless de Lord! bless de Lord!" "And what duz he call his paper boat?" "Maria Theresa," I replied. "Maria Truss Her," cried the orator. "He calls her Maria Truss Her. Berry good, berry good name; kase he truss his life in her ebry day, and dat's why he calls his little boat Truss Her. Yes, de Yankee-mans makes de gunboats and de paper boats. Has de gemmin from de norf any bacca for dis yere chile?"

As the women had become very piously inclined, and were in just·the state of nervous excitement to commence "de shoutings," old Uncle Seba rudely informed them that "de Yankee-mans wants sleep," and cleared the room of the crowd, to my great relief, for the state of the atmosphere was beyond description. Seba had a closet where he kept onions, muskrat skins, and other pieces of personal property. He now set his wife to sweeping it out, and I spread my clean blankets with a sigh upon the black floor, knowing I should carry away in the morning more than I had brought into Seba's dwelling.

I will not now expatiate upon the small annoyances of travel; but to the canoeist who may follow the southern watercourses traversed by the paper canoe, I would quietly say, "Keep away from cabins of all kinds, and you will by so doing travel with a light heart and even temper."

When I cast up my account with old Seba the next morning, he said that by trading the rice he raised he could obtain "bout ebbry ting he wanted, 'cept rum." Rum was his medicine. So long as he kept a little stowed away, he admitted he was often sick. Having been destitute of cash, and consequently of rum for some time, he acknowledged his state of health remarkable; and he was a model of strength and manly development. All the other negroes were dwarfish-looking specimens, while their hair was so very short that it gave them the appearance of being bald.

When the canoe was taken out of the storehouse to be put into the canal, these half-naked, ebony-skinned creatures swarmed about it like bees. Not a trace of white blood could be detected in them. Each tried to put a finger upon the boat. They seemed to regard it as a Fetich; and, I believe, had it been placed upon an end they would have bowed down and paid their African devotions to it. Only the oldest ones could speak English well enough to be understood. The youths chattered in African tongue, and wore talismans about their necks. They were, to say the least, verging on barbarism. The experience gathered among the blacks of other lands impressed me with the well-founded belief, that in more than one place in the south would the African Fetich be set up and worshipped before long, unless the church bestirs herself to look well to her *home* missions.

In all my travels, outside of the cities, in the south it has not been my good fortune to find an educated white man preaching to negroes, yet everywhere the poor blacks gather in the log-cabin, or rudely constructed church, to listen to ignorant preachers of their own color. The blind leading the blind.

A few men of negro extraction, with white blood in their veins, not any more negro than white man, consequently *not* negroes in the true sense of the word, are sent from the negro colleges of the south to lecture northern congregations upon the needs of *their* race; and these one-quarter, or perhaps three-quarters, white men are, with their intelligence, and sometimes brilliant oratory, held up as true types of the negro race by northerners; while there is, in fact, as much difference between the pure-blooded negro of the rice-field and this false representative of " his needs," as can well be imagined.

An Irishman, just from the old country, listened one evening to the fascinating eloquence of a mulatto freedman. The good Irishman had never seen a pure-blooded black man. The orator said, "I am only half a black man. My mother was a slave, my father a white planter." "Be jabbers," shouted the excited Irishman, who was charmed with the lecturer, "if you arc only half a nigger, what must a *whole one* be like!"

The blacks were kind and civil, as they usually are when fairly treated. They stood upon the dike and shouted unintelligible farewells as I descended the canal to Alligator Creek. This thoroughfare soon carried me on its salt-water current to the sea; for I missed a narrow entrance to the marshes, called the Eye of the Needle (a steamboat thoroughfare), and found myself upon the calm sea, which pulsated in long swells. To the south was the low island of Cape Roman, which, like a protecting arm, guarded the quiet bay behind it. The marshes extended from the main almost to the cape, while upon the edge of the rushy meadows, upon an island just inside of the cape, rose the tower of Roman Light.

This was the first time my tiny shell had floated upon the ocean. I coasted the sandy beach of the muddy lowlands, towards the lighthouse, until I found a creek debouching from

the marsh, which I entered, and from one watercourse to another, without a chart, found my
way at dusk into Bull's Bay. The sea was rolling in and breaking upon the shore, which I was
forced to hug closely, as the old disturbers of my
peace, the porpoises, were visible, fishing in
numbers. To escape the dangerous raccoon
oyster reefs of the shoal water the canoe was
forced into a deeper channel, when the lively
porpoises chased the boat and drove me back
again on to the sharp-lipped shells. It was fast
growing dark, and no place of refuge nearer
than the upland, a long distance across the soft
marsh, which was even now wet with the sea.

The rough water of the sound, the oyster reefs
which threatened to pierce my boat, and a coast
which would be submerged by the next flood-
tide, all seemed to conspire against me. Suddenly my anxiety was relieved, and gratitude
filled my heart, as the tall masts of a schooner
rose out of the marshes not far from the upland,
telling me that a friendly creek was near at hand.
Its wide mouth soon opened invitingly before
me, and I rowed towards the beautiful craft
anchored in its current, the trim rig of which
plainly said — the property of the United States.
An officer stood on the quarterdeck watching
my approach through his glass; and, as I was
passing the vessel, a sailor remarked to his
mates, " That is the paper canoe. I was in Nor-

folk, last December, when it reached the Eliza-beth River."

The officer kindly hailed me, and offered me the hospitality of the Coast-Survey schooner " Caswell." In the cosiest of cabins, Mr. W. H. Dennis, with his co-laborers Messrs. Ogden and Bond, with their interesting conversation soon made me forget the discomforts of the last three days spent in the muddy flats among the lowland negroes. From poor, kind Seba Gillings' black cabin-floor, to the neat state-room, with its snowy sheets and clean towels, where fresh, pure water could be used without stint, was indeed a transi-tion. The party expected to complete their work as far as Charleston harbor before the season closed.

The Sunday spent on the " Caswell" greatly refreshed me. On Saturday evening Mr. Dennis traced upon a sheet of paper my route through the interior coast watercourses to Charleston harbor; and I left the pretty schooner on Mon-day, fully posted for my voyage. The tide com-menced flooding at eleven A. M., and the flats soon afforded me water for their passage in the vicinity of the shore. Heavy forests covered the uplands, where a few houses were visible. Bull's Island, with pines and a few cabbage palms, was on my left as I reached the entrance of the southern thoroughfare at the end of the bay. Here, in the intricacies of creeks and passages through the islands, and made careless by the possession of Mr. Dennis' chart, I several times blundered into the wrong course; and got no further that afternoon than Price's Inlet, though I rowed more than twenty miles. Some eight miles of the distance rowed was lost by ascending and descending creeks by mistake.

After a weary day's work shelter was found in a house close by the sea, on the shores of Price's Inlet; where, in company with a young fisherman, who was in the employ of Mr. Magwood, of Charleston, I slept upon the floor in my blankets. Charles Hucks, the fisherman, asserted that three albino deer were killed on Caper's Island the previous winter. Two were shot by a negro, while he killed the third. Messrs. Magwood, Terry, and Noland, of Charleston, one summer penned beside the water one thousand old terrapin, to hold them over for the winter season. These "diamond-backs" would consume five bushels of shrimps in one hour when fed. A tide of unusual height washed out the terrapins from their "crawl," and with them disappeared all anticipated results of the experiment.

The next day, Caper's Island and Inlet, Dewees' Inlet, Long Island, and Breach Inlet were successively passed, on 'strong tidal currents. Sullivan's Island is separated from Long Island by Breach Inlet. While following the creeks in the marshes back of Sullivan's Island, the compact mass of buildings of Moultrieville, at its western end, at the entrance of Charleston harbor, rose imposingly to view.

The gloomy mantle of darkness was settling over the harbor as the paper canoe stole quietly into its historic waters. Before me lay the quiet bay, with old Fort Sumter rising from the watery plain like a spectral giant, as though to remind one that this had been the scene of mighty struggles. The tranquil waters softly rippled a response to the touch of my oars; all was peace and quiet here, where, only a few short years before, the thunder of cannon woke a thousand echoes, and the waves were stained with the life-blood of America, — where war, with her iron throat, poured out destruction, and God's creatures, men, made after his own image, destroyed each other ruthlessly, having never, in all that civilization had done for them, discovered any other way of settling their difficulties than by this wholesale murder.

The actors in this scene were scattered now; they had returned to the farm, the workshop, the desk, and the pulpit. The old flag again floated upon the ramparts of Sumter, and a government was trying to reconstruct itself, so that the Great Republic should become more thoroughly a government of the people, founded upon equal rights to all men.

A sharp, scraping sound under my boat roused

me from my revery, for I had leaned upon my oars while the tide had carried me slowly but surely upon the oyster-reefs, from which I escaped with some slight damage to my paper shell. Newspaper reading had impressed upon me a belief that the citizens of the city which played so important a part in the late civil war might not treat kindly a Massachusetts man. I therefore decided to go up to the city upon the ferry-boat for the large mail which awaited my arrival at the Charleston post-office, after receiving which I intended to return to Mount Pleasant, and cross the bay to the entrance of the southern watercourses, leaving the city as quietly as I entered it.

My curiosity was, however, aroused to see how, under the new reconstruction rule, things were conducted in the once proud city of Charleston. As I stood at the window of the post-office delivery, and inquired through the narrow window for my letters, a heavy shadow seemed to fall upon me as the head of a negro appeared. The black post-office official's features underwent a sudden change as I pronounced my name, and, while a warm glow of affection lighted up his dark face, he thrust his whole arm through the window, and grasped my hand with a vigorous shake in the most friendly manner, as though upon his shoulders rested the good name of the people.

Reception at Charleston Post-Office

"*Welcome* to Charleston, Mr. B——, *welcome* to our beautiful city," he exclaimed. So *this* was Charleston under reconstruction.

After handing me my mail, the postmaster graciously remarked, "Our rule is to close the office at five o'clock P. M., but if you are belated any day, tap at the door, and I will attend you."

This was my first welcome to Charleston; but before I could return to my quarters at Mount Pleasant, members of the Chamber of Commerce, the Carolina Club, and others, pressed upon me kind attentions and hospitalities, while Mr. James L. Frazer, of the South Carolina Regatta Association, sent for the Maria Theresa, and placed it in charge of the wharfinger of the Southern Wharf, where many ladies and gentlemen visited it.

When I left the old city, a few days later, I blushed to think how I had doubted these people, whose reputation for hospitality to strangers had been world-wide for more than half a century.

While here I was the guest of Rev. G. R. Brackett, the well-loved pastor of one of Charleston's churches. It was with feelings of regret I turned my tiny craft towards untried waters, leaving behind me the beautiful city of Charleston, and the friends who had so kindly cared for the lonely canoeist.

Route of Paper-Canoe
MARIA THERESA
From Bull's Bay, S.C. to St. Simon's Sound, Ga.
Followed by N.H. Bishop
in 1875

N.H.Bishop's Route
Light House
Scale, 1:1600000
Statute Miles

Copyright, 1878, by Lee & Shepard

Bull's Bay
Bull's I.
Price's Inlet
Caper's Inlet
Dewees Inlet
Breach Inlet
Charleston
Charleston Hbr.
Stono Inlet
N. Edisto R.
S. Edisto R.
St. Helena Sound
St. Helena Sound
Dawho R.
Ashepoo
Combahee
Coosaw R.
Beaufort
Beaufort R.
Broad R.
Port Royal Sound
Hilton Head I.
Calibogue Sd.
Tybee Roads
May R.
Wassaw Sound
Savannah R.
Savannah
Ossabaw Sound
Ossabaw I.
Ogeechee R.
St. Catherine's Sd.
St. Catherine's I.
Medway R.
S. Newport
Sapelo R.
Sapelo Sound
Sapelo Island
Doboy Sound
Altamaha Sound
St. Simon's I.
St. Simon's Sd.
Darien
Altamaha R.

SOUTH CAROLINA
GEORGIA

CHAPTER XII.

FROM CHARLESTON TO SAVANNAH, GEORGIA.

THE INTERIOR WATER ROUTE TO JEHOSSEE ISLAND. — GOVERNOR
AIKEN'S MODEL RICE PLANTATION. — LOST IN THE HORNS. —
ST. HELENA SOUND. — LOST IN THE NIGHT. — THE PHANTOM
SHIP. — A FINLANDER'S WELCOME. — A NIGHT ON THE EM-
PEROR'S OLD YACHT. — THE PHOSPHATE MINES. — COOSAW
AND BROAD RIVERS. — PORT ROYAL SOUND AND CALIBOQUE
SOUND. — CUFFY'S HOME. — ARRIVAL IN GEORGIA. — RECEP-
TIONS AT GREENWICH SHOOTING-PARK.

CAPTAIN N. L. COSTE, and several other
Charleston pilots, drew and presented to
me charts of the route to be followed by the
paper canoe through the Sea Island passages,
from the Ashley to the Savannah River, as some
of the smaller watercourses near the upland were
not, in 1875, upon any engraved chart of the
Coast Survey.

Ex-Governor William Aiken, whose rice plantation on Jehossee Island was considered, before
the late war, the model one of the south, invited
me to pass the following Sunday with him upon
his estate, which was about sixty-five miles from
Charleston, and along one of the interior water
routes to Savannah. He proposed to leave his
city residence and travel by land, while I paddled

my canoe southward to meet him. The genial editor of the " News and Courier " promised to notify the people of my departure, and have the citizens assembled to give me a South Carolina adieu. To avoid this publicity, — so kindly meant, — I quietly left the city from the south side on Friday, February 12th, and ascended the Ashley to Wappoo Creek, on the opposite bank of the river.

A steamboat sent me a screaming salute as the mouth of the Wappoo was reached, which made me feel that, though in strange waters, friends were all around me. I was now following one of the salt-water, steamboat passages through the great marshes of South Carolina. From Wappoo Creek I took the " Elliot Cut " into the broad Stono River, from behind the marshes of which forests rose upon the low bluffs of the upland, and rowed steadily on to Church Flats, where Wide Awake, with its landing and store, nestled on the bank.

A little further on the tides divided, one ebbing through the Stono to the sea, the other towards the North Edisto. " New Cut " connects Church Flats with Wadmelaw Sound, a sheet of water not over two miles in width and the same distance in length. From the sound the Wadmelaw River runs to the mouth of the Dahoo. Vessels drawing eight and a half feet of water can pass on full tides from Charleston over the course I was following to the North Edisto River.

Leaving Wadmelaw Sound, a deep bend of the river was entered, when the bluffs of Enterprise Landing, with its store and the ruins of a burnt saw-mill, came into view on the left. Having rowed more than thirty miles from the Ashley, and finding that the proprietor of Enterprise, a Connecticut gentleman, had made preparations to entertain me, this day of pleasant journeying ended.

The Cardinal-bird was carolling his matin song when the members of this little New England colony watched my departure down the Wadmelaw the next morning. The course was for the most part over the submerged phosphate beds of South Carolina, where the remains of extinct species were now excavated, furnishing food for the worn-out soils of America and Europe, and interesting studies and speculations for men of science. The Dahoo River was reached soon after leaving Enterprise. Here the North Edisto, a broad river, passes the mouth of the Dahoo, in its descent to the sea, which is about ten miles distant.

For two miles along the Dahoo the porpoises gave me strong proof of their knowledge of the presence of the paper canoe by their rough gambols, but being now in quiet inland waters, I could laugh at these strange creatures as they

broke from the water around the boat. At four
o'clock P. M. the extensive marshes of Jehossee
Island were reached, and I approached the village of the plantation through a short canal.

Out of the rice-fields of rich, black alluvium
rose an area of higher land, upon which were
situated the mansion and village of Governor
Aiken, where he, in 1830, commenced his duties
as rice-planter. A hedge of bright green casino
surrounded the well-kept garden, within which
magnolias and live-oaks enveloped the solid old
house, screening it with their heavy foliage from
the strong winds of the ocean, while flowering
shrubs of all descriptions added their bright and
vivid coloring to the picturesque beauty of the
scene.

The governor had arrived at Jehossee before
me, and Saturday being pay-day, the faces of the
negroes were wreathed in smiles. Here, in his
quiet island home, I remained until Monday with
this most excellent man and patriot, whose soul
had been tried as by fire during the disturbances
caused by the war.

As we sat together in that room where, in
years gone by, Governor Aiken had entertained
his northern guests, with Englishmen of noble
blood, — a room full of reminiscences both
pleasant and painful, — my kind host freely told
me the story of his busy life, which sounded like
a tale of romance. He had tried to stay the wild

storm of secession when the war-cloud hung gloomily over his state.   It broke, and his un-heeded warnings were drowned in the thunders of the political tempest that swept over the fair south.   Before the war he owned one thousand slaves.   He organized schools to teach his ne-groes to read and write.   The improvement of their moral condition was his great study.

The life he had entered upon, though at first distasteful, had been forced upon him, and he met his peculiar responsibilities with a true Christian desire to benefit all within his reach. When a young man, having returned from the tour of Europe, his father presented him with Jehossee Island, an estate of five thousand acres, around which it required four stout negro oars-men to row him in a day.   " Here," said the father to the future governor of South Carolina, as he presented the domain to his son, — " here are the means; now go to work and develop them."

William Aiken applied himself industriously to the task of improving the talents given him. His well-directed efforts bore good fruit, as year after year Jehossee Island, from a half sub-merged, sedgy, boggy waste, grew into one of the finest rice-plantations in the south.   The new lord of the manor ditched the marshes, and walled in his new rice-fields with dikes, to keep out the freshets from the upland and the tides from the ocean, perfecting a complete system of drainage and irrigation. He built comfortable quarters for his slaves, and erected a church and schoolhouse for their use. From the original two hundred and eighty acres of cultivated rice land, the new proprietor developed the wild morass into sixteen hundred acres of rice-fields, and six hundred acres of vegetable, corn, and provender producing land.

For several seasons prior to the war, Jehossee yielded a rice crop which sold for seventy thousand dollars, and netted annually fifty thousand dollars income to the owner. At that time Governor Aiken had eight hundred and seventy-three slaves on the island, and about one hundred working as mechanics, &c., in Charleston. The eight hundred and seventy-three Jehossee slaves, men, women, and children, furnished a working force of three hundred for the rice-fields.

Mr. Aiken would not tolerate the loose matrimonial ways of negro life, but compelled his slaves to accept the marriage ceremony; and herein lay one of his chief difficulties, for, to whatever cause we attribute it, the fact remains the same, namely, that the ordinary negro has no sense of morality. After all the attempts made on this plantation to improve the moral nature of these men and women, Governor Aiken, during a yellow-fever season in Savannah after the war, while visiting the poor sufferers, intent upon charitable works, found in the lowest quarter of the city, sunk in the most abject depths of vice, men and women who had once been good servants on his plantations.

In old times Jehossee was a happy place for master and for slave. The governor rarely locked the door of his mansion. The family plate, valued at fifteen thousand dollars, was stored in a chest in a room on the ground-floor of the house, which had for its occupants, during four months of the year, two or three negro servants. Though all the negroes at the quarters, which were only a quarter of a mile from the mansion, knew the valuable contents of the chest, it was never disturbed. They stole small things, but seemed incapable of committing a burglary.

When the Union army marched through another part of South Carolina, where Governor Aiken had buried these old family heirlooms and had added to the original plate thirty thousand dollars' worth of his own purchasing, the soldiers dug up this treasure-trove, and forty-five thousand dollars' worth of fine silver went to enrich the spoils of the Union army. Soon after, three thousand eight hundred bottles of fine old wines, worth from eight to nine dollars a bottle, were dug up and destroyed by a Confederate officer's order, to prevent the Union army from capturing them. Thus was plundered an old and revered governor of South Carolina — one who was a kind neighbor, a true patriot, and a Christian gentleman.

The persecutions of the owner of Jehossee did not, however, terminate with the war; for when the struggle was virtually ended, and the fair mansion of the rice-plantation retained its heirlooms and its furniture, Beaufort, of South Carolina, was still under the influence of the Freedman's Bureau; and when it was whispered that Aiken's house was full of nice old furniture, and that a few faithful servants of the good old master were its only guards, covetous thoughts at once stirred the evil minds of those who were the representatives of law and order. This house was left almost without protection. The war was over. South Carolina had bent her proud head in agony over her burned plantations and desolate homes. The victorious army was now proclaiming peace, and generous treatment to a fallen foe. Then to what an almost unimaginable state of demoralization must some of the freedmen's protectors have fallen, when they sent a gunboat to Jehossee Island, and rifled the old house of all its treasures!

To-day, the governor's favorite sideboard stands in the house of a citizen of Boston, as a relic of the war. O, people of the north, hold no longer to your relics of the war, stolen from the firesides of the south! Restore them to their owners, or else bury them out of the sight of your children, that they may not be led to believe that the war for the preservation of the Great Republic was a war for *plunder;* — else did brave men fight, and good women pray in vain.   Away with stolen pianos, " captured " sideboards, and purloined silver!   What but this petty plundering could be expected of men who robbed by wholesale the poor negro, to protect whose rights they were sent south?

The great political party of the north became the pledged conservator of the black man's rights, and established a Freedman's Bureau, and Freedman's banks to guard his humble earnings.   All know something of the workings of those banks; and to everlasting infamy must be consigned the names of many of those conducting them, — men who robbed every one of these depositories of negro savings, and left the poor, child-like freedman in a physical state of destitution, and in a perfect bewilderment of mind as to who his true friend really was.

A faithful negro of Jehossee Island was but one among thousands of such cases.   While the tumult of war vexed the land, the faithful negro overseer remained at his post to guard his late master's property, supporting himself by the manufacture of salt, and living in the most frugal manner to be able to " lay by " a sum for his old age.   Having saved five hundred dollars, he deposited them in the nearest Freedman's bank, which, though *fathered* by the United States government, failed; and the now destitute negro found himself stripped in the same moment of his hard-earned savings, and his confidence in his new protectors.

As the war of the rebellion was slowly drawing to its close, Mr. Lincoln's kind heart was drawn towards his erring countrymen, and he made a list of the names of the wisest and best men of the south, who, not having taken an active part in the strife, might be intrusted with the task of bringing back the unruly states to their constitutional relations with the national government. Governor Aiken was informed that his name was upon that list; and he would gladly have accepted the onerous position, and labored in the true interests of the whole people, but the pistol of an assassin closed the life of the President, whose generous plans of reconstruction were never realized.

In the birth of our new Centennial let us eschew the political charlatan, and bring forward our statesmen to serve and govern a people, who, to become a unit of strength, must ever bear in mind the words of the great southern statesman, who said he knew " no north, no south, no east, no west; but one undivided country."

On Monday, at ten A. M., two negroes assisted

me to launch my craft from the river's bank at the mouth of the canal, for the tide was very low. As I settled myself for a long pull at the oars, the face of one of the blacks was seemingly rent in twain, as a huge mouth opened, and a pair of strong lungs sent forth these parting words: *"Bully for Massachusetts!"*

" How did you know I came from Massachusetts?" I called out from the river.

"I knows de cuts ob dem. I suffered at Fort Wagner. Dis chile knows Massachusetts."

Two miles further on, Bull Creek served me as a " cut-off," and half an hour after entering it the tide was flooding against me. When Goat Island Creek was passed on the left hand, knots of pine forests rose picturesquely in places out of the bottom-lands, and an hour later, at Bennett's Point, on the right, I found the watercourse a quarter of a mile in width.

The surroundings were of a lovely nature during this day's journey. Here marshes, diversified by occasional hammocks of timber dotting their uninteresting wastes; there humble habitations of whites and blacks appearing at intervals in the forest growth. As I was destitute of a finished chart of the Coast Survey, after rowing along one side of Hutchinson's Island I became bewildered in the maze of creeks which penetrate the marshes that lie between Bennett's Point and the coast.

Making a rough topographical sketch of the country as I descended Hutchinson's Creek, or Big River, — the latter appellation being the most appropriate, as it is a very wide watercourse, — I came upon a group of low islands, and found upon one of them a plantation which had been abandoned to the negroes, and the little bluff upon which two or three rickety buildings were situated was the last land which remained unsubmerged during a high tide between the plantation and the sea.

I was now in a quandary. I had left the hospitable residence of Governor Aiken at ten o'clock A. M., when I should have departed at sunrise in order to have had time to enter and pass through St. Helena Sound before night came on. The prospect of obtaining shelter was indeed dismal. Just at this time a loud shout from the negroes on shore attracted my attention, and I rested upon my oars, while a boat-load of women and children paddled out to me.

"Is *dat* de *little* boat?" they asked, viewing my craft with curious eyes. "And is dat boat made of paper?" they continued, showing that negro runners had posted the people, even in these solitary regions, of the approach of the paper canoe. I questioned these negro women about the route, but each gave a different answer as to the passage through the Horns to St. Helena Sound. Hurrying on through tortuous creeks, the deserted tract called "the Horns" was entered, and until sunset I followed one short stream after another, to its source in the reedy plain, constantly retracing the route, with the tide not yet ebbing strong enough to show me a course to the sound. Presently it ebbed more rapidly, and I followed the tide from one intricacy to another, but never found the principal thoroughfare.

While I was enveloped in reeds, and at a loss which way to go, the soft ripple of breaking waves struck my ear like sweet music. The sea was telling me of its proximity. Carefully balancing myself, I stood up in the cranky canoe, and peering over the grassy thickets, saw before me the broad waters of Helena Sound. The fresh salt breeze from the ocean struck upon my forehead, and nerved me to a renewal of my efforts to get within a region of higher land, and to a place of shelter.

The ebbing tide was yet high, and through the forest of vegetation, and over the submerged coast, I pushed the canoe into the sound. Now I rowed as though for my life, closely skirting the marshes, and soon entered waters covered by a chart in my possession. My course was to skirt the coast of the sound from where I had entered it, and cross the mouths of the Combahee and Bull rivers to the entrance of the broad Coosaw. This last river I would ascend seven miles to the first upland, and camp thereon until morning. The tide was now against me, and the night was growing darker, as the faithful craft was forced along the marshes four miles to the mouth of the Combahee River, which I had to ascend half a mile to get rid of a shoal of frisky porpoises, who were fishing in the current.

Then descending it on the opposite shore, I rowed two miles further in the dark, but for half an hour previous to my reaching the wide debouchure of Bull River, some enormous blackfish surged about me in the tideway and sounded their nasal calls, while their more demonstrative porpoise neighbors leaped from the water in the misty atmosphere, and so alarmed me and occupied my attention, that instead of crossing to the Coosaw River, I unwittingly ascended the Bull, and was soon lost in the contours of the river.

As I hugged the marshy borders of the stream to escape the strong current of its channel, and rowed on and on in the gloom, eagerly scanning the high, sedge-fringed flats to find one little spot of firm upland upon which I might land my canoe and obtain a resting-spot for myself for the night, the feeling that I was lost was not the most cheerful to be imagined. In the thin fog which arose from the warm water into the cool night air, objects on the marshes assumed fantastical shapes. A few reeds, taller than the rest, had the appearance of trees twenty feet high.

So real did these unreal images seem, that I drove my canoe against the soft, muddy bank, repeatedly prompted to land in what seemed a copse of low trees, but in every instance I was deceived. Still I pulled up that mysterious river, ignorant at the time of even its name, praying only for one little spot of upland where I might camp.

While thus employed, I peered over my shoulder into the gloom, and beheld what seemed to be a vision; for, out of a cloud of mist rose the skeleton lines of a large ship, with all its sails furled to the yards. "A ship at anchor, and in this out-of-the-way place!" I ejaculated, scarcely believing my eyes; but when I pointed the canoe towards it, and again looked over my shoulder, the vision of hope was gone.

Again I saw tall masts cutting through the mists, but the ship's hull could not be distinguished, and as I rowed towards the objects, first the lower masts disappeared, then the topmasts dissolved, and later, the topgallant and royal masts faded away. For half an hour I rowed and rowed for that mysterious vessel, which was veiled and unveiled to my sight. Never did so spectral an object haunt or thwart me. It seemed to change its position on the water, as well as in the atmosphere, and I was too busily employed in trying to reach it to discover in the darkness that the current, which I could not distinguish from smooth water, was whirling me down stream as fast as I would approach the weird vessel.

Drawing once more from the current, I followed the marsh until the canoe was opposite the anchorage of a real ship; then, with hearty pulls, I shot around its stern, and shouted: " Ship ahoy! "

No one answered the hail. The vessel looked like a man-of-war, but not of American build. Not a light gleamed from her ports, not a footfall came from her decks. She seemed to be deserted in the middle of the river, surrounded by a desolate waste of marshes. The current gurgled and sucked about her run, as the ebb-tide washed her black hull on its way to the sea. The spectacle seemed now even more mysterious than when, mirage-like, it peered forth from a cloud of mist. But it was real, and not fantastic. Another hail, louder than the first, went forth into the night air, and penetrated to the ship's forecastle, for a sailor answered my call, and reported to the captain in the cabin the presence of a boat at the ship's side.

A quick, firm tread sounded upon the deck; then, with a light bound, a powerfully-built young man landed upon the high rail of the vessel. He peered down from his stately ship upon the little speck which floated upon the gurgling current; then, with a voice " filled with the fogs of the ocean," he thundered forth, as though he were hailing a man-of-war: "What boat's that?"

"Paper canoe Maria Theresa," I replied, in as foggy a voice as I could assume.

"Where from, and where bound?" again roared the captain.

"*From* Quebec, Canada, and *bound* to sleep on board your vessel, if I can ever get up there," I politely responded, in a more subdued voice, for I soon discovered that nature had never intended me for a fog-trumpet.

"Ah, is it you?" cheerily responded the captain, suddenly dispensing with all his fogginess; "I've been looking for you this long time. Got a Charleston paper on board; your trip all in it. Come up, and break a bottle of wine with me."

"All hands" came from the forecastle, and Finland mates and Finland sailors, speaking both English and Russian, crowded to the rail to receive the paper canoe, which had first been described to them by English newspapers when the vessel lay in a British port, awaiting the charter-party which afterwards sent them to Bull River, South Carolina, for a load of phosphates.

The jolly crew lowered buntlines and clew-lines, to which I attached my boat's stores. These were hoisted up the high sides of the ship, and, after bending on a line to the bow and stern rings of the canoe, I ascended by the ladder, while Captain Johs. Bergelund and his mates claimed the pleasure of landing the paper canoe on the deck of the Rurik. The tiny shell looked very small as she rested on the broad, white decks of the emperor of Russia's old steam yacht, which bore the name of the founder of the Russian empire. Though now a bark and not a steamer, though a freighter and not a royal yacht, the Rurik looked every inch a government vessel, for her young captain, with a sailor's pride, kept her in a thorough state of cleanliness and order. We went to supper. The captain, his mates, and the stranger gathered around the board, while the generous sailor brought out his curious bottles and put them by the side of the still more curious dishes of food.

All my surroundings were those of the country of the midnight sun, and I should have felt more bewildered than when in the fog I viewed and chased this spectral-looking ship, had not Captain Bergelund, in most excellent English, entertained me with a flow of conversation which put me at my ease. He discoursed of Finland, where lakes covered the country from near Abo, its chief city, to the far north, where the summer days are " nearly all night long."

Painting in high colors the delights of his native land, he begged me to visit it. Finally, as midnight drew near, this genial sailor insisted upon putting me in his own comfortable stateroom, while he slept upon a lounge in the cabin.

One mile above the Rurik's anchorage was the phosphate-mill of the Pacific Company, which was supplying Captain Bergelund, by lighters, with his freight of unground fertilizer.

The next morning I took leave of the Rurik, but, instead of descending the Bull River to the Coosaw, I determined to save time by crossing the peninsula between the two rivers by means of two short creeks which were connected at their sources by a very short canal near "the mines" of the Phosphate Company. When I entered Horse Island Creek, at eleven o'clock, the tide was on the last of the ebb, and I sat in the canoe a long time awaiting the flood to float me up the wide ditch, which would conduct me to the creek that emptied into the Coosaw. Upon the banks of the canal three hours were lost waiting for the tide to give me one foot of water, when I rowed into the second water-course, and late in the afternoon entered the wide Coosaw. The two creeks and the connecting canal are called the Haulover Creek.

As I turned up the Coosaw, and skirted the now submerged marshes of its left bank, two dredging-machines were at work up the river raising the remains of the marine monsters of antiquity. The strong wind and swashing seas being in my favor, the canoe soon arrived opposite the spot of upland I had so longed to reach the previous night.

This was Chisolm's Landing, back of which were the phosphate works of the Coosaw Mine Company. The inspector of phosphates, Mr. John Hunn, offered me the hospitality of Alligator Hall, where he and some of the gentlemen employed by the company resided in bachelor retirement. My host described a mammal's tooth that weighed nearly fourteen pounds, which had been taken from a phosphate mine; it had been sent to a public room at Beaufort, South Carolina. A fossil shark's tooth, weighing four and a half pounds, was also found, and a learned ichthyologist has asserted that the owner of this remarkable relic of the past must have been one hundred feet in length.

Beaufort was near at hand, and could be easily reached by entering Brickyard Creek, the entrance of which was on the right bank of the Coosaw, nearly opposite Chisolm's Landing. It was nearly six miles by this creek to Beaufort, and from that town to Port Royal Sound, by following Beaufort River, was a distance of eleven miles. The mouth of Beaufort River is only two miles from the sea. Preferring to follow a more interior water route than the Beaufort one, the canoe was rowed up the Coosaw five miles to Whale Branch, which is crossed by the Port Royal railroad bridge. Whale Branch, five miles in length, empties into Broad River, which I descended thirteen miles, to the lower end of Daw Island, on its right bank.   Here, in this region of marshy shores, the Chechessee River and the Broad River mingle their strong currents in Port Royal Sound. It was dusk when the sound was entered from the extreme end of Daw Island, where it became necessary to cross immediately to Skull Creek, at Hilton Head Island, or go into camp for the night.

I looked down the sound six miles to the broad Atlantic, which was sending in clouds of mist on a fresh breeze.   I gazed across the mouth of the Chechessee, and the sound at the entrance of the port of refuge.   I desired to traverse nearly three miles of this rough water.   I would gladly have camped, but the shore I was about to leave offered to submerge me with the next high water.   No friendly hammock of trees could be seen as I glided from the shadow of the high rushes of Daw Island.   Circumstances. decided the point in debate, and I rowed rapidly into the sound. The canoe had not gone half a mile when the Chechessee River opened fully to view, and a pretty little hammock, with two or three shanties beneath its trees, could be plainly seen on Daw's Island.

It was now too late to return and ascend the river to the hammock, for the sound was disturbed by the freshening breeze from the sea blowing against the ebb-tide, which was increased in power by the outflowing volume of water from the wide Chechessee.   It required all the energy

I possessed to keep the canoe from being over-run by the swashy, sharp-pointed seas. Once or twice I thought my last struggle for life had come, but a merciful Power gave me the strength and coolness that this trying ordeal required, and I somehow weathered the dangerous oyster reefs above Skull Creek, and landed at " Seabrook Plantation," upon Hilton Head Island, near two or three old houses, one of which was being fitted up as a store by Mr. Kleim, of the First New York Volunteers, who had lived on the island since 1861. Mr. Kleim took me to his bachelor quarters, where the wet cargo of the Maria Theresa was dried by the kitchen fireplace.

The next day, February 18, I left Seabrook and followed Skull Creek to Mackay's Creek, and, passing the mouth of May River, entered Calibogue Sound, where a sudden tempest arose and drove me into a creek which flowed out of the marshes of Bull Island. A few negro huts were discovered on a low mound of earth. The blacks told me their hammock was called Bird Island.

The tempest lasted all day, and as no shelter could be found on the creek, a darky hauled my canoe on a cart a couple of miles to Bull Creek, which enters into Cooper River, one of the water-courses I was to enter from Calibogue Sound. Upon reaching the wooded shores of Bull Creek, my carter introduced me to the head man of the

settlement, a weazened-looking little old creature called Cuffy, who, though respectful in his
demeanor to " de Yankee-mans," was cross and
overbearing to the few families occupying the
shanties in the magnificent grove of live-oaks
which shaded them.

Cuffy's cook-house, or kitchen, which was a
log structure measuring nine by ten feet, with
posts only three feet high, was the only building
which could be emptied of its contents for my
accommodation.   Our contract or lease was a
verbal one, Cuffy's terms being "whateber de
white man likes to gib an ole nigger."   Cuffy
cut a big switch, and sent in his "darter," a girl
of about fourteen years, to clean out the shanty.
When she did not move fast enough to suit the
old man's wishes, he switched her over the
shoulders till it excited my pity; but the girl
seemed to take the beating as an every-day
amusement, for it made no impression on her
hard skull and thick skin.

After commencing to "keep house," the old
women came to sell me eggs and beg for
"bacca." They requested me never to throw
away my coffee-grounds, as it made coffee "good
'nuf for black folks."   I distributed some of my
stores among them, and, after cutting rushes and
boughs for my bed, turned in for the night.

These negroes had been raising Sea-Island
cotton, but the price having declined to five

cents a pound, they could not get twenty-five cents a day for their labor by cultivating it.

The fierce wind subsided before dawn, but a heavy fog covered the marshes and the creek. Cuffy's "settlement" turned out before sunrise to see me off; and the canoe soon reached the broad Cooper River, which I ascended in the misty darkness by following close to the left bank. Four miles up the Cooper River from Calibogue Sound there is a passage through the marshes from the Cooper to New River, which is called Ram's Horn Creek. On the right of its entrance a well-wooded hammock rises from the marsh, and is called Page Island. About midway between the two rivers and along this crooked thoroughfare is another piece of upland called Pine Island, inhabited by the families of two boat-builders.

While navigating Cooper River, as the heavy mists rolled in clouds over the quiet waters, a sail-boat, rowed by negroes, emerged from the gloom and as suddenly disappeared. I shouted after them: "Please tell me the name of the next creek." A hoarse voice came back to me from the cloud: "Pull and be d—d." Then all was still as night again. To solve this seemingly uncourteous reply, so unusual in the south, I consulted the manuscript charts which the Charleston pilots had kindly drawn for my use, and found that the negroes had spoken geographically as well as truthfully, for Pine Island Creek is known to the watermen as " Pull and be d—d Creek," on account of its tortuous character, and chiefly because, as the tides head in it, if a boat enters it from one river with a favorable tide, it has a strong head current on the other side of the middle ground to oppose it. Thus pulling at the oars at some parts of the creek becomes hard work for the boatmen; hence this name, which, though profane, may be considered geographical.

After leaving the Cooper River, the watercourses to Savannah were discolored by red or yellow mud. From Pine Island I descended New River two miles and a half to Wall's Cut, which is only a quarter of a mile in length, and through which I entered Wright's River, following it a couple of miles to the broad, yellow, turbulent current of the Savannah.

My thoughts now naturally turned to the early days of steamboat enterprise, when this river, as well as the Hudson, was conspicuous; for though the steamer Savannah was not the first steam-propelled vessel which cut the waves of the Atlantic, she was the first steamer that ever crossed it. Let us examine historical data. Colonel John Stevens, of New York, built the steamboat Phœnix about the year 1808, and was prevented from using it upon the Hudson River by the Fulton and Livingston monopoly charter.

The Phœnix made an ocean voyage to the Delaware River. The first English venture was that of the steamer Caledonia, which made a passage to Holland in 1817. The London Times of May 11, 1819, printed in its issue of that date the following item:

"GREAT EXPERIMENT. — A new vessel of three hundred tons has been built at New York for the express purpose of carrying passengers across the Atlantic. She is to come to Liverpool direct."

This ship-rigged steamer was the " Savannah," and the bold projector of this experiment of sending a steamboat across the Atlantic was Daniel Dodd. The Savannah was built in New York, by Francis Ficket, for Mr. Dodd. Stephen Vail, of Morristown, New Jersey, built her engines, and on the 22d of August, 1818, she was launched, gliding gracefully into the element which was to bear her to foreign lands, there to be crowned with the laurels of success. On May 25th this purely American-built vessel left Savannah, and glided out from this waste of marshes, under the command of Captain Moses Rogers, with Stephen Rogers as navigator. The port of New London, Conn., had furnished these able seamen.

The steamer reached Liverpool June 20th, the passage having occupied twenty-six days, upon eighteen of which she had used her paddles. A son of Mr. Dodd once told me of the sensation produced by the arrival of a smoking vessel on the coast of Ireland, and how Lieutenant John Bowie, of the king's cutter Kite, sent a boat-load of sailors to board the Savannah to assist her crew to extinguish the fires of what his Majesty's officers supposed to be a burning ship.

The Savannah, after visiting Liverpool, continued her voyage on July 23d, and reached St. Petersburg in safety. Leaving the latter port on October 10th, this adventurous craft completed the round voyage upon her arrival at Savannah, November 30th.

I pulled up the Savannah until within five miles of the city, and then left the river on its south side, where old rice-plantations are first met, and entered St. Augustine Creek, which is the steamboat thoroughfare of the inland route to Florida. Just outside the city of Savannah, near its beautiful cemetery, where tall trees with their graceful drapery of Spanish moss screen from wind and sun the quiet resting-places of the dead, my canoe was landed, and stored in a building of the German Greenwich Shooting Park, where Mr. John Hellwig, in a most hospitable manner, cared for it and its owner.

While awaiting the arrival of letters at the Savannah post-office, many of the ladies of that beautiful city came out to see the paper canoe. They seemed to have the mistaken idea that my little craft had come from the distant Dominion of Canada over the Atlantic Ocean. They also looked upon the voyage of the paper canoe as a very sentimental thing, while the canoeist had found it an intensely practical affair, though occasionally relieved by incidents of romantic or amusing character. As the ladies clustered round the boat while it rested upon the centre-table of Mr. Hellwig's parlor, they questioned me freely.

" Tell us," they said, " what were your thoughts while you rowed upon the broad ocean in the lonely hours of night? "

Though unwilling to break their pleasing illusions, I was obliged to inform them that a sensible canoeist is usually enjoying his needed rest in some camp, or sleeping in some sheltered place, — under a roof if possible, — after it is too dark to travel in safety; and as to ocean travelling, the canoe had only once entered upon the Atlantic Ocean, and then through a mistake.

" But what subjects occupy your thoughts as you row, and row, and row all day by yourself, in this little ship? " a motherly lady inquired.

" To tell you honestly, ladies, I must say that when I am in shallow watercourses, with the tides usually ebbing at the wrong time for my convenience, I am so full of anxiety about getting wrecked on the reefs of sharp coon-oysters, that I am wishing myself in deep water; and when my route forces me into the deep water of sounds, and the surface becomes tossed into wild disorder by strong currents and stronger winds, and the porpoises pay me their little attentions, chasing the canoe, flapping their tails, and showing their sportive dispositions, I think longingly of those same shoal creeks, and wish I was once more in their shallow waters."

" We ladies have prayed for your safety," said a kind-looking German lady, " and we will pray that your voyage may have a happy and success- ful end."

When the ladies left, two Irish laborers, dressed in sombre black, with high hats worn with the air of dignity, examined the boat. There was an absence of the sparkle of fun usually seen in the Irish face, for this was a serious occasion. They did not see any romance or sentiment in the voyage, but took a broad, geographical view of the matter. They stood silently gazing at the canoe with the same air of solemnity they would have given a corpse. Then one addressed the other, as though the owner of the craft was entirely out of the hearing of their conversation.

Said No. 1, " And what did I tell ye, Pater?" " And so ye did," replied No. 2. " And didn't I say so?" continued No. 1. " Of course ye did; and wasn't me of the same mind, to be sure?" responded No. 2. " Yes, I told ye as how it is the men of *these* times is greater than the men of ould times. There was the great Coolumbus, who came over in three ships to see Americky. What did he know about *paper* boats?   Nothing at all, at all.   He cum over in big ships, while this young feller has cum all the way from Canada.   I tell ye the men of ould times was not up to the men of these times.   Thin there's Captain Boyton, who don't use any boat or ship at all, at all, but goes a-*swimming* in rubber clothes to keep him dry all over the Atlantic Oshin.   Jis' look, man, how he landed on the shores of ould Ireland not long since. Now what's Coolumbus, or any other man of the past ages, to him?   Coolumbus could not hold a candle to Boyton!   No, I tell ye agen that the men of this age is greater than the men of the past ages."   "And," broke in No. 2, "there's a Britisher who's gone to the River Niles in a canoe."   "The *River Niles!*" hotly exclaimed No. 1;   "don't waste your breath on that thing. It's no *new* thing at all, at all.   It was diskivered a long time ago, and nobody cares a fig for it now."   "Yet," responded No. 2, "some of those old-times people were very enterprising.   There was that great traveller Robinson Crusoe: ye must confess he was a great man for *his* time."   "The same who wint to the South Sea Islands and settled there?" asked the first biographer.   "The *very same man,*" replied No. 2, with animation.

This instructive conversation was here interrupted by a party of ladies and gentlemen, who in turn gave their views of canoe and canoeist.

CHAPTER XIII.

FROM THE SAVANNAH RIVER TO FLORIDA.

ROUTE TO THE SEA ISLANDS OF GEORGIA. — STORM-BOUND ON
GREEN ISLAND. — OSSABAW ISLAND. — ST. CATHERINE'S SOUND.
— SAPELO ISLAND. — THE MUD OF MUD RIVER. — NIGHT IN A
NEGRO CABIN. — "DE SHOUTINGS" ON DOBOY ISLAND. —
BROUGHTON ISLAND. — ST. SIMON'S AND JEKYL ISLANDS. —
INTERVIEW WITH AN ALLIGATOR. — A NIGHT IN JOINTER
HAMMOCK. — CUMBERLAND ISLAND AND ST. MARY'S RIVER. —
FAREWELL TO THE SEA.

ON February 24th, the voyage was again resumed. My route lay through the coast
islands of Georgia, as far south as the state
boundary, Cumberland Sound, and the St. Mary's River. This part of the coast is very interesting, and is beautifully delineated on the Coast
Charts No. 56–57 of the United States Coast
Survey, which were published the year after my
voyage ended.

Steamers run from Savannah through these
interesting interior water-ways to the ports of
the St. John's River, Florida, and by taking this
route the traveller can escape a most uninteresting railroad journey from Savannah to Jacksonville, where sandy soils and pine forests present

an uninviting prospect to the eye. A little dredging, in a few places along the steamboat route, should be done at national cost, to make this a more convenient and expeditious tidal route for vessels.

Leaving Greenwich, Bonaventure, and Thunderbolt behind me on the upland, the canoe entered the great marshy district of the coast along the Wilmington and Skiddaway rivers to Skiddaway Narrows, which is a contracted, crooked watercourse connecting the Skiddaway with the Burnside River. The low lands were made picturesque by hammocks, some of which were cultivated.

In leaving the Burnside for the broad Vernon River, as the canoe approached the sea, one of the sudden tempests which frequently vex these coast-waters arose, and drove me to a hammock in the marshes of Green Island, on the left bank and opposite the mouth of the Little Ogeechee River. Green Island has been well cultivated in the past, but is now only the summer home of Mr. Styles, its owner. Two or three families of negroes inhabited the cabins and looked after the property of the absent proprietor.

I waded to my knees in the mud before the canoe could be landed, and, as it stormed all night, I slept on the floor of the humble cot of the negro Echard Holmes, having first treated the household to crackers and coffee. The ne-

groes gathered from other points to examine the
canoe, and, hearing that I was from the north,
one grizzly old darky begged me to "carry"
his complaints to Washington.

"De goberment," he said, "has been berry
good to wees black folks. It gib us our freedom, — all berry well; but dar is an noder ting
wees wants; dat is, wees wants General Grant to
make tings *stashionary*. De storekeeper gibs a
poor nigger only one dollar fur bushel corn, sometimes not so much. Den he makes poor nigger
gib him tree dollars fur bag hominy, sometimes
more 'n dat. Wees wants de goberment to make
tings *stashionary*. Make de storekeeper gib
black man one dollar and quarter fur de bushel
of corn, and make him sell de poor nigger de
bag hominy fur much less dan tree dollars.
Make all tings *stashionary*. Den dar's one ting
more. Tell de goberment to do fur poor darky
'nodder ting, — make de ole massa say to me,
'You's been good slave in ole times, — *berry*
good slave; now I gib you one, two, tree, *five*
acres of land for yoursef.' Den ole nigger be
happy, and massa be happy too; den bof of um
bees happy. Hab you a leetle bacca fur dis ole
man?"

From the Styles mansion it was but three
miles to Ossabaw Sound. Little Don Island
and Raccoon Key are in the mouth of the Vernon. Between the two flat islands is a deep

passage through which the tides rush with great force; it is called Hell Gate. On the south side of Raccoon Key the Great Ogeechee River pours its strong volume of water into Ossabaw Sound.

I entered the Great Ogeechee through the Don Island passage, and saw sturgeon-fishermen at work with their nets along the shores of Ossabaw, one of the sea islands. Ossabaw Island lies between Ossabaw and St. Catherine's sounds, and is eight miles long and six miles wide. The side towards the sea is firm upland, diversified with glades, while the western portion is principally marshes cut up by numerous creeks. All the sea islands produce the long staple cotton known as sea-island cotton, and before the war a very valuable variety. A few negroes occupy the places abandoned by the proprietor, and eke out a scanty livelihood.

There are many deer in the forests of Ossabaw Island. One of its late proprietors informed me that there must be at least ten thousand wild hogs there, as they have been multiplying for many years, and but few were shot by the negroes. The domestic hog becomes a very shy animal if left to himself for two or three years. The hunter may search for him without a dog almost in vain, though the woods may contain large numbers of these creatures.

The weather was now delightful, and had I

possessed a light tent I would not have sought shelter at night in a human habitation anywhere along the route. The malaria which arises from fresh-water sinks in many of the sea islands during the summer months, did not now make camping-out dangerous to the health. Crossing the Great Ogeechee above Middle Marsh Island, I followed the river to the creek called Florida Passage, through which I reached Bear River, with its wide and long reaches, and descended it to St. Catherine's Sound.

Now the sea opened to full view as the canoe crossed the tidal ocean gateway two miles to North Newport River. When four miles up the Newport I entered Johnson's Creek, which flows from North to South Newport rivers. By means of the creek and the South Newport River, my little craft was navigated down to the southern end of St. Catherine's Island to the sound of the same name, and here another inlet was crossed at sunset, and High Point of Sapelo Island was reached.

From among the green trees of the high bluff a mansion, which exhibited the taste of its builder, rose imposingly. This was, however, but one of the many edifices that are tombs of buried hopes. The proprietor, a northern gentleman, after the war purchased one-third of Sapelo Island for fifty-five thousand dollars in gold. He attempted, as many other enterprising

northerners had done, to give the late slave a
chance to prove his worth as a freedman to the
world.

"Pay the negro wages; treat him as you
would treat a white man, and he will reward
your confidence with industry and gratitude."
So thought and so acted the large-hearted northern colonel. He built a large mansion, engaged
his freedmen, paid them for their work, and
treated them like *men*. The result was ruin,
and simply because he had not paused to consider that the negro had not been *born* a freedman, and that the demoralization of slavery was
still upon him. Beside which facts we must
also place certain ethnological and moral principles which exist in the pure negro type, and
which are entirely overlooked by those philan-
thropic persons who have rarely, if ever, seen a
full-blooded negro, but affect to understand him
through his *half*-white brother, the mulatto.

Mud River opened its wide mouth before me
as I left the inlet, but the tide was very low, and
Mud River is a sticking-point in the passage of
the Florida steamers. It became so dark that I
was obliged to get near the shore to make a
landing. My attempt was made opposite a negro's house which was on a bluff, but the water
had receded into the very narrow channel of
Mud River, and I was soon stuck fast on a flat.
Getting overboard, I sank to my knees in the

soft mud. I called for help, and was answered
by a tall darky, who, with a double-barrelled gun,
left his house and stood in a threatening manner
on the shore. I appealed for help, and said I
wished to go ashore. "Den cum de best way
you can," he answered in a surly manner. "What
duz you want 'bout here, any way? What duz
you want on Choc'late Plantation, anyhow?"

I explained to this ugly black that I was a
northern man, travelling to see the country, and
wished to camp near his house for protection,
and promised, if he would aid me to land, that I
would convince him of my honest purpose by
showing him the contents of my canoe, and
would prove to him that I was no enemy to the
colored man. I told him of the maps, the letters, and the blankets which were in the little
canoe now so fast in the mud, and what a loss it
would be if some marauder, passing on the next
high tide, should steal my boat.

The fellow slowly lowered his gun, which had
been held in a threatening position, and said:

"Nobody knows his friends in dese times. I'se
had a boat stealed by some white man, and spose
you was cumin to steal sumting else. Dese folks
on de riber can't be trussed. Dey steals ebryting. Heaps o' bad white men 'bout nowadays
sens de war. Steals a nigger's chickens, boats,
and ebryting dey lays hands on. Up at de big
house on High Pint (norfen gemmin built him,

and den got gusted wid cotton-planting and went home) de white folks goes and steals all de cheers and beds, and ebryting out ob de house. Sens de war all rascals."

It was a wearisome and dangerous job for me to navigate the canoe over the soft, slippery mud to the firm shore, as there were unfathomed places in the flats which might ingulf or entomb me at any step; but the task was completed, and I stood face to face with the now half tranquillized negro. Before removing the mud that hung upon me to the waist in heavy clods, I showed the darky my chart-case, and explained the object of my mission. He was very intelligent, and, after asking a few questions, said to his son:

"Take dis gun to de house;" and then turning to me, continued: "Dis is de sort ob man I'se am. I'se knows how to treat a friend like a white man, and I'se can fight wid my knife or my fist or my gun anybody who 'poses on me. Now I'se knows you is a gemmin I'se won't treat you like a nigger. Gib you best I'se got. Cum to de house."

When inside of the house of this resolute black, every attention was paid to my comfort. The cargo of the paper canoe was piled up in one corner of the room. The wife and children sat before the bright fire and listened to the story of my cruise. I doctored the sick pickaninny of my host, and made the family a pot of strong coffee. This negro could read, but he asked me to

address a label he wished to attach to a bag of
Sea-Island cotton of one hundred and sixty
pounds' weight, which he had raised, and was
to ship by the steamboat Lizzie Baker to a mer-
cantile house in Savannah.

As I rested upon my blankets, which were
spread upon the floor of the only comfortable
room in the house, at intervals during the night
the large form of the black stole softly in and bent
over me to see if I were well covered up, and he
as noiselessly piled live-oak sticks upon the dying
embers to dry up the dampness which rose from
the river.

He brought me a basin of cold water in the
morning, and not possessing a towel clean enough
for a white man, he insisted that I should use his
wife's newly starched calico apron to wipe my
face and hands upon. When I offered him
money for the night's accommodation and the
excellent oyster breakfast that his wife prepared
for me, he said: "You may gib my wife whateber pleases you for *her cooking*, but nuffin for
de food or de lodgings. I'se no nigger, ef I is
a cullud man."

It was now Saturday, and as I rowed through
the marsh thoroughfare called New Tea Kettle
Creek, which connects Mud River with Doboy
Sound near the southern end of Sapelo Island, I
calculated the chances of finding a resting-place
for Sunday. If I went up to the mainland

through North and Darien rivers to the town of Darien, my past experience taught me that instead of enjoying rest I would become a forced exhibiter of the paper canoe to crowds of people. To avoid this, I determined to pass the day in the first hammock that would afford shelter and fire-wood; but as the canoe entered Doboy Sound, which, with its inlet, separates Sapelo from the almost treeless Wolf Island, the wind rose with such violence that I was driven to take refuge upon Doboy Island, a small marshy territory, the few firm acres of which were occupied by the settlement and steam saw-mill of Messrs. Hiltons, Foster & Gibson, a northern lumber firm.

Foreign and American vessels were anchored under the lee of protecting marshes, awaiting their cargoes of sawed deals and hewn timber; while rafts of logs, which had been borne upon the currents of the Altamaha and other streams from the far interior regions of pine forests, were collected here and manufactured into lumber.

One of the proprietors, a northern gentleman, occupied with his family a very comfortable cottage near the store and steam saw-mill. As the Doboy people had learned of the approach of the paper canoe from southern newspapers, the little craft was identified as soon as it touched the low shores of the island.

I could not find any kind of hotel or lodging-place in this settlement of Yankees, Canadians,

and negroes, and was about to leave it in search
of some lone hammock, when a mechanic kindly
offered me the floor of an unfinished room in an
unfinished house, in which I passed my Sunday
trying to rest, and obtaining my meals at a restaurant kept by a negro.

A member of the Spaulding family, the owners of a part of Sapelo Island, called upon me,
and seeing me in such inhospitable quarters,
with fleas in hundreds invading my blankets,
urged me to return with him to his island domain, where he might have an opportunity to
make me comfortable. The kind gentleman
little knew how hardened I had become to such
annoyances as hard floors and the active flea.
Such inconveniences had been robbed of their
discomforts by the kind voices of welcome
which, with few exceptions, came from every
southern gentleman whose territory had been
invaded by the paper canoe.

There was but one place of worship on the
island, and that was under the charge of the negroes. Accepting the invitation of a nephew of
the resident New England proprietor of Doboy
Island to attend " de shoutings," we set out on
Sunday evening for the temporary place of negro
worship. A negro girl, decked with ribbons,
called across the street to a young colored delin-
quent: "You no goes to de shoutings, Sam!
Why fur? You neber hears me shout, honey,

and dey *do* say I shouts *so* pretty. Cum 'long' wid me now."

A few blacks had collected in the small shanty, and the preacher, an old freedman, was about to read a hymn as we entered. At first the singing was low and monotonous, but it gradually swelled to a high pitch as the negroes became excited. Praying followed the singing. Then the black preacher set aside " de shouting " part of the service for what he considered more important interests, and discoursed upon things spiritual and temporal in this wise:

" Now I'se got someting to tell all of yese berry 'portant." Here two young blacks got up to leave the room, but were rudely stopped by a negro putting his back against the door. " No, no," chuckled the preacher, " yese don't git off dat a-way. I'se prepared fur de ockasun. No-body gits out ob dis room till I'se had my say. Jes you set down dar. Now I'se goin' to do one ting, and it's dis: I'se goin' to spread de Gospel all ober dis yere island of Doboy. Now's de time; talked long 'nuf, too long, 'bout buildin' de church. Whar's yere pride? whar is it? Got none! Look at dis room for a church! Look at dis pulpit — one flour-barrel wid one candle stickin' out ob a bottle! Dat's yere pulpit. Got no pride! Shamed o' yeresefs! Here white men comes way from New York to hear de Gospel in dis yere room wid flour-barrel fur pulpit, and empty bottle fur candlestick. No more talk now. All go to work. De mill people will gib us lumber fur de new church; odders mus' gib *money*. Tell ebbry cullud pusson on de island to cum on Tuesday and carry lumber, and gib ebbry one what he can, — one dollar apiece, or ten cents ·if got no more. De white gemmins we knows whar to find when we wants dar money, but de cullud ones is berry slippery when de hat am passed round."

At the termination of the preacher's exhortation, I proposed to my companion that I should present the minister with a dollar for his new church, but, with a look of dismay, he replied: " Oh, don't give it to the *preacher*. Hand it to that other negro sitting near him. We never trust the *preacher* with money; he always spends the church-money. We only trust him for *preaching*."

Monday, March 1st, opened fair, but the wind arose when the canoe reached Three Mile Cut, which connects the Darien with Altamaha River. I went through this narrow steamboat passage, and being prevented by the wind from entering the wide Altamaha, returned to the Darien River and ascended it to General's Cut, which, with Butler River, affords a passage to the Altamaha River. Before entering, General's Cut, mistaking a large, half submerged alligator for a log on a mud bank, the canoe nearly touched the saurian before he was roused from his nap to retire into the water. General's Cut penetrates a rice plantation opposite the town of Darien, to Butler's Island, the estate of the late Pierce Butler, at its southern end. Rice-planting, since the war, had not proved a very profitable business to the present proprietors, who deserve much praise for the efforts they have made to educate their freedmen. A profitable crop of oranges is gathered some seasons from the groves upon Butler's Island.

From the mouth of General's Cut down Butler River to the Altamaha was but a short row. The latter stream would have taken me to Altamaha Sound, to avoid which I passed through Wood's Cut into the South Altamaha River, and proceeded through the lowland rice-plantations towards St. Simon's Island, which is by the sea. About the middle of the afternoon, when close to Broughton Island, where the South Altamaha presented a wide area to the strong head-wind which was sending little waves over my canoe, a white plantation-house, under the veranda of which an elderly gentleman was sitting, attracted my attention. Here was what seemed to be the last camping-ground on a route of several miles to St. Simon's Island.

If the wind continued to blow from the same quarter, the canoe could not cross Buttermilk Sound that night; so I went ashore to inquire if there were any hammocks in the marshes by the river-banks between the plantation and the sound.

The bachelor proprietor of Broughton Island, Captain Richard A. Akin, posted me as to the route to St. Simon's Island, but insisted that the canoe traveller should share his comfortable quarters until the next day; and when the next day came round, and the warm sun and smooth current of the wide Altamaha invited me to continue the voyage, the hospitable rice-planter thought the weather not settled enough for me to venture down to the sound. In fact, he held me a rather willing captive for several days, and then let me off on the condition that I should return at some future time, and spend a month with him in examining the sea islands and game resources of the vicinity.

Captain Akin was a successful rice-planter on the new system of employing freedmen on wages, but while he protected the ignorant blacks in all their newly-found rights, he was a thorough disciplinarian. The negroes seemed to like their employer, and stuck to him with greater tenacity than they did to those planters who allowed them to do as they pleased. The result of lax treatment with these people is always a failure of crops. The rivers and swamps near Broughton Island abound in fine fishes and terrapin, while the marshes and flats of the sea islands afford excellent opportunities for the sportsman to try his skill upon the feathered tribe.

On Monday, March 9th, the Maria Theresa left Broughton Island well provisioned with the stores the generous captain had pressed upon my acceptance. The atmosphere was softened by balmy breezes, and the bright sunlight played with the shadows of the clouds upon the wide marshes, which were now growing green with the warmth of returning spring. The fish sprang from the water as I touched it with my light oars.

St. Simon's Island, — where Mr. Pierce Butler once cultivated sea-island cotton, and to which he took his English bride, Miss Kemble, — with its almost abandoned plantation, was reached before ten o'clock. Frederica River carried me along the whole length of the island to St. Simon's Sound. When midway the island, I paused to survey what remains of the old town of Frederica, of which but few vestiges can be discovered. History informs us that Frederica was the first town built by the English in Georgia, and was founded by General Oglethorpe, who began and established the colony.

The fortress was regular and beautiful, and was the largest, most regular, and perhaps most costly of any in North America of British construction. Pursuing my journey southward, the canoe entered the exposed area of St. Simon's

Sound, which, with its ocean inlet, was easily crossed to the wild and picturesque Jekyl Island, upon which the two bachelor brothers Dubignon live and hunt the deer, enjoying the free life of lords of the forest. Their old family mansion, once a haven of hospitality, where the northern tourist and shipwrecked sailor shared alike the good things of this life with the kind host, was used for a target by a gunboat during the late war, and is now in ruins.

Here, twenty years ago, at midnight, the slave-yacht "Wanderer" landed her cargo of African negroes, the capital for the enterprise being supplied by three southern gentlemen, and the execution of the work being intrusted, under carefully drawn contracts, to Boston parties.

The calm weather greatly facilitated my progress, and had I not missed Jekyl Creek, which is the steamboat thoroughfare through the marshes to Jekyl and St. Andrew's Sound, that whole day's experience would have been a most happy one. The mouth of Jekyl Creek was a narrow entrance, and being off in the sound, I passed it as I approached the lowlands, which were skirted until a passage at Cedar Hammock through the marsh was found, some distance from the one I was seeking. Into this I entered, and winding about for some time over its tortuous course, at a late hour in the afternoon the canoe emerged into a broad watercourse, down which I could look across Jekyl Sound to the sea.

This broad stream was Jointer Creek, and I ascended it to find a spot of high ground upon which to camp. It was now low water, and the surface of the marshes was three or four feet above my head. After much anxious searching, and a great deal of rowing against the last of the ebb, a forest of pines and palmetto-trees was reached on Colonel's Island, at a point about four miles — across the marshes and Brunswick River — from the interesting old town of Brunswick, Georgia.

The soft, muddy shores of the hammock were in one place enveloped in a thicket of reeds, and here I rested upon my oars to select a convenient landing-place. The rustling of the reeds suddenly attracted my attention. Some animal was crawling through the thicket in the direction of the boat. My eyes became fixed upon the mysterious shaking and waving of the tops of the reeds, and my hearing was strained to detect the cause of the crackling of the dry rushes over which this unseen creature was moving. A moment later my curiosity was satisfied, for there emerged slowly from the covert an alligator nearly as large as my canoe. The brute's head was as long as a barrel; his rough coat of mail was besmeared with mud, and his dull eyes were fixed steadily upon me. I was so surprised and fascinated by the appearance of this huge reptile that I remained immovable in my boat, while he in a deliberate manner entered the water within a few feet of me. The hammock suddenly lost all its inviting aspect, and I pulled away from it faster than I had approached. In the gloom I observed two little hammocks, between Colonel's Island and the Brunswick River, which seemed to be near Jointer's Creek, so I followed the tortuous thoroughfares until I was within a quarter of a mile of one of them.

Pulling my canoe up a narrow creek towards the largest hammock, until the creek ended in the lowland, I was cheered by the sight of a small house in a grove of live-oaks, to reach which I was obliged to abandon my canoe and attempt to cross the soft marsh. The tide was now rising rapidly, and it might be necessary for me to swim some inland creek before I could arrive at the upland.

An oar was driven into the soft mud of the marsh and the canoe tied to it, for I knew that the whole country, with the exception of the hammock near by, would be under water at flood-tide. Floundering through mud and pressing aside the tall, wire-like grass of the lowland, which entangled my feet, frequently leaping natural ditches, and going down with a thud in the mud on the other side, I finally struck the firm ground of the largest Jointer Hammock, when the voice of its owner, Mr. R. F. Williams, sounded most cheerfully in my ears as he exclaimed: "Where *did* you come from? How did you get across the marsh?"

The unfortunate position of my boat was explained while the family gathered round me, after which we sat down to supper. Mr. Williams felt anxious about the cargo of my boat. "The coons," he said, "will scent your provisions, and tear everything to pieces in the boat. We must go look after it immediately." To go to the canoe we were obliged to follow a creek which swept past the side of the hammock, opposite to my landing-place, and row two or three miles on Jointer Creek. At nine o'clock we reached the locality where I had abandoned the paper canoe. Everything had changed in appearance; the land was under water; not a landmark remained except the top of the oar, which rose out of the lake-like expanse of water, while near it gracefully floated my little companion. We towed her to the hammock; and after the tedious labor of divesting myself of the marsh mud, which clung to my clothes, had been crowned with success, the comfortable bed furnished by my host gave rest to limbs and nerves which had been severely overtaxed since sunset.

The following day opened cloudy and windy. The ocean inlet of Jekyl and St. Andrew's sounds is three miles wide. From the mouth of Jointer Creek, across these unprotected sounds, to High Point of Cumberland Island, is eight miles. The route from the creek to Cumberland Island was a risky one for so small a boat as the paper canoe while the weather continued unpropitious. After entering the sounds there was but one spot of upland, near the mouth of the Satilla River, that could be used for camping purposes on the vast area of marshes.

During the month of March rainy and windy weather prevail on this coast. I could ill afford to lose any time shut up in Jointer's Hammock by bad weather, as the low regions of Okefenokee Swamp were to be penetrated before the warm season could make the task a disagreeable one. After holding a consultation with Mr. Williams, he contracted to take the canoe and its captain across St. Andrew's Sound to High Point of Cumberland Island that day. His little sloop was soon under way, and though the short, breaking waves of the sound, and the furious blasts of wind, made the navigation of the shoals disagreeable, we landed quietly at Mr. Chubbs' Oriental Hotel, at High Point, soon after noon.

Mr. Martin, the surveyor of the island, welcomed me to Cumberland, and gave me much information pertaining to local matters. The next morning the canoe left the high bluffs of this beautiful sea island so filled with historic

associations, and threaded the marshy thoroughfare of Cumberland and Brickhill River to Cumberland Sound.   As I approached the mouth of
the St. Mary's River, the picturesque ruins of
Dungeness towered above the live-oak forest
of the southern end of Cumberland Island.
It was with regret I turned my back upon that
sea, the sounds of which had so long struck
upon my ear with their sweet melody.   It
seemed almost a moan that was borne to me
now as the soft waves laved the sides of my
graceful craft, as though to give her a last,
loving farewell.

CHAPTER XIV.

ST. MARY'S RIVER AND THE SUWANEE WILDER-
NESS.

A PORTAGE TO DUTTON. — DESCENT OF THE ST. MARY'S RIVER.
— FÊTE GIVEN BY THE CITIZENS TO THE PAPER CANOE. —
THE PROPOSED CANAL ROUTE ACROSS FLORIDA. — A PORTAGE
TO THE SUWANEE RIVER. — A NEGRO SPEAKS ON ELECTRIC-
ITY AND THE TELEGRAPH. — A FREEDMAN'S SERMON.

I NOW ascended the beautiful St. Mary's River,
which flows from the great Okefenokee
Swamp. The state of Georgia was on my right
hand, and Florida on my left. Pretty hammocks
dotted the marshes, while the country presented
peculiar and interesting characteristics. When
four miles from Cumberland Sound, the little city
of St. Mary's, situated on the Georgia side of
the river, was before me; and I went ashore to
make inquiries concerning the route to Okefenokee Swamp.

My object was to get information about the
upper St. Mary's River, from which I proposed
to make a portage of thirty-five or forty miles in
a westerly direction to the Suwanee River,
upon arriving at which I would descend to the

Gulf of Mexico. My efforts, both at St. Mary's and Fernandina, on the Florida side of Cumberland Sound, to obtain any reliable information upon this matter, were unsuccessful. A settlement at Trader's Hill, about seventy-five miles up the St. Mary's River, was the geographical limit of local knowledge, while I wished to ascend the river at least one hundred miles beyond that point.

Believing that if I explored the uninhabited sources of the St. Mary's, I should be compelled to return without finding any settler upon its banks at the proper point of departure for a portage to the Suwanee, it became necessary to abandon all idea of ascending this river. I could not, however, give up the exploration of the route. In this dilemma, a kindly written letter seemed to solve the difficulties. Messrs. Dutton & Rixford, northern gentlemen, who possessed large facilities for the manufacture of resin and turpentine at their new settlements of Dutton, six miles from the St. Mary's River, and at Rixford, near the Suwanee, kindly proposed that I should take my canoe by railroad from Cumberland Sound to Dutton. From that station Mr. Dutton offered to transport the boat through the wilderness to the St. Mary's River, which could be from that point easily descended to the sea. The Suwanee River, at Rixford, could be reached by rail, and the voyage would end at its debouchure on the marshy coast of the Gulf of Mexico.

Hon. David Yulee, president and one-third owner of the A. G. & W. I. T. C. Railroad, which connects the Atlantic coast at Fernandina with the Gulf coast at Cedar Keys, offered me the free use of his long railroad, for any purpose of exploration, &c., while his son, Mr. C. Wickliffe Yulee, exerted himself to remove all impediments to delay.

These gentlemen, being native Floridians, have done much towards encouraging all legitimate exploration of the peninsula, and have also done something towards putting a check on the outrageous impositions practised on northern agricultural emigrants to Florida, by encouraging the organization of a railroad land-company, which offers a forty-acre homestead for fifty dollars, to be selected out of nearly six hundred thousand acres of land along their highway across the state. A man of comparatively small means can now try the experiment of making a home in the mild climate of Florida, and if he afterwards abandons the enterprise there will have been but a small investment of capital, and consequently little loss.

The turpentine distillery of Dutton was situated in a heavy forest of lofty pines. Major C. K. Dutton furnished a team of mules to haul the Maria Theresa to the St. Mary's River, the morning after my arrival by rail at Dutton Station. The warm sunshine shot aslant the tall pines as the teamster followed a faintly developed trail towards the swamps. Before noon the flashing waters of the stream were discernible, and a little later, with paddle in hand, I was urging the canoe towards the Atlantic coast. A luxurious growth of trees and shrubs fringed the low, and in some places submerged, river shores. Back, on the higher, sandy soils, the yellow pine forests, in almost primeval grandeur, arose, shutting out all view of the horizon. Low bluffs, with white, sandy beaches of a few rods in extent, offered excellent camping-grounds.

When the Cracker of Okefenokee Swamp is asked why he lives in so desolate a region, with only a few cattle and hogs for companions, with mosquitoes, fleas, and vermin about him, with alligators, catamounts, and owls on all sides, making night hideous, he usually replies, " Wal, stranger, wood and water is so *powerful* handy. Sich privileges ain't met with everywhar."

As I glided swiftly down the dark current I peered into the dense woods, hoping to be cheered by the sight of a settler's cabin; but in all that day's search not a clearing could be found, nor could I discern rising from the tree-tops of the solitary forest a little cloud of smoke issuing from the chimney of civilized man. I was alone in the vast wilds through which the beautiful river flowed noiselessly but swiftly to the sea. Thoreau loved a swamp, and so do all lovers of nature, for nowhere else does she so bountifully show her vigorous powers of growth, her varied wealth of botanical wonders. Here the birds resort in flocks when weary of the hot, sandy uplands, for here they find pure water, cool shade, and many a curious glossy berry for their dainty appetites.

As the little Maria Theresa sped onward through the open forest and tangled wild-wood, through wet morass and piny upland, my thoughts dwelt upon the humble life of the Concord naturalist and philosopher. How he would have enjoyed the descent of this wild river from the swamp to the sea! He had left us for purer delights; but I could enjoy his "Walden" as though he still lived, and read of his studies of nature with ever-increasing interest.

Swamps have their peculiar features. Those of the Waccamaw were indeed desolate, while the swamps of the St. Mary's were full of sunshine for the traveller. Soon after the canoe had commenced her river journey, a sharp sound, like that produced by a man striking the water with a broad, flat stick, reached my ears. As this sound was frequently repeated, and always in advance of my boat, it roused my curiosity. It proved to come from alligators. One after another slipped off the banks, striking the water

with their tails as they took refuge in the river
from the disturber of their peace. To observe
the movements of these reptiles I ran the canoe
within two rods of the left shore, and by rapid
paddling was enabled to arrive opposite a creature as he entered the water. When thus con-
fronted, the alligator would depress his ugly
head, lash the water once with his tail, and dive
under the canoe, a most thoroughly alarmed animal. All these alligators were mere babies,
very few being over four feet long. Had they
been as large as the one which greeted me at
Colonel's Island, I should not have investigated
their dispositions, but would have considered
discretion the better part of valor, and left them
undisturbed in their sun-baths on the banks.

In all my experience with the hundreds of
alligators I have seen in the southern rivers
and swamps of North America, every one, both
large and small, fled at the approach of man.
The experience of some of my friends in their
acquaintance with American alligators has been
of a more serious nature. It is well to exercise
care about camping at night close to the water
infested with large saurians, as one of these
strong fellows could easily seize a sleeping man
by the leg and draw him into the river. They
do not seem to fear a recumbent or bowed figure, but, like most wild animals, flee before the
upright form of man.

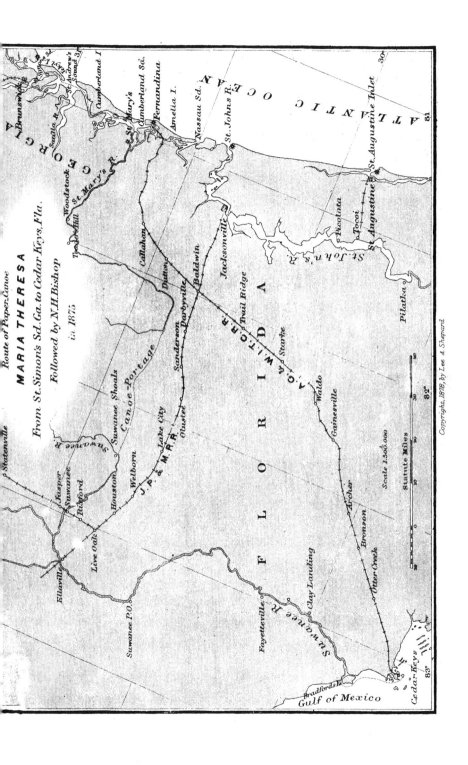

Route of Paper Canoe

MARIA THERESA

From St. Simon's Sd. Ga. to Cedar Keys, Fla.

Followed by N. H. Bishop

in 1875

Scale 1,500,000

Statute Miles

Copyright, 1878, by Lee & Shepard.

Late in the afternoon I passed an island, made by a " cut-off " through a bend of the river, and, according to previous directions, counted fourteen bends or reaches in the river which was to guide me to Stewart's Ferry, the owner of which lived back in the woods, his cabin not being discernible from the river. Near this spot, which is occasionally visited by lumbermen and pinywoods settlers, I drew my canoe on to a sandy beach one rod in length. A little bluff, five or six feet above the water, furnished me with the broad leaves of the saw-palmetto, a dwarfish sort of palm, which I arranged for a bed. The provision-basket was placed at my head. A little fire of light-wood cheered me for a while, but its bright flame soon attracted winged insects in large numbers. Having made a cup of chocolate, and eaten some of Captain Akin's chipped beef and crackers, I continued my preparations for the night. Feeling somewhat nervous about large alligators, I covered myself with a piece of painted canvas, which was stiff and strong, and placed the little revolver, my only weapon, under my blanket.

As I fully realized the novelty of my strange position in this desolate region, it was some time before I could compose myself and sleep. It was a night of dreams. Sounds indistinct but numerous troubled my brain, until I was fully roused to wakefulness by horrible visions and doleful cries. The chuck-will's-widow, which in the south supplies the place of our whip-poorwill, repeated his oft-told tale of "chuck-will's-widow, chuck-will's-widow," with untiring earnestness. The owls hooted wildly, with a chorus of cries from animals and reptiles not recognizable by me, excepting the snarling voices of the coons fighting in the forest. These last were old acquaintances, however, as they frequently gathered round my camp at night to pick up the remains of supper.

While I listened, there rose a cry so hideous in its character and so belligerent in its tone, that I trembled with fear upon my palm-leaf mattress. It resembled the bellowing of an infuriated bull, but was louder and more penetrating in its effect. The proximity of this animal was indeed unpleasant, for he had planted himself on the river's edge, near the little bluff upon which my camp had been constructed. The loud roar was answered by a similar bellow from the other side of the river, and for a long time did these two male alligators keep up their challenging cries, without coming to combat. Numerous wood-mice attacked my provision-basket, and even worked their way through the leaves of my palmetto mattress.

Thus with an endless variety of annoyances the night wore wearily away, but the light of the rising sun did not penetrate the thick fog which enveloped the river until after eight o'clock, when I embarked for a second day's journey upon the stream, which had now attained a width of five or six rods. Rafts of logs blocked the river as I approached the settlement of Trader's Hill, and upon a most insecure footing the canoe was dragged over a quarter of a mile of logs, and put into the water on the lower side of the "jam." Crossing several of these log "jams," which covered the entire width of the St. Mary's, I became weary of the task, and, after the last was reached, determined to go into camp until the next day, when suddenly the voices of men in the woods were heard.

Soon a gentleman, with two raftsmen, appeared and kindly greeted me. They had been notified of my approach at Trader's Hill by a courier sent from Dutton across the woods, and these men, whose knowledge of wood-craft is wonderful, had timed my movements so correctly that they had arrived just in time to meet me at this point. The two raftsmen rubbed the canoe all over with their hands, and expressed delight at its beautiful finish in their own peculiar vernacular.

"She's the dog-gonedest thing I ever seed, and jist as putty as a new coffin!" exclaimed one.

"Indeed, she's the handsomest trick I ever did blink on," said the second.

The two stalwart lumbermen lifted the boat as

though she were but a feather, and carried her, jumping from log to log, the whole length of the raft. They then put her gently in the water, and added to their farewell the cheering intelligence that "there's no more jams nor rafts 'twixt here and the sea, and you can go clar on to New York if you like."

Trader's Hill, on a very high bluff on the left bank, was soon passed, when the current seemed suddenly to cease, and I felt the first tidal effect of the sea, though many miles from the coast. The tide was flooding. I now laid aside the paddle, and putting the light steel outriggers in their sockets, rapidly rowed down the now broad river until the shadows of night fell upon forest and stream, when the comfortable residence of Mr. Lewis Davis, with his steam saw-mill, came into sight upon Orange Bluff, on the Florida side of the river. Here a kind welcome greeted me from host and hostess, who had dwelt twenty years in this romantic but secluded spot. There were orange-trees forty years old on this property, and all in fine bearing order. There was also a fine sulphur spring near the house.

Mr. Davis stated that, during a residence of twenty years in this charming locality, he had experienced but one attack of chills. He considered the St. Mary's River, on account of the purity of its waters, one of the healthiest of southern streams. The descent of this beautiful river now became a holiday pastime. Though there were but few signs of the existence of man, the scenery was of a cheering character. A brick-kiln, a few saw-mills, and an abandoned rice-plantation were passed, while the low salt-marshes, extending into the river from the forest-covered upland, gave evidence of the proximity to the sea. Large alligators were frequently seen sunning themselves upon the edges of the banks.

At dusk the town of St. Mary's, in its wealth of foliage, opened to my view from across the lowlands, and soon after the paper canoe was carefully stored in a building belonging to one of its hospitable citizens, while local authority asserted that I had traversed one hundred and seventy-five miles of the river.

One evening, while enjoying the hospitality of Mr. Silas Fordam, at his beautiful winter home, " Orange Hall," situated in the heart of St. Mary's, a note, signed by the Hon. J. M. Arnow, mayor of the city, was handed me. Mr. Arnow, in the name of the city government, invited my presence at the Spencer House. Upon arriving at the hotel, a surprise awaited me. The citizens of the place had gathered to welcome the paper canoe and its owner, and to express the kindly feelings they, as southern citizens, held towards their northern friends. The hotel was decorated with flags and floral emblems, one of which expressed, in its ingeniously constructed words, wrought in flowers, "*One hundred thousand Welcomes.*"

The mayor and his friends received me upon the veranda of the hotel with kind words of welcome. Bright lights glimmered at this moment through the long avenue of trees, and music arose upon the night air. It was a torchlight procession coming from the river, bearing upon a framework structure, from which hung Chinese lanterns and wreaths of laurel, the little paper canoe. The Base-ball Club of the city, dressed in their handsome uniform, carried the "Maria Theresa," while the sailors from the lumber fleet in the river, with the flags of several nationalities, brought up the rear.

When the procession arrived in front of the hotel, three hearty cheers were given by the people, and the mayor read the city's address of welcome to me; to which I made reply, not only in behalf of myself, but of all those of my countrymen who desired the establishment of a pure and good government in every portion of our dear land.

Mayor Arnow presented me with an engrossed copy of his speech of welcome, in which he invited all industrious northerners to come to his native city, promising that city ordinances should be passed to encourage the erection of manufactories, &c., by northern capital and northern labor. After the address, the wife of the mayor presented me with two memorial banners, in the name of the ladies of the city. These were made for the occasion, and being the handiwork of the ladies themselves, were highly appreciated by the recipient. When these graceful tributes had been received, each lady and child present deposited a bouquet of flowers, grown in the gardens of St. Mary's, in my little craft, till it contained about four hundred of these refined expressions of the good-will of these kind people. Not only did the native population of the town vie with each other to accord the lonely voyager a true southern welcome, but Mr. A. Curtis, an English gentleman, who, becoming fascinated with the fine climate of this part of Georgia, had settled here, did all he could to show his appreciation of canoe-travelling, and superintended the marine display and flag corps of the procession.

I left St. Mary's with a strange longing to return to its interesting environs, and to study here the climatology of southern Georgia, for, strange to say, cases of local "fever and chills" have never originated in the city. It is reached from Savannah by the inside steamboat route, or by rail, to Fernandina, with which it is connected by a steamboat ferry eight miles in length. Speculation not having yet affected the low valuation placed upon property around St. Mary's, northern men can obtain winter homes in this attractive town at a very low cost. This city is a port of entry. Mr. Joseph Shepard, a most faithful government officer, has filled the position of collector of customs for several years.

As vessels of considerable tonnage can ascend the St. Mary's River from the sea on a full tide to the wharves of the city, its citizens prophesy a future growth and development for the place when a river and canal route across the peninsula between the Atlantic Ocean and the Gulf of Mexico shall have been completed. For many years Colonel Raiford has been elaborating his plan " for elongating the western and southern inland system of navigation to harbors of the Atlantic Ocean." He proposes to unite the natural watercourses of the coast of the Gulf of Mexico by short canals, so that barges drawing seven feet of water, and freighted with the produce of the Mississippi River and its tributaries, may pass from New Orleans eastward to the southern ports of the Atlantic States. The great peninsula of Florida would be crossed by these vessels from the Suwanee to the St. Mary's River by means of a canal cut through the Okefenokee Swamp, and this route would save several hundred miles of navigation upon open ocean waters. The dangerous coral reefs of the Florida and Bahama shores would be avoided, and a land-locked channel of thirty thousand miles of navigable watercourses would be united in one system.

Lieutenant-Colonel Q. A. Gilmore's report on

"Water Line for Transportation from the Mouth of the St. Mary's River, on the Atlantic Coast, through Okefenokee Swamp and the State of Florida to the Gulf of Mexico," in which the able inquirer discusses this water route, has recently been published. I traversed a portion of this route in 1875–6, from the head of the Ohio River to New Orleans, and along the shores of the Gulf of Mexico to Cedar Keys, in a cedar duck-boat; and as the results of my observations may some day be made public, I will at this time refer the reader, if he be interested in the important enterprise, to the Congressional reports which describe the feasibility of the plan.

Another portage by rail was made in order to complete my journey to the Gulf of Mexico, and Rixford, near the Suwanee River, was reached via the A. G. & W. I. T. C. Railroad to Baldwin, thence over the J. P. & M. Railroad to Live Oak, where another railroad from the north connects, and along which, a few miles from Live Oak, Messrs. Dutton & Rixford had recently established their turpentine and resin works.

At Rixford I found myself near the summit, or backbone of Florida, from which the tributaries of the water-shed flow on one side to the Atlantic Ocean, and on the other to the Gulf of Mexico. It was a high region of rolling country, heavily wooded with magnificent pine forests, rich in terebinthine resources. The residence of the proprietor, the store and the distillery, with a few log cabins inhabited by negroes and white employés, made up the establishment of Rixford.

The Crackers and negroes came from long distances to see the paper boat. One afternoon, when a number of people had gathered at Rixford to behold the little craft, I placed it on one of those curious sheets of water of crystal purity called in that region a *sink;* and though this nameless, mirror-like lakelet did not cover over an acre in extent, the movements of the little craft, when propelled by the double paddle, excited an enthusiasm which is seldom exhibited by the piny-woods people.

As the boat was carefully lifted from the silvery tarn, one woman called out in a loud voice, " Lake Theresa! " and thus, by mutual consent of every one present, did this lakelet of crystal waters receive its name.

The blacks crowded around the canoe, and while feeling its firm texture, and wondering at the long distance it had traversed, expressed themselves in their peculiar and original way. One of their number, known as a " tonguey nigger," volunteered to explain the wonder to the somewhat confused intellects of his companions. To a question from one negro as to " How did dis yere Yankee-man cum all dis fur way in de *paper* canoe, all hissef lone? " the " *educated*" negro replied: " It's all de Lord.   No man ken cum so fur in a *paper* boat ef de Lord didn't help him. De Lord does eberyting. He puts de tings in de Yankee-man's heads to du um, an' dey duz um. Dar was de big Franklin up norf, dat made de telegraf. Did ye eber har tell ob him?"

"Neber, neber!" responded all the negroes.

Then, with a look of supreme contempt for the ignorance of his audience, the orator proceeded: "Dis great Franklin, *Cap'n* Franklin, he tort he'd kotch de litening and make de telegraf; so he flies a big kite way'up to de heabens, an' he puts de string in de bottle dat hab nufing in it. Den he holds de bottle in one hand, an' he holds de cork in de udder hand. Down cums de litening and fills de bottle *full up*, and Cap'n Franklin he dun cork him up mighty quick, and kotched de litening an' made de telegraf. But it was de Lord—de Lord, not Cap'n Franklin— dat did all dis."

It was amusing to watch the varied expression of the negroes, as they listened to this description of the discovery of electricity, and the origin of the telegraph. Their eyes dilated with wonder, and their thick lips parted till the mouth, growing wider and wider, seemed to cover more than its share of the face. The momentary silence was soon broken by a deep gurgle proceeding from a stolid-looking negro, as he exclaimed: "Did he kotch de bottle *full* ob litening, and *cork* him up. Golly! I tort he wud hab *busted* hissef!"

"So he wud! so he wud!" roared the orator, "but ye see 'twas all de Lord — de Lord's a-doing it."

While in Florida I paid some attention to the negro method of conducting praise meetings, which they very appropriately call "de shout-ings." If I give some verbatim reports of the negro's curious and undignified clerical efforts, it is not done for the purpose of caricaturing him, nor with a desire to make him appear desti-tute of mental calibre; but rather with the hope that the picture given may draw some sympathy from the liberal churches of the north, which do not forget the African in his native jungle, nor the barbarous islanders of the South Seas. A well-informed Roman Catholic priest told me that he had been disappointed with the progress his powerfully organized church had made in con-verting the freedmen. Before going among them I had supposed that the simple-minded black, now no longer a slave, would be easily attracted to the impressive ceremonies of the Church of Rome; but after witnessing the activity of their devotions, and observing how anxious they are to take a conspicuous and a leading part in all religious services, it seemed to me that the free black of the south would take more naturally to Methodism than to any other form of Chris-tianity.

The appointment of *local preachers* would be

especially acceptable to the negro, as he would then be permitted to have ministers of his own color, and of his own neighborhood, to lead the meetings; while the Roman Catholic priest would probably treat him more like a child, and would therefore exercise a strong discipline over him.

In one of their places of worship, at my request, a New York lady, well skilled in rapid writing and familiar with the negro vernacular, reported verbatim the negro preacher's sermon. The text was the parable of the ten virgins; and as the preacher went on, he said: "Five ob dem war wise an' five of dem war foolish. De wise jes gone an' dun git dar lamps *full up ob oil*, and git rite in and see de bridegoom; an' de foolish dey sot dem rite down on de stool ob do-noting, an' dar dey sot till de call cum; den dey run, pick up der ole lamps and try to push door in, but de Lord say to dem, ' Git out dar! you jes git out dar!' an' shut door rite in dar face.

" My brudders and my sisters, yer must fill de lamps wid de gospel an' de edication ob Moses, fur Moses war a larned man, an' edication is de *mos estaminable blessin'* a pusson kin hab in dis world.

" Hole-on to de gospel! Ef you see dat de flag am tore, get hole somewhar, keep a grabblin until ye git hole ob de stick, an' nebah gib up de stick, but grabble, grabble till ye die; for dough

yer sins be as black as scarlet, dey shall be white
as snow."

The sermon over, the assembled negroes then
sung in slow measure:

> " Lit-tell chil-ern, you'd bet-tar be-a-lieve —
> Lit-tell chil-ern, you'd bet-tar be-a-lieve —
> Lit-tell chil-ern, you'd bet-tar be-a-lieve —
>   I'll git home to heav-en when I die.
>
> Sweet heav-en ain-a-my-ain,
> Sweet heav-en ain-a-my-ain,
> Sweet heav-en ain-a-my-ain,
>   I'll git home to *heav-en* when I die.
>
> Lord wish-ed I was in heav-en,
> Fur to see my mudder when she enter,
> Fur to see her tri-als an' long white robes :
>   She'll shine like cristul in de sun.
>
> Sweet heav-en ain-a-my-ain,
> Sweet heav-en ain-a-my-ain,
> Sweet heav-en ain-a-my-ain,
>   I'll git home to heav-en when I die."

While visiting a town in Georgia, where the
negroes had made some effort to improve their
condition, I made a few notes relating to the
freedman's debating society of the place. Affect-
ing high-sounding words, they called their organization, " De Lycenum," and its doings were
directed by a committee of two persons, called
respectively, " de disputaceous visitor," and " de
lachrymal visitor." What particular duties de-
volved upon the " lachrymal visitor," I could

never clearly ascertain. One evening these negroes debated upon the following theme, " Which is de best — when ye are out ob a ting, or when ye hab got it? " which was another form of expressing the old question, " Is there more pleasure in possession than in anticipation? " Another night the colored orators became intensely excited over the query, " Which is de best, *Spring Water* or Matches? "

The freedmen, for so unfortunate a class, seem to be remarkably well behaved. During several journeys through the southern states I found them usually temperate, and very civil in their intercourse with the whites, though it must be confessed that but few of them can apply themselves steadily and persistently to manual labor, either for themselves or their employers.

CHAPTER XV.

DOWN UPON THE SUWANEE RIVER.

THE RICH FOLIAGE OF THE RIVER. — COLUMBUS. — ROLINS'
BLUFF. — OLD TOWN HAMMOCK. — A HUNTER KILLED BY A
PANTHER. — DANGEROUS SERPENTS. — CLAY LANDING. — THE
MARSHES OF THE COAST. — BRADFORD'S ISLAND. — MY LAST
CAMP. — THE VOYAGE ENDED.

SOME friends, among whom were Colonel
George W. Nason, Jr., of Massachusetts,
and Major John Purviance, Commissioner of
Suwanee County, offered to escort the paper
canoe down "the river of song" to the Gulf of
Mexico, a distance, according to local authority,
of two hundred and thirty-five miles. While
the members of the party were preparing for the
journey, Colonel Nason accompanied me to the
river, which was less than three miles from Rixford, the proprietors of which sent the canoe
after us on a wagon drawn by mules. The point
of embarkation was the Lower Mineral Springs,
the property of Judge Bryson.

The Suwanee, which was swollen by some
recent rains in Okefenokee Swamp, was a wild,
dark, turbulent current, which went coursing
through the woods on its tortuous route with

great rapidity.   The luxuriant foliage of the river-banks was remarkable.   Maples were in blossom, beech-trees in bloom, while the buck-eye was covered with its heavy festoons of red flowers.   Pines, willows, cotton-wood, two kinds of hickory, water-oak, live-oak, sweet-gum, magnolia, the red and white bay-tree, a few red-cedars, and haw-bushes, with many species not known to me, made up a rich wall of verdure on either side, as I sped along with a light heart to Columbus, where my *compagnons de voyage* were to meet me.   Wood-ducks and egrets, in small flocks, inhabited the forest.   The lime-stone banks of the river were not visible, as the water was eighteen feet above its low summer level.

I now passed under the railroad bridge which connects Live Oak with Savannah.   After a steady row of some hours, my progress was checked by a great boom, stretched across the river to catch the logs which floated down from the upper country.   I was obliged to disembark and haul the canoe around this obstacle, when, after passing a few clearings, the long bridge of the J. P. & M. Railroad came into view, stretching across the now wide river from one wilderness to the other.   On the left bank was all that remained of the once flourishing town of Colum-bus, consisting now of a store, kept by Mr. Allen, and a few buildings.   Before the railroad

was built, Columbus possessed a population of
five hundred souls, and it was reached, during
favorable stages of water, by light-draught steamboats from Cedar Keys, on the Gulf of Mexico.
The building of railroads in the south has
diverted trade from one locality to another, and
many towns, once prosperous, have gone to
decay.

The steam saw-mills and village of Ellaville
were located on the river-bank opposite Columbus, and this lumber establishment is the only
place of importance between it and Cedar Keys.
This far-famed river, to which the heart of the
minstrel's darky " is turning eber," is, in fact,
almost without the " one little hut among de
bushes," for it is a wild and lonely stream.
Even in the most prosperous times there were
but few plantations upon its shores. Wild animals roam its great forests, and vile reptiles
infest the dense swamps. It is a country well
fitted for the hunter and lumberman, for the
naturalist or canoeist; but the majority of people
would, I am sure, rather hear of it poured forth
in song from the sweet lips of Christina Nilsson,
than to be themselves " way down upon the
Suwanee Ribber."

On Monday, March 22d, Messrs. Nason, Purviance, and Henderson joined me. The party
had obtained a northern-built shad-boat, which
had been brought by rail from Savannah. It

was sloop-rigged, and was decked forward, so that the enthusiastic tourists possessed a weatherproof covering for their provisions and blankets. With the strong current of the river, a pair of long oars, and a sail to be used when favorable· winds blew, the party in the shad-boat could make easy and rapid progress towards the Gulf, while my lightly dancing craft needed scarcely a touch of the oar to send her forward.

On Tuesday, the 23d, we left Columbus, while a crowd of people assembled to see us off, many of them seeming to consider this simple and delightful way of travelling too dangerous to be attempted. The smooth but swift current rolled on its course like a sea of molten glass, as the soft sunlight trembled through the foliage and shimmered over its broad surface.

Our boats glided safely over the rapids, which for a mile and a half impede the navigation of the river during the summer months, but which were now made safe by the great depth of water caused by the freshet. The weather was charming, and our little party, fully alive to all the beautiful surroundings, woke many an echo with sounds meant to be sweet. Of course the good old song was not forgotten. Our best voice sang:

> "Way down up-on de Suwanee Rib-ber,
> Far, far away,
> Dere's whar my heart is turn-ing eb-ber,
> Dere's whar de old folks stay.

All up and down de whole creation
Sadly I roam,
Still longing for de old plantation,
And for de old folks at home.

" All round de little farm I wander'd
When I was young ;
Den many happy days I squan-der'd —
Many de songs I sung.
When I was playing wid my brud-der,
Hap-py was I.
O ! take me to my kind old mud-der,
Dere let me live and die !

" One little hut among de bushes, —
One dat I love, —
Still sadly to my mem'ry rushes,
No matter where I rove.
When will I see de bees a-hum-ming
All round de comb ?
When will I hear de ban-jo tum-ming
Down in my good old home ? "

We all joined in the chorus at the end of each verse:

" All de world am sad and dreary
Eb-ry-whar I roam.
O, darkies, how my heart grows weary,
Far from de old folks at home."

We soon entered forests primeval which were quiet, save for the sound of the axe of the log-thief, for timber-stealing is a profession which reaches its greatest perfection on the Florida state lands and United States naval reserves. Uncle Sam's territory is being constantly plundered to supply the steam saw-mills of private individuals in Florida. Several of the party told interesting stories of the way in which log-thieves managed to steal from the government *legally*.

"There," said one, "is X, who runs his mill on the largest tract of pine timber Uncle Sam has got. He once bought a few acres' claim adjacent to a fine naval reserve. He was not, of course, able to discover the boundary line which separated his little tract from the rich government reserve, so he kept a large force of men cutting down Uncle Sam's immense pines, and, hauling them to the Suwanee, floated them to his mill. This thing went on for some time, till the government agent made his appearance and demanded a settlement.

"The wholesale timber-thief now showed a fair face, and very frankly explained that he supposed he had been cutting logs from his own territory, but quite recently he had discovered that he had really been trespassing on the property of his much-loved country, and as he was truly a loyal citizen, he desired to make restitution, and was now ready to settle.

"The government agent was astonished at the seeming candor of the man, who so worked upon his sympathy that he promised to be as *easy* upon him as the law allowed. The agent settled upon a valuation of fifty cents an acre for all the territory that had been cut over. 'And now,' said he, 'how many acres of land have you "logged" since you put your lumbermen into the forest?'

" Mr. X declared himself unable to answer this question, but generously offered to permit the agent to put down any number of acres he thought would represent a fair thing between a kind government and one of its unfortunate citizens. Intending to do his duty faithfully, the officer settled upon two thousand acres as having been trespassed upon; but to his astonishment the incomprehensible offender stoutly affirmed that he had logged fully five thousand acres, and at once settled the matter in full by paying twenty-five hundred dollars, taking a receipt for the same.

" When this enterprising business-man visited Jacksonville, his friends rallied him upon confessing judgment to government for three thousand acres of timber more than had been claimed by the agent. This true *patriot* winked as he replied:

"'It is true I hold a receipt from the government for the timber on five thousand acres at the very low rate of fifty cents an acre. As I have not yet cut logs from more than one-fifth of the tract, *I intend to work off the timber on the other four thousand acres at my leisure*, and no power can stop me now I have the government receipt to show it's paid for.'"

The sloop and the canoe had left Columbus a little before noon, and at six P. M. we passed

Charles' Ferry, where the old St. Augustine and Tallahassee forest road crosses the river. At this lonely place an old man, now dead, owned a subterranean spring, which he called " Mediterranean passage." This spring is powerful enough to run a rickety, " up-and-down " saw-mill. The great height of the water allowed me to paddle into the mill with my canoe.

At half past seven o'clock a deserted log cabin at Barrington's Ferry offered us shelter for the night. The whole of the next day we rowed through the same immense forests, finding no more cultivated land than during our first day's voyage. We landed at a log cabin in a small clearing to purchase eggs of a poor woman, whose husband had shot her brother a few days before. As the wife's brother had visited the cabin with the intention of killing the husband, the woman seemed to think the murdered man had " got his desarts," and, as a coroner's jury had returned a verdict of " justifiable homicide," the affair was considered settled.

Below this cabin we came to Island No. 1, where rapids trouble boatmen in the summer months. Now we glided gently but swiftly over the deep current. The few inhabitants we met along the banks of the Suwanee seemed to carry with them an air of repose while awake. To rouse them from mid-day slumbers we would call loudly as we passed a cabin in the woods, and after considerable delay a man would appear at the door, rubbing his eyes as though the genial sunlight was oppressive to his vision. It was indeed a quiet, restful region, this great wilderness of the Suwanee.

We passed Mrs. Goodman's farm and log buildings on the left bank, just below Island No. 8, before noon, and about this time Major Purviance shot at a large wild turkey (*Meleagris gallopavo*), knocking it off a bank into the water. The gobbler got back to land, and led us a fruitless chase into the thicket of saw-palmetto. He knew his ground better than we, for, though wounded, he made good his escape. We stopped a few moments at Troy, which, though dignified in name, consists only of a store and some half dozen buildings.

A few miles below this place, on the left bank of the river, is an uninhabited elevation called Rolins' Bluff, from which a line running north 22° east, twenty-three miles and a half in length, will strike Live Oak. A charter to connect Live Oak with this region of the Suwanee by means of a railroad had just passed the Florida legislature, but had been killed by the veto of the governor. After sunset the boats were secured in safe positions in front of a deserted cabin, round which a luxuriant growth of bitter-orange trees showed what nature could do for this neglected grove. The night air was balmy, and tremulous with insect life, while the alligators in the swamps kept up their bellowings till morning.

After breakfast we descended to the mouth of the Santa Fé River, which was on the left bank of the Suwanee. The piny-woods people called it the Santaffy. The wilderness below the Santa Fé is rich in associations of the Seminole Indian war. Many relics have been found, and, among others, on the site of an old Indian town, entombed in a hollow tree, the skeletons of an Indian adult and child, decked with beads, were discovered. Fort Fanning is on the left bank, and Old Town Hammock on the right bank of the Suwanee.

During the Seminole war, the hammock and the neighboring fastnesses became the hiding-places of the persecuted Indians, and so wild and undisturbed is this region, even at this time, that the bear, lynx, and panther take refuge from man in its jungles.

Colonel J. L. F. Cottrell left his native Virginia in 1854, and commenced the cultivation of the virgin soil of Old Town Hammock. Each state has its peculiar mode of dividing its land, and here in Florida this old plantation was in township 10, section 24, range 13. The estate included about two thousand acres of land, of which nearly eleven hundred were under cultivation. The slaves whom the colonel brought from Virginia were now his tenants, and he leased them portions of his arable acres. He considered this locality as healthy as any in the Suwanee country. The old planter's home, with its hospitable doors ever open to the stranger, was embowered in live-oaks and other trees, from the branches of which the graceful festoons of Spanish moss waved in the soft air, telling of a warm, moist atmosphere.

A large screw cotton-press and corn-cribs, with smoke-house and other plantation buildings, were conveniently grouped under the spreading branches of the protecting oaks. The estate produced cotton, corn, sweet potatoes, cattle, hogs, and poultry. Deer sometimes approached the enclosed fields, while the early morning call of the wild turkey came from the thickets of the hammock. In this retired part of Florida, cheered by the society of a devoted wife and four lovely daughters, lived the kind-hearted gentleman who not only pressed upon us the comforts of his well-ordered house, but also insisted upon accompanying the paper canoe from his forest home to the sea.

When gathered around the firesides of the backwoods people, the conversation generally runs into hunting stories, Indian reminiscences, and wild tales of what the pioneers suffered while establishing themselves in their forest homes. One event of startling interest had oc-

curred in the Suwanee country a few weeks before the paper canoe entered its confines. Two hunters went by night to the woods to shoot deer by firelight. As they stalked about, with light-wood torches held above their heads, they came upon a herd of deer, which, being bewildered by the glare of the lights, made no attempt to escape. Sticking their torches in the ground, the hunters stretched themselves flat upon the grass, to hide their forms from the animals they hoped to kill at their leisure. One of the men was stationed beneath the branches of a large tree; the other was a few yards distant.

Before the preconcerted signal for discharging their rifles could be given, the sound of a heavy body falling to the ground, and an accompanying smothered shriek, startled the hunter who was farthest from the tree. Starting up in alarm, he flew to the assistance of his friend, whose prostrate form was covered by a large panther, which had pounced upon him from the overhanging limb of the great oak. It had been but the work of an instant for the powerful cougar to break with his strong jaws the neck of the poor backwoodsman.

In this rare case of a panther (*Felis concolor*) voluntarily attacking man, it will be noted by the student of natural history that the victim was lying upon the ground. Probably the animal would not have left his perch among the branches of the oak, where he was evidently waiting for the approach of the deer, if the *up-right* form of the man had been seen. Go to a southern bayou, which is rarely, if ever, visited by man, and where its saurian inhabitants have never been annoyed by him, — place your body in a recumbent position on the margin of the lagoon, and wait until some large alligator slowly rises to the surface of the water. He will eye you for a moment with evident curiosity, and will in some cases steadily approach you. When the monster reptile is within two or three rods of your position, rise slowly upon your feet to your full height, and the alligator of the southern states — the *A. Mississippiensis* — will, in nine cases out of ten, retire with precipitation.

There are but few wild animals that will attack man willingly when face to face with him; they quail before his erect form. In every case of the animals of North America showing fight to man, which has been investigated by me, the beasts have had no opportunity to escape, or have had their young to defend, or have been wounded by the hunter.

It was nearly ten o'clock A. M. on Friday, March 26th, when our merry party left Old Town Hammock. This day was to see the end of the voyage of the paper canoe, for my tiny craft was to arrive at the waters of the great southern sea before midnight. The wife and

daughters of our host, like true women of the forest, offered no forebodings at the departure of
the head of their household, but wished him, with
cheerful looks, a pleasant voyage to the Gulf.
The gulf port of Cedar Keys is but a few miles
from the mouth of the Suwanee River.   The
railroad which terminates at Cedar Keys would,
with its connection with other routes, carry the
members of our party to their several homes.

The bright day animated our spirits, as we
swept swiftly down the river.   The party in the
shad-boat, now called "Adventurer," rowed mer-
rily on with song and laughter, while I made an
attempt to examine more closely the character
of the water-moccasin — the *Trigono cephalus-
piscivorus* of Lacepede, — which I had more
cause to fear than the alligators of the river.
The water-moccasin is about two feet in length,
and has a circumference of five or six inches.
The tail possesses a horny point about half an
inch in length, which is harmless, though the
Crackers and negroes stoutly affirm that when
it strikes a tree the tree withers and dies, and
when it enters the flesh of a man he is poisoned
unto death.   The color of the reptile is a dirty
brown.   Never found far from water, it is common in the swamps, and is the terror of the rice-
field negroes.   The bite of the water-moccasin
is exceedingly venomous, and it is considered
more poisonous than that of the rattlesnake, which

warns man of his approach by sounding his rattle.

The moccasin does not, like the rattlesnake, wait to be attacked, but assumes the offensive whenever opportunity offers, striking with its fangs at every animated object in its vicinity. All other species of snakes flee from its presence. It is found as far north as the Peedee River of South Carolina, and is abundant in all low districts of the southern states. As the Suwanee had overflowed its banks below Old Town Hammock, the snakes had taken to the low limbs of the trees and to the tops of bushes, where they seemed to be sleeping in the warmth of the bright sunlight; but as I glided along the shore a few feet from their aerial beds, they discovered my presence, and dropped sluggishly into the water. It would not be an exaggeration to say that we passed thousands of these dangerous reptiles while descending the Suwanee. Raftsmen told me that when traversing lagoons in their log canoes, if a moccasin is met some distance from land he will frequently enter the canoe for refuge or for rest, and instances have been known where the occupant has been so alarmed as to jump overboard and swim ashore in order to escape from this malignant reptile.

The only place worthy of notice between Old Town Hammock and the gulf marshes is Clay Landing, on the left bank of the river, where

Mrs. Tresper formerly lived in a very comfortable house.   Clay Landing was used during the Confederate war as a place of deposit for blockade goods.· Archer, a railroad station, is but twenty miles distant, and to it over rough roads the contraband imports were hauled by mule teams, after having been landed from the fleet blockade-runner.

As the sun was sinking to rest, and the tree-shadows grew long on the wide river's bosom, we tasted the saltness in the air as the briny breezes were wafted to us over the forests from the Gulf of Mexico.   After darkness had cast its sombre mantle upon us, we left the " East Pass " entrance to the left, and our boats hurried on the rapidly ebbing tide down the broad " West Pass " into the great marshes of the coast. An hour later we emerged from the dark forest into the smooth savannas.   The freshness of the sea-air was exhilarating   The stars were shining softly, and the ripple of the tide, the call of the heron, or the whirr of the frightened duck, and the leaping of fishes from the water, were the only sounds nature offered us.   It was like entering another world.   In these lowlands, near the mouth of the river, there seemed to be but one place above the high-tide level.   It was a little hammock, covered by a few trees, called Bradford's Island, and rose like an oasis in the desert. The swift tide hurried along its shores, and a

little farther on mingled the waters of the great
wilderness with that of the sea.

Our tired party landed on a shelly beach, and
burned a grassy area to destroy sand-fleas.   This
done, some built a large camp-fire, while others
spread blankets upon the ground.   I drew the
faithful sharer of my long voyage near a thicket
of prickly-pears, and slept beside it for the last
time, never thinking or dreaming that one year
later I should approach the mouth of the Suwanee from the west, after a long voyage of twenty-
five hundred miles from the head of the Ohio
River, and would again seek shelter on its banks.
It was a night of sweet repose.   The camp-fire
dissipated the damps, and the long row made
rest welcome.

A glorious morning broke upon our party as
we breakfasted under the shady palms of the
island.   Behind us rose the compact wall of
dark green of the heavy forests, and along the
coast, from east to west, as far as the eye could
reach, were the brownish-green savanna-like
lowlands, against which beat, in soft murmurs,
the waves of that sea I had so longed to reach.
From out the broad marshes arose low hammocks, green with pines and feathery with palmetto-trees.   Clouds of mist were rising, and
while I watched them melt away in the warm
beams of the morning sun, I thought they were
like the dark doubts which curled themselves

about me so long ago in the cold St. Lawrence, now all melted by the joy of success. The snow-clad north was now behind me. The Maria Theresa danced in the shimmering waters of the great southern sea, and my heart was light, for my voyage was over.

No. 14. THE VOYAGE ENDED.